Microsoft®

PowerPoint® 97

Illustrated Standard Edition

Microsoft®

PowerPoint® 97

Illustrated Standard Edition

David W. Beskeen

COURSE
TECHNOLOGY

ONE MAIN STREET, CAMBRIDGE, MA 02142

an International Thomson Publishing company I(T)P®

Cambridge • Albany • Bonn • Boston • Cincinnati • London • Madrid • Melbourne • Mexico City
New York • Paris • San Francisco • Singapore • Tokyo • Toronto • Washington

Microsoft PowerPoint 97—Illustrated Standard Edition is published by Course Technology

Managing Editor:	Nicole Jones Pinard
Product Manager:	Jeanne Herring
Production Editor:	Nancy Ray, Elena Montillo
Developmental Editor:	Katherine T. Pinard
Composition House:	GEX, Inc.
QA Manuscript Reviewers:	John McCarthy, Brian McCooey
Text Designer:	Joseph Lee
Cover Designer:	Joseph Lee

© 1999 by Course Technology — I(T)P®

For more information contact:

Course Technology
One Main Street
Cambridge, MA 02142

ITP Europe
Berkshire House 168-173
High Holborn
London WCIV 7AA
England

Nelson ITP, Australia
102 Dodds Street
South Melbourne, 3205
Victoria, Australia

ITP Nelson Canada
1120 Birchmount Road
Scarborough, Ontario
Canada M1K 5G4

International Thomson Editores
Seneca, 53
Colonia Polanco
11560 Mexico D.F. Mexico

ITP GmbH
Königswinterer Strasse 418
53227 Bonn
Germany

ITP Asia
60 Albert Street, #15-01
Albert Complex
Singapore 189969

ITP Japan
Hirakawacho Kyowa Building, 3F
2-2-1 Hirakawacho
Chiyoda-ku, Tokyo 102
Japan

ISBN 0-7600-6164-5

Printed in the United States of America

1 2 3 4 5 6 7 8 9 BM 02 01 00 99 98

From the

Illustrated Series™ Team

At Course Technology we believe that technology will transform the way that people teach and learn. We are very excited about bringing you, instructors and students, the most practical and affordable technology-related products available.

► The Development Process

Our development process is unparalleled in the educational publishing industry. Every product we create goes through an exacting process of design, development, review, and testing.

Reviewers give us direction and insight that shape our manuscripts and bring them up to the latest standards. Every manuscript is quality tested. Students whose backgrounds match the intended audience work through every keystroke, carefully checking for clarity and pointing out errors in logic and sequence. Together with our own technical reviewers, these testers help us ensure that everything that carries our name is as error-free and easy to use as possible.

► The Products

We show both how and why technology is critical to solving problems in the classroom and in whatever field you choose to teach or pursue. Our time-tested, step-by-step instructions provide unparalleled clarity. Examples and applications are chosen and crafted to motivate students.

► The Illustrated Series™ Team

The Illustrated Series™ Team is committed to providing you with the most visual introduction to microcomputer applications. No other series of books will get you up to speed faster in today's changing software environment. This book will suit your needs because it was delivered quickly, efficiently, and affordably. In every aspect of business, we rely on a commitment to quality and the use of technology. Each member of the Illustrated Series™ Team contributes to this process. The names of all our team members are listed below.

The Team

Cynthia Anderson	Mary-Terese Cozzola	Jeanne Herring	Elizabeth Eisner Reding
Chia-Ling Barker	Carol Cram	Meta Chaya Hirschl	Art Rotberg
Donald Barker	Kim T. M. Crowley	Jane Hosie-Bounar	Neil Salkind
Ann Barron	Catherine DiMassa	Steven Johnson	Gregory Schultz
David Beskeen	Stan Dobrawa	Bill Lisowski	Ann Shaffer
Ann Marie Buconjic	Shelley Dyer	Chet Lyskawa	Dan Swanson
Rachel Bunin	Linda Eriksen	Kristine O'Brien	Marie Swanson
Joan Carey	Jessica Evans	Tara O'Keefe	Jennifer Thompson
Patrick Carey	Lisa Friedrichsen	Harry Phillips	Sasha Vodnik
Sheralyn Carroll	Jeff Goding	Nicole Jones Pinard	Jan Weingarten
Brad Conlin	Michael Halvorson	Katherine T. Pinard	Christie Williams
Pam Conrad	Jamie Harper	Kevin Proot	Janet Wilson

Preface

Welcome to *Microsoft PowerPoint 97 – Illustrated Standard Edition*! This book in our highly visual new design offers new users a hands-on introduction to Microsoft PowerPoint 97 and also serves as an excellent reference for future use.

▶ Organization and Coverage

This text contains nine units that cover basic PowerPoint skills. In these units students learn how to design, create, edit, and enhance PowerPoint presentations. They also work with text and objects and create an on-screen slide show.

▶ Microsoft Office User Specialist Program

This book has been approved by Microsoft as courseware for the Microsoft Office User Specialist program. After completing the units in this book, you will be prepared to take the Expert level Microsoft Office User Specialist exam for Microsoft PowerPoint 97. By passing the certification exam for a Microsoft software program, you demonstrate your proficiency in that program to employers. Microsoft Office User Specialist exams are offered at participating test centers, participating corporations, and participating employment agencies. For more information about the Microsoft Office User Specialist program, visit Microsoft's Web site at http://www.microsoft.com/office/train_cert/.

▶ About this Approach

What makes the Illustrated approach so effective at teaching software skills? It's quite simple. Each skill is presented on two facing pages, with the step-by-step instructions on the left page, and large screen illustrations on the right. Students can focus on a single skill without having to turn the page. This unique design makes information extremely accessible and easy to absorb, and provides a great reference for after the course is over. This hands-on approach also makes it ideal for both self-paced or instructor-led classes. The modular structure of the book also allows for great flexibility; you can cover the units in any order you choose.

Each lesson, or "information display," contains the following elements:

This icon indicates a CourseHelp 97 slide show is available for this lesson. See the Instructor's Resource Kit page for more information.

Each 2-page spread focuses on a single skill

Concise text that introduces the basic principles in the lesson and integrates the brief case study.

Excel 97

Changing Attributes and Alignment of Labels

Attributes are font styling features such as bold, italics, and underlining. You can apply bold, italics, and underlining from the Formatting toolbar or from the Font tab in the Format Cells dialog box. You can also change the alignment of text in cells. Left, right, or center alignment can be applied from the Formatting toolbar, or from the Alignment tab in the Format Cells dialog box. See Table C-2 for a description of the available attribute and alignment buttons on the Formatting toolbar. Excel also has predefined worksheet formats to make formatting easier. ◆ Now that he has applied the appropriate fonts and font sizes to his worksheet labels, Evan wants to further enhance his worksheet's appearance by adding bold and underline formatting and centering some of the labels.

Steps

CourseHelp
The camera icon indicates there is a CourseHelp available with this lesson. Click the Start button, point to programs, point to CourseHelp, then click Word 97 Illustrated. Choose the CourseHelp that corresponds to this lesson.

QuickTip
Highlighting information on a worksheet can be useful, but overuse of any attribute can be distracting and make a document less readable. Be consistent by adding emphasis the same way throughout a workbook.

Time To
✔ Save

1. Press [Ctrl][Home] to select cell A1, then click the Bold button **B** on the Formatting toolbar
   The title "Advertising Expenses" appears in bold.

2. Select the range A3:J3, then click the Underline button **U** on the Formatting toolbar
   Excel underlines the column headings in the selected range.

3. Click cell A3, click the Italics button **I** on the Formatting toolbar, then click **B**
   The word "Type" appears in boldface, italic type. Notice that the Bold, Italics, and Underline buttons on the Formatting toolbar are indented. You decide you don't like the italic formatting. You remove it by clicking **I** again.

4. Click **I**
   Excel removes italics from cell A3.

5. Add bold formatting to the rest of the labels in the range B3:J3
   You want to center the title over the data.

6. Select the range A1:F1, then click the Merge and Center button **⊞** on the Formatting toolbar
   The title Advertising Expenses is centered across six columns. Now you center the column headings in their cells.

7. Select the range A3:J3 then click the Center button **≡** on the Formatting toolbar
   You are satisfied with the formatting in the worksheet. Compare your screen to Figure C-8.

TABLE C-2: Attribute and Alignment buttons on the Formatting toolbar

icon	description	icon	description
B	Adds boldface	≣	Aligns left
I	Italicizes	≣	Aligns center
U	Underlines	≣	Aligns right
	Adds lines or borders	⊞	Centers across columns, and combines two or more selected adjacent cells into one cell.

▶ EX C-6 **FORMATTING A WORKSHEET**

Quickly accessible summaries of key terms, toolbar buttons, or keyboard alternatives connected with the lesson material. Students can refer easily to this information when working on their own projects at a later time.

Hints as well as trouble-shooting advice right where you need it – next to the step itself.

Clear step-by-step directions, with what students are to type in red, explain how to complete the specific task.

Every lesson features large, full-color representations of what the screen should look like as students complete the numbered steps.

The innovative design draws the students' eyes to important areas of the screens.

Brightly colored tabs above the program name indicate which section of the book you are in. Students should find these tabs useful for finding your place within the book and for referencing information from the index.

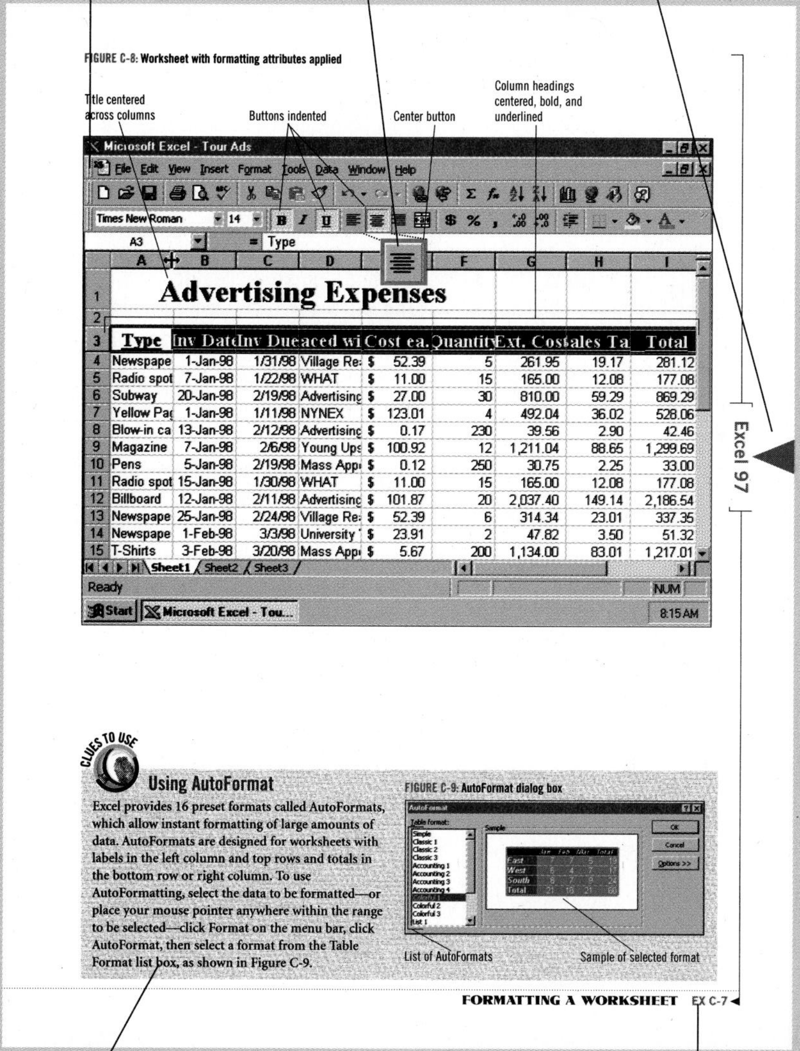

Other Features

The two-page lesson format featured in this book provides the new user with a powerful learning experience. Additionally, this book contains the following features:

▶ **Real-World Case**
The case study used throughout the textbook, a fictitious company called Nomad Ltd, is designed to be "real-world" in nature and introduces the kinds of activities that students will encounter when working with Microsoft PowerPoint 97. With a real-world case, the process of solving problems will be more meaningful to students.

▶ **End of Unit Material**
Each unit concludes with a Concepts Review that tests students' understanding of what they learned in the unit. A Skills Review follows the Concepts Review and provides students with additional hands-on practice of the skills they learned in the unit. The Skills Review is followed by Independent Challenges, which pose case problems for students to solve. At least one Independent Challenge in each unit asks students to use the World Wide Web to solve the problem as indicated by a Web Work icon. The Visual Workshops that follow the Independent Challenges help students to develop critical thinking skills. Students are shown completed documents and are asked to recreate them from scratch.

FIGURE C-8: Worksheet with formatting attributes applied

Title centered across columns

Buttons indented

Center button

Column headings centered, bold, and underlined

Excel 97

Using AutoFormat

Excel provides 16 preset formats called AutoFormats, which allow instant formatting of large amounts of data. AutoFormats are designed for worksheets with labels in the left column and top rows and totals in the bottom row or right column. To use AutoFormatting, select the data to be formatted—or place your mouse pointer anywhere within the range to be selected—click Format on the menu bar, click AutoFormat, then select a format from the Table Format list box, as shown in Figure C-9.

FIGURE C-9: AutoFormat dialog box

List of AutoFormats

Sample of selected format

FORMATTING A WORKSHEET EX C-7

Clues to Use Boxes provide concise information that either expands on of the major lesson skill or describes an independent task that in some way relates to the major lesson skill.

The page numbers are designed like a road map. EX indicates the Excel section, C indicates Excel Unit C, and 7 indicates the page within the unit. This map allows for the greatest flexibility in content – each unit stands completely on its own.

Instructor's Resource Kit

The Instructor's Resource Kit is Course Technology's way of putting the resources and information needed to teach and learn effectively into your hands. With an integrated array of teaching and learning tools that offer you and your students a broad range of instructional options, we believe this kit represents the highest quality and most cutting edge resources available to instructors today. Many of these resources are available online at www.course.com. The resources available with this book are:

CourseHelp 97
CourseHelp 97 is a student reinforcement tool offering online annotated tutorials that are accessible directly from the Start menu in Windows 95. These on-screen "slide shows" help students understand the most difficult concepts in a specific program. Students are encouraged to view a CourseHelp 97 slide show before completing that lesson. This text includes the following CourseHelp 97 slide shows:
- Aligning, Grouping, and Stacking Objects
- Screen Show Effects

Adopters of this text are granted the right to post the CourseHelp 97 files on any standalone computer or network.

Course Test Manager
Designed by Course Technology, this cutting edge Windows-based testing software helps instructors design and administer tests and pre-tests.   This full-featured program also has an online testing component that allows students to take tests at the computer and have their exams automatically graded.

Course Faculty Online Companion
This new World Wide Web site offers Course Technology customers a password-protected Faculty Lounge where you can find everything you need to prepare for class. These periodically updated items include lesson plans, graphic files for the figures in the text, additional problems, updates and revisions to the text, links to other Web sites, and access to Student Disk files. This new site is an ongoing project and will continue to evolve throughout the semester. Contact your Customer Service Representative for the site address and password.

Course Student Online Companion
This book features its own Online Companion where students can go to access Web sites that will help them complete the WebWork Independent Challenges. This page also contains links to other Course Technology student pages where students can find task references for each of the Microsoft Office 97 programs, a graphical glossary of terms found in the text, an archive of meaningful templates, software, hot tips, and Web links to other sites that contain pertinent information. These new sites are also ongoing projects and will continue to evolve throughout the semester.

Student Files
To use this book students must have the Student Files. See the inside front or inside back cover for more information on the Student Files. Adopters of this text are granted the right to post the Student Files on any stand-alone computer or network.

Instructor's Manual
This is quality assurance tested and includes:
- Solutions to all lessons and end-of-unit material
- Unit notes with teaching tips from the author
- Extra Independent Challenges
- Transparency Masters of key concepts
- Student Files
- CourseHelp 97

The Illustrated Family of Products

This book that you are holding fits in the Illustrated Series – one series of three in the Illustrated family of products. The other two series are the Illustrated Projects Series and the Illustrated Interactive Series. The Illustrated Projects Series is a supplemental series designed to reinforce the skills learned in any skills-based book through the creation of meaningful and engaging projects. The Illustrated Interactive Series is a line of computer-based training multimedia products that offer the novice user a quick and interactive learning experience. All three series are committed to providing you with the most visual and enriching instructional materials.

Brief Contents

Contents

 ▶ PowerPoint 97

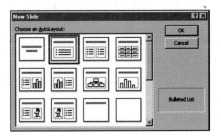

Contents

Modifying a Presentation   PP C-1

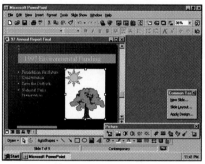

Contents

Enhancing Charts   PP F-1

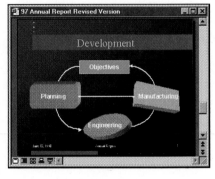

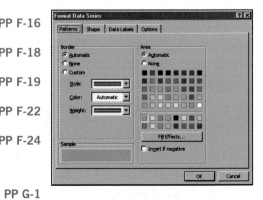

Working with Embedded and Linked Objects and Hyperlinks   PP G-1

Using Slide Show Features PP H-1

Contents

Working with Special PowerPoint Features

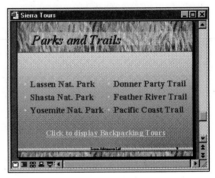

Getting
Started with PowerPoint 97

Objectives

► **Define presentation software**
► **Start PowerPoint 97**
► **Use the AutoContent Wizard**
► **View the PowerPoint window**
► **View your presentation**
► **Save your presentation**
► **Get Help**
► **Print and close the file, and exit PowerPoint**

Microsoft PowerPoint 97 is a presentation graphics program that transforms your ideas into professional, compelling presentations. With PowerPoint, you can create slides to display as an electronic slide show or as 35-mm slides and transparency masters to display on an overhead projector. Carrie Armstrong is a new executive assistant to the president of Nomad Ltd, an outdoor sporting gear and adventure travel company. She needs to familiarize herself with the basics of PowerPoint and learn how to use PowerPoint to create professional presentations.

Defining Presentation Software

A **presentation graphics program** is a computer program you use to organize and present information. Whether you are giving a sales pitch or explaining your company's goals and accomplishments, a presentation graphics program can help make your presentation effective and professional. You can use PowerPoint to create 35-mm slides, overheads, speaker's notes, audience handouts, outline pages, or on-screen presentations, depending on your specific presentation needs. Table A-1 explains the PowerPoint output capabilities. Carrie's boss, Lynn Shaw, has asked her to create a brief presentation about Nomad's new initiative to expand its business during the next year as part of Carrie's training. The company president will use the presentation at Nomad Ltd's next company meeting. Carrie is not familiar with PowerPoint so she gets right to work exploring its capabilities. Figure A-1 shows an overhead created using a word processor for the president's most recent presentation. Figure A-2 shows how the same overhead might look in PowerPoint. Carrie can easily complete the following tasks using PowerPoint:

Details

 Create slides to display information
With PowerPoint, information is presented on full-color slides with interesting backgrounds, layouts, and clipart. The impact of a full-color slide is more powerful than a traditional black and white overhead.

 Enter and edit data easily
Using PowerPoint, you can enter and edit data quickly and efficiently. When you need to change a part of your presentation, you can use the advanced word processing and outlining capabilities of PowerPoint to edit your content rather than re-create your presentation.

 Change the appearance of information
By exploring the capabilities of PowerPoint, you will discover how easy it is to change the appearance of your presentation. PowerPoint has many features that can transform the way text, graphics, and slides look.

 Organize and arrange information
Once you start using PowerPoint, you won't have to spend a lot of time making sure your information is correct and in the right order. With PowerPoint, you can quickly and easily rearrange and modify any piece of information in your presentation.

 Incorporate information from other sources
Often, when you create presentations, you will use information from other people. With PowerPoint, you can import information from a variety of sources, including spreadsheets, graphics, and word-processed files from programs such as Microsoft Excel, Microsoft Access, Microsoft Word, and WordPerfect.

 Show a presentation on any Windows 95 computer
PowerPoint has a powerful feature called the PowerPoint Viewer that you can use to show your presentation on computers running Windows 95 that do not have PowerPoint installed. The PowerPoint Viewer displays a presentation as an on-screen slide show.

FIGURE A-1: Traditional overhead

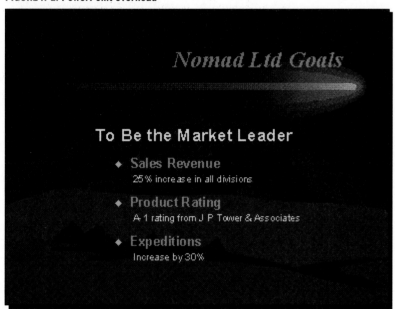

Nomad Ltd Goals

To Be the Market Leader
- Sales Revenue
  - 25% increase in all divisions
- Product Rating
  - A-1 rating from J P Tower & Associates
- Expeditions
  - Increase by 30%

FIGURE A-2: PowerPoint overhead

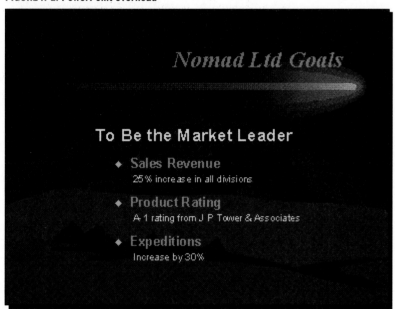

Nomad Ltd Goals

To Be the Market Leader
- Sales Revenue
  - 25% increase in all divisions
- Product Rating
  - A-1 rating from J P Tower & Associates
- Expeditions
  - Increase by 30%

TABLE A-1: PowerPoint output capabilities

output	method
On-screen presentations	Run a slide show directly from your computer.
35-mm slides	Use a film-processing bureau to convert PowerPoint slides to 35-mm slides.
Black-and-white overheads	Print PowerPoint slides directly to transparencies on your black-and-white printer.
Color overheads	Print PowerPoint slides directly to transparencies on your color printer.
Speaker notes	Print notes that help you remember points about each slide when you speak to a group.
Audience handouts	Print handouts with two, three, or six slides on a page.
Outline pages	Print the outline of your presentation to show the main points.

Starting PowerPoint 97

To start PowerPoint, you must first start Windows, then click Start on the taskbar and point to the Programs folder, which contains the PowerPoint program icon. PowerPoint is usually in the Programs folder, but on your computer it might be in a different location. If you are using a computer on a network, you might need to use a different starting procedure. You also can customize your starting procedure. Carrie starts PowerPoint to familiarize herself with the program.

Steps

1. Make sure your computer is on and the Windows desktop is visible
If any application windows are open, close them.

2. Click the Start button on the taskbar, then point to Programs
The Programs menu opens, displaying icons and names for all your programs, as shown in Figure A-3. Your screen might look different, depending on which programs are installed on your computer.

Trouble?
If you have trouble finding Microsoft PowerPoint on the Programs menu, check with your instructor or technical support person.

3. Click Microsoft PowerPoint on the Programs menu
PowerPoint starts, and the PowerPoint startup dialog box appears, as shown in Figure A-4. This allows you to choose how you want to create your presentation or to open an existing presentation. Don't worry if the animated character, called the Office Assistant, and the small window containing a list of Common Tasks do not appear on your screen. A previous user might have closed them. In the next lesson, you choose the AutoContent Wizard option in the PowerPoint startup dialog box to see how wizards can help you develop a presentation.

4. If a dialog box connected to the Office Assistant appears, click Close to close it.

FIGURE A-3: Programs menu

Your list of programs
might be different

Microsoft
PowerPoint program

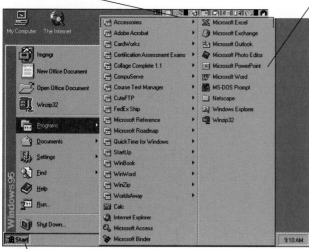

Start button

FIGURE A-4: Screen after starting PowerPoint

Common Tasks toolbar

Startup dialog box

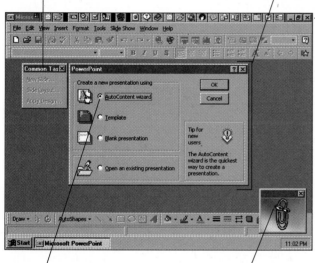

If you had a previous installation
of Office on your computer, your
screen may contain the Office 97
shortcut bar.

AutoContent Wizard
option button

Your screen may show
a different animated
character as the
Office Assistant

CLUES TO USE

Moving the PowerPoint shortcut to the desktop

PowerPoint comes with a shortcut that you can use to start it. To move this shortcut to the desktop, click Start, point to Programs, then click Windows Explorer. In the left section of the Exploring window, click the plus sign next to My Computer. The plus sign changes to a minus sign, and the drives and files on the computer are listed below it. Click the plus sign next to the icon representing the C: drive, then click the plus sign next to the Program Files folder.

(You might need to scroll down to see this folder.) Double-click the Microsoft Office folder. The list of files in the Microsoft Office folder opens in the right section of the window. Drag the PowerPoint shortcut directly to the desktop or to the icon representing the desktop in the left section of the Exploring window. Now you can start PowerPoint by double-clicking the icon on the desktop, without having to navigate through the Programs menu.

PowerPoint 97

Using the AutoContent Wizard

When PowerPoint first starts, the startup dialog box appears. The startup dialog box gives you four options for starting your presentation. See Table A-2 for an explanation of all the options in the PowerPoint startup dialog box. The first option, the AutoContent Wizard, is the quickest way to create a presentation. A **wizard** is a series of steps that guides you through a task (in this case, creating a presentation). Using the AutoContent Wizard, you choose a presentation type from the wizard's list of sample presentations. Then you indicate how the presentation will be used and what type of output you will need. Next, you type the information for the title slide. The AutoContent Wizard then creates a presentation with sample text you can use as a guide to help formulate the major points of your presentation.  Carrie decides to start her presentation by opening the AutoContent Wizard.

Steps

Trouble?

If the Office Assistant dialog box appears asking you if you want help with this feature, click No. If the Office Assistant is in the way, drag it over to the side of the screen.

1. **Click the AutoContent Wizard option button to select it, then click OK**
   The AutoContent Wizard dialog box opens, as shown in Figure A-5. The left section outlines the sections of the AutoContent Wizard and highlights the current screen name, and the text on the right side explains the purpose of the wizard.

2. **Click Next**
   The AutoContent Wizard dialog box opens the Presentation type screen. This screen contains categories and types of presentations. Each presentation type contains suggested text based on that particular use. By default, the category All is selected, and all the presentation types are listed.

3. **Click the category Projects, click Project Overview in the list box, then click Next**
   The Output options screen appears, asking how this presentation will be used.

4. **Click the Presentations, informal meetings, handouts option button to select it, then click Next**
   The Presentation style screen appears, asking you to indicate the type of output you would like.

5. **If necessary, click the On-screen presentation option button to select it, click the Yes option button to specify printed handouts, then click Next**
   The Presentation options screen requests information that will appear on the title slide of the presentation. Enter the presentation title and the president's name.

Trouble?

If the Office Assistant and the Common Tasks are in front of the slide, drag them to the positions shown in Figure A-6. If the Common Tasks commands (New Slide, Slide Layout, and Apply Design) appear in a bar at the bottom of the window, drag the bar up by the double lines on its left side until it becomes a window to the right of the slide.

6. **Click and drag the pointer over the text Title goes here to select it, type Nomad Business Expansion Project, press [Tab], type Bill Davidson, press [Tab], type Nomad Ltd, click Next, then click Finish at the bottom of the dialog box**
   The AutoContent Wizard displays the presentation outline with sample text based on the Project Overview presentation type you chose. Slide 1, containing the title slide information you just entered, is highlighted in the Outline. A reduced color version of Slide 1, called a **slide miniature**, appears on the right side of the screen in a window titled Color. Look at the slide more closely.

7. **Right-click the slide miniature, then click Go To Slide View on the pop-up menu**
   The presentation displays in Slide view, which shows one slide at a time. Finish the lesson by making sure your slide display matches the figures in this book.

8. **Click the Restore Window button in the Presentation window (in the menu bar), click the percentage number in the Zoom text box on the Standard toolbar, type 36, then press [Enter]**

9. **Click Window on the menu bar, then click Fit to Page**
   Compare your screen with Figure A-6.

FIGURE A-5: AutoContent Wizard opening dialog box

Current screen
name

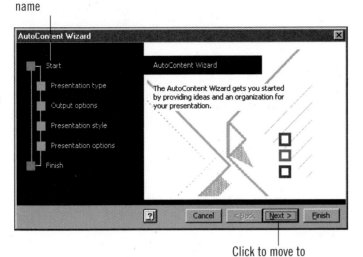

Click to move to
next screen

FIGURE A-6: Presentation window

Presentation window

Zoom text box

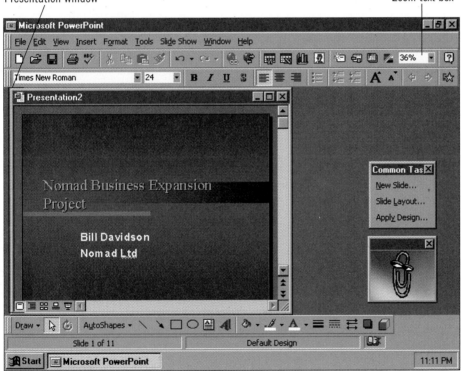

TABLE A-2: PowerPoint startup dialog box options

option	description
AutoContent Wizard	Helps you determine the content and organization of your presentation by creating a title slide and an outline using ready-made text for the category you choose.
Template	Opens the New Presentation dialog box, displaying PowerPoint presentation design templates and preformatted presentations. You can click a template to see a preview of it.
Blank presentation	Opens the New Slide dialog box, allowing you to choose a predesigned slide layout.
Open an existing presentation	Opens the Open dialog box, allowing you to open a previously created presentation. You can see a preview of a selected presentation before you open it.

Viewing the PowerPoint Window

After you make your selection in the PowerPoint startup dialog box, the Presentation window appears within the PowerPoint window, displaying the presentation you just created or opened. You use the toolbars, buttons, and menus in the PowerPoint window to view and develop your presentation. PowerPoint has different **views** that allow you to see your presentation in different forms. You move around in these views by using the scroll bars. You'll learn more about PowerPoint views in the next lesson. Carrie examines the elements of the PowerPoint window. Find and compare the elements described below, using Figure A-7 as a guide.

Details

 The title bar displays the program name and contains a program Control Menu button, resizing buttons, and the program Close button. The Office toolbar appears in the title bar.

 The menu bar contains the names of the menus you use to choose PowerPoint commands. Clicking a menu name on the menu bar displays a list of commands from which you can choose.

 The Standard toolbar contains buttons for the most frequently used commands, such as copying and pasting. Clicking buttons on a toolbar is often faster than using the menu. However, in some cases, using the menu offers additional options not available by clicking a button.

 The Formatting toolbar contains buttons for the most frequently used formatting commands, such as changing font type and size.

 The Presentation window is the "canvas" where you type text, work with lines and shapes, and view your presentation.

 The Common Tasks toolbar displays a menu of three common tasks typically performed in PowerPoint. These three commands have corresponding buttons on the Standard toolbar. The default position for this toolbar is floating, that is, not attached to one side of the window.

 The Office Assistant is an animated character that provides online Help. The character on your screen might be different. You can close the Assistant window, but it will reappear if you use online Help. If another user closed the Assistant, it may not appear on your screen.

 The Drawing toolbar, located below the Presentation window, contains buttons and menus that let you create lines, shapes, and special effects.

 The view buttons, to the left of the horizontal scroll bar, allow you to quickly switch between PowerPoint views.

 The status bar, located at the bottom of the PowerPoint window, displays messages about what you are doing and seeing in PowerPoint, including which slide you are viewing.

FIGURE A-7: Presentation window in Slide view

Title bar   Menu bar   Standard toolbar   Formatting toolbar   Presentation window

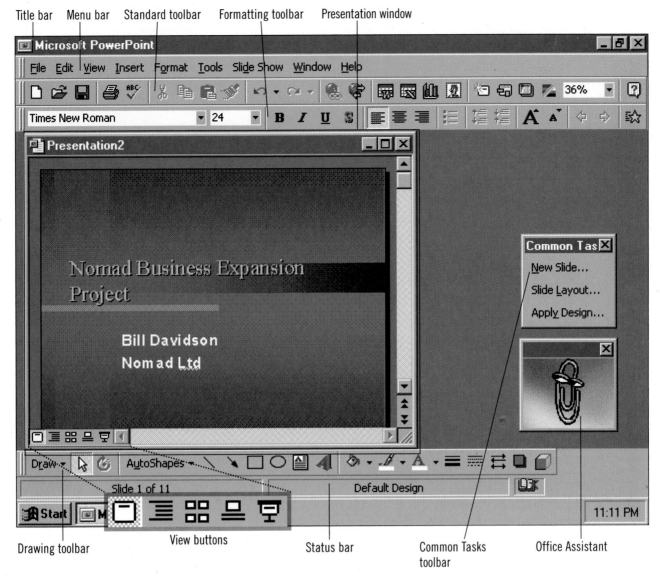

Drawing toolbar   View buttons   Status bar   Common Tasks toolbar   Office Assistant

Using the scroll bars

If you cannot see an entire slide on the screen, you need to **scroll**, or move, within a window to see more of the window contents. There are three ways to scroll in PowerPoint: click the scroll arrows to move one line at a time; click above or below the vertical scroll box or to the left or right of the horizontal scroll box to move one screen at a time; or drag the scroll boxes to move quickly to any point in the window.

Viewing Your Presentation

This lesson introduces you to the five PowerPoint views: Slide view, Outline view, Slide Sorter view, Notes Page view, and Slide Show view. Each PowerPoint view displays your presentation in a different way and allows you to manipulate your presentation differently. To move easily among the PowerPoint views, you use view buttons located at the bottom of the Presentation window, to the left of the horizontal scroll bar, as shown in Figure A-8. See Table A-3 for a brief description of the PowerPoint views and the view buttons. ◤━━ Carrie practices scrolling through her presentation and then switches to each PowerPoint view.

1. Drag the **scroll box** down the vertical scroll bar until the slide indicator box displays "Slide: 5 of 11, Competitive Analysis, cont.", then release the mouse button
See Figure A-8. The **slide indicator box** tells you which slide will appear when you release the mouse button. Now use the Previous Slide button to go to Slide 1.

2. Click the **Previous Slide button** ⚊ at the bottom of the vertical scroll bar until Slide 1 appears
The scroll box in the vertical scroll bar moves back up the scroll bar. The status bar indicates the view name and the number of the slide you are viewing. As you scroll through the presentation, notice the sample text on each slide created by the AutoContent Wizard.

QuickTip

You can also click view on the menu bar, then click the name of the view you want.

3. Click the **Outline View button** ▤ to the left of the horizontal scroll bar
PowerPoint switches to Outline view, displaying the outline of the presentation with Slide 1 selected. The slide miniature of the selected slide appears in the Color window. Compare your screen with Figure A-9. Notice that the name of the view appears in the status bar. To see the rest of the outline, scroll to the bottom of the outline.

4. Click the **down scroll arrow** until you reach the bottom of the outline
As you scroll through the presentation, notice that each of the 11 slides in the presentation is identified by a number along the left side of the outline.

5. Click the **Notes Page View button** ▣ to the left of the horizontal scroll bar
Outline view changes to Notes Page view, showing a reduced image of the title slide above a large box. You can enter text in this box and then print the notes page for your own use to help you remember important points about your presentation.

6. Click the **Slide Sorter View button** ▦ to the left of the horizontal scroll bar
A miniature image of each slide in the presentation appears in this view. You can examine the flow of your slides and easily move them to change their order.

7. Click the **Slide Show View button** ▱ to the left of the horizontal scroll bar
The first slide fills the entire screen. In this view, you can practice running through your slides so the presentation can be shown as an electronic slide show.

8. Click the **left mouse button** to advance to the next slide

QuickTip

To end a slide show before you reach the last slide, press [Esc] or right-click anywhere on the screen, then click End Show on the pop-up menu.

9. Press **[Spacebar]** or **[Enter]** to advance through the slides one at a time until you return to Slide Sorter view
After you view the last slide in Slide Show view, you are automatically returned to Slide Sorter view you were in before you ran the slide show.

FIGURE A-8: Slide view with slide indicator box

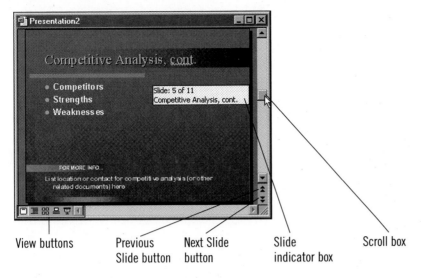

View buttons   Previous   Next Slide   Slide   Scroll box
                Slide button button   indicator box

FIGURE A-9: Outline view

Up scroll arrow   Slide miniature

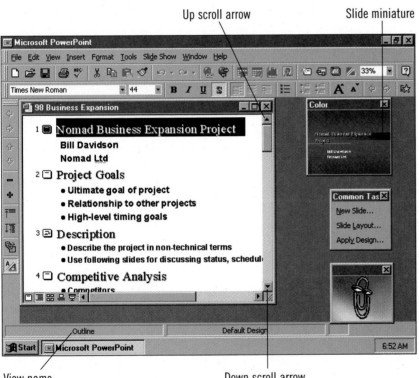

View name   Down scroll arrow

TABLE A-3: View buttons

button	button name	description
▫	Slide View	Displays one slide at a time; use this view to modify and enhance a slide's appearance.
≣	Outline View	Displays the title and main topics in the form of an outline; use this view to enter and edit the text of your presentation.
🔡	Slide Sorter View	Displays a miniature picture of each slide in the order in which they appear in your presentation; use this view to rearrange and add special effects to your slides.
🖳	Notes Page View	Displays a reduced slide image and a box to type notes; use this view to take notes on your slides that you can use during your presentation.
🖵	Slide Show View	Displays your presentation as an electronic slide show.

PowerPoint 97

Saving Your Presentation

To store your presentation permanently, you must save it as a file on a disk. As a general rule, you should save your work about every 10 or 15 minutes and before printing. In this lesson, you will save your presentation to your Student Disk. ◄▬▬▬ Carrie saves her presentation as 98 Business Expansion.

QuickTip

Make a copy of your Student Disk before you use it.

1. Click **File** on the menu bar, then click **Save As**
The Save As dialog box opens. See Figure A-10.

2. Make sure your Student Disk is in the appropriate drive, click the **Save in list arrow**, then click the drive that contains your Student Disk
A list of files on your Student Disk appears in the Look in list box, with the default filename placeholder in the Filename text box already selected.

Trouble?

If you see the three-letter extension .PPT on the filenames in the Save As dialog box, don't worry. Windows can be set up to display or not to display the file extensions.

3. Click in the File name text box to place the blinking insertion point, type **98 Business Expansion**, then click **Save**
PowerPoint adds the .PPT extension to the filename, even if it does not appear in the Save As dialog box. The Save As dialog box closes, and the new filename appears in the title bar at the top of the Presentation window. You decide you want to save the presentation in Outline view instead of in Slide Sorter view.

4. Click the **Outline View button** 🔲
The presentation view changes from Slide Sorter view to Outline view.

QuickTip

You also can press the shortcut key combination [Ctrl][S] to save a file quickly.

5. Click the **Save button** 🔲 on the Standard toolbar
The Save command saves any changes you made to the file to the same location you specified when you used the Save As command. Save your file frequently while working with it to protect the presentation.

FIGURE A-10: Save As dialog box

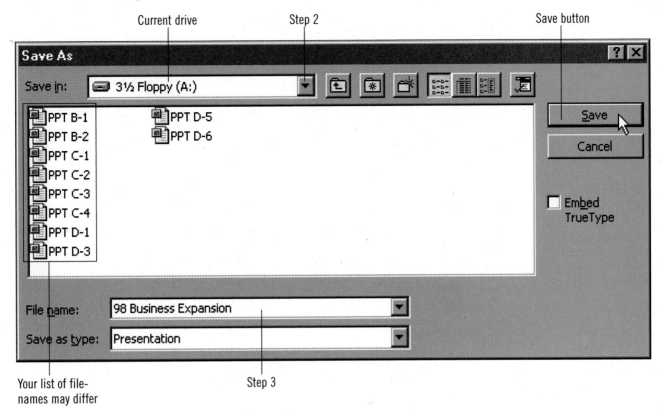

Current drive   Step 2   Save button

Your list of file-
names may differ   Step 3

Filenames and extensions

When you save a file, PowerPoint automatically adds the extension .PPT to the filename. However, the PowerPoint file extension does not appear in dialog boxes or in Windows Explorer unless you change the DOS file extension setting in the Windows Explorer Options dialog box (on the View menu in the Exploring window). Windows 95 allows you to have filenames up to 255 characters long and permits you to use lower or uppercase letters, symbols, numbers, and spaces.

Getting Help

PowerPoint has an extensive online Help system that gives you immediate access to definitions, reference information, and feature explanations. Help information appears in a separate window that you can move and resize. Carrie likes the way the AutoContent Wizard helped her create a presentation quickly, and she decides to find out more about it.

Steps

QuickTip

To quickly access the Office Assistant dialog box, click the Assistant animated character, click the Office Assistant button 🔃 on the Standard toolbar, or press [F1].

1. Click Help on the menu bar, then click Microsoft PowerPoint Help

If the Office Assistant wasn't already open, it opens. A balloon-shaped dialog box opens next to the Office Assistant, similar to Figure A-11. At the top of the dialog box, under the question "What would you like to do?" are topics related to what is on-screen and the last few commands you executed. Below the list of topics is a space for you to type a specific question. At the bottom of the dialog box are four buttons. Refer to Table A-4 for a description of these buttons. A lightbulb appears in the Assistant window whenever the Assistant has a context-sensitive tip.

2. Type AutoContent Wizard, then click Search

The dialog box closes and reopens with four topics related to the AutoContent Wizard listed under the head, "What would you like to do?"

3. Click Create a new presentation

A new Help window opens containing information about creating a new presentation. Read the information in the window, using the scroll bar as necessary.

4. Click Create a presentation based on suggested content and design under the head "What do you want to do?" at the bottom of the window

Another Help window opens listing the steps to follow for using the AutoContent Wizard. Read through the steps, scrolling as necessary. See Figure A-12.

5. Click the Help Topics button

The window closes, and a Help Topics dialog box opens. This dialog box contains three tabs: Contents, Index, and Find. The Contents tab contains Help topic organized in outline form. To open a Help window about a topic, double-click it. The Index tab contains an alphabetical list of Help topics. Type the word you want help on, and the list scrolls to that word. On the Find tab, you can search for a key word in all the Help topics. This is similar to how the Office Assistant works.

6. Click the Close button in the Help Topics dialog box to close it

The Help Topics dialog box closes, and you return to your presentation. Now close the Office Assistant window.

7. Click the Close button in the Office Assistant

The rest of the figures in this text will not show the Office Assistant.

QuickTip

You can quickly identify any item on-screen by clicking Help on the menu bar, then clicking What's This? The cursor turns to a help icon ℝ❓. The next screen item you click will display a definition of that item.

FIGURE A-11: Office Assistant dialog box

Topics related to current screen

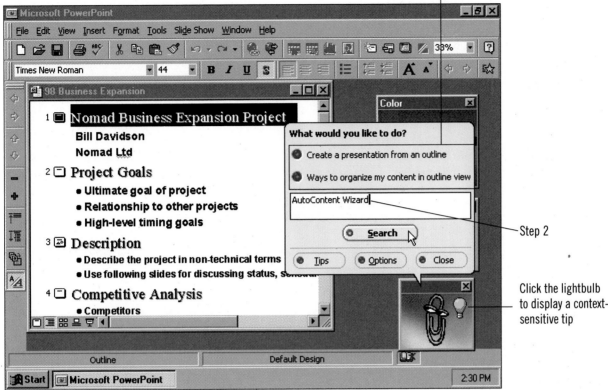

Step 2

Click the lightbulb to display a context-sensitive tip

FIGURE A-12: Help window

Close button

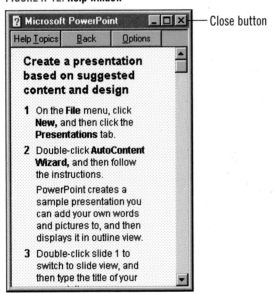

TABLE A-4: Buttons in the Office Assistant dialog box

button	description
Search	Searches all the PowerPoint Help topics for topics related to the words you type.
Tips	Displays the PowerPoint tips, starting with the Tip of the Day.
Options	Opens a dialog box allowing you to change Office Assistant options or change the animated character.
Close	Closes the Office Assistant dialog box.

Printing and Closing the File, and Exiting PowerPoint

You print your presentation when you have completed it or when you want to review your work. Reviewing hard copies of your presentation at different stages of production is helpful and gives you an overall perspective of your presentation's content and look. When you are finished working on your presentation, close the file containing your presentation and exit PowerPoint. Carrie needs to go to a meeting, so after saving her presentation, she prints the slides and notes pages of the presentation so she can review them later, and then closes the file and exits PowerPoint.

Steps

QuickTip

The options you choose in the Print dialog box are saved when you save your presentation. To quickly print the presentation with the most recently saved options, click the Print button 🖨 on the Standard toolbar.

1. Click File on the menu bar, then click Print

The Print dialog box opens, as shown in Figure A-13. In this dialog box, you can specify which parts of your presentation you want to print (slides, handouts, notes pages, etc.) as well as the number of pages to print and other print options.

2. Make sure the All option button is selected in the Print range section

3. Click the Print what list arrow and click Handouts (6 slides per page)

4. Click the Black & white check box to select it

If you have a black and white printer, the presentation will print in black and white, even if you don't check this option; however, checking this option causes PowerPoint to prepare the color slides for black and white output.

5. Click OK

The presentation prints on two pages. Now, print the notes pages.

6. Click File on the menu bar, then click Print

The Print dialog box opens again.

7. Click the Print what list arrow, click Notes Pages, then click OK

The Print dialog box closes, now close the presentation file; the note pages of your presentation prints.

QuickTip

Clicking the Close button in the Presentation window title bar closes the presentation. Clicking the Close button in the PowerPoint window title bar exits the program.

8. Click File on the menu bar, then click Close

If you have made changes to your presentation, a Microsoft PowerPoint alert box opens asking you if you want to save changes you have made to 98 Business Expansion, as shown in Figure A-14.

9. Click Yes to close the alert box

The Presentation window closes. Next, exit the PowerPoint program.

QuickTip

To exit PowerPoint and close the presentation at the same time, click File on the menu bar, then click Exit.

10. Click File on the menu bar, then click Exit

The PowerPoint program closes, and you return to the Windows desktop.

FIGURE A-13: **Print dialog box**

Step 2

Your printer name
may be different

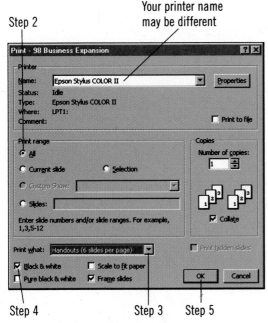

Step 4   Step 3   Step 5

FIGURE A-14: **Save changes alert box**

Presentation window
Close button

PowerPoint window
Close button

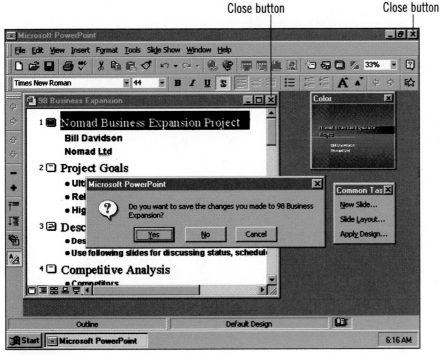

Viewing your presentation in black and white

Viewing your presentation in black and white is very useful when you will be printing a presentation on a black and white or grayscale printer. To see how your color presentation looks in black and white when you are in Outline view, right-click the slide miniature, then click Black and White view on the pop-up menu. In other views, click the Black and White View button ![icon] on the Standard toolbar. In Slide view and Notes Pages view, the slide miniature appears in color so you can compare the black and white version with the color version. To remove the slide miniature from the screen, click View, Slide Miniature or click the Close button in the slide miniature window.

Practice

► Concepts Review

Label the PowerPoint window elements shown in Figure A-15.

FIGURE A-15

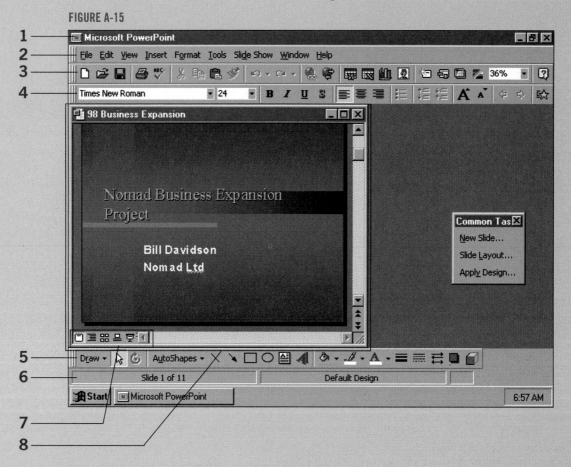

Match each term with the statement that describes its function.

a. AutoContent Wizard
b. Presentation window
c. Zoom box
d. Fit to Page
e. Slide indicator box

9. The area where you work on your presentation.
10. Identifies slide title and number.
11. Series of dialog boxes that guides you through creating a presentation and produces a presentation with suggestions for content.
12. Command that automatically sizes the Presentation window on the screen.
13. Lets you change the magnification of a slide.

Select the best answer from the list of choices.

14. **PowerPoint can help you create all of the following, *except:***
    a. 35-mm slides.
    b. Movies.
    c. An on-screen presentation.
    d. Outline pages.

15. **The buttons you use to switch between the PowerPoint views are called:**
    a. PowerPoint buttons.
    b. View buttons.
    c. Screen buttons.
    d. Toolbar buttons.

16. **All of these are PowerPoint views, *except:***
    a. Slide view.
    b. Notes Pages view.
    c. Outline view.
    d. Current Page view.

17. **The animated character that appears on the screen when you click the Help button is the:**
    a. Office Helper.
    b. Office Assistant.
    c. Assistant Paper Clip.
    d. PowerPoint Assistant.

18. **The view that allows you to view your electronic slide show with each slide filling the entire screen is called:**
    a. Electronic view.
    b. Slide Sorter view.
    c. Presentation view.
    d. Slide Show view.

19. **Which wizard helps you create and outline your presentation?**
    a. Pick a Look Wizard
    b. Presentation Wizard
    c. AutoContent Wizard
    d. OrgContent Wizard

20. **How do you switch to Slide view?**
    a. Click the Slide View button to the left of the horizontal scroll bar.
    b. Click View on the menu bar, then click Slide.
    c. Right-click the slide miniature in Outline view, then click Go To Slide View on the pop-up menu.
    d. All of the above are true.

21. **How do you save your presentation after you have saved it for the first time?**
    a. Click Save As on the File menu, then assign it a new name.
    b. Click the Save button on the toolbar.
    c. Click Save As on the File menu, then click Save.
    d. Click Save As on the File menu, specify a new location and filename, then click Save.

Skills Review

1. **Start PowerPoint and use the AutoContent Wizard to create a sample presentation on a topic of your choice.**
   a. Click the Start button on the Taskbar, then point to the Programs folder.
   b. Click Microsoft PowerPoint.
   c. If the Tip of the Day dialog box appears, click Close.
   d. Click the AutoContent Wizard option button, then click OK.
   e. Read the information in the AutoContent Wizard dialog box, then click Next.
   f. Select a presentation category and type, then click Next.
   g. Click the output options of your choice, then click Next.
   h. Click the presentation style of your choice, then click Next.
   i. Enter a presentation title and your name and any additional information you want to appear on the title slide, then click Next.
   j. Click Finish.

2. **View the PowerPoint window and explore the PowerPoint views.**
   a. Click the Slide View button and adjust the Zoom to 36%, click the Restore button in the Presentation window, click Window on the menu bar, then click Fit to Page.
   b. Identify as many elements of the PowerPoint window as you can without referring to the unit material.
   c. Use the Next and Previous Slide buttons to move up and down the slides of your presentation to view its content.
   d. When you are finished, drag the scroll box in the vertical scroll bar up to Slide 1.
   e. Click the Outline View button.
   f. Use the down scroll arrow to view the contents of all your slides.
   g. Click the Notes Page View button, then click the Next Slide button repeatedly to view all your notes pages.
   h. After you finish exploring the presentation, drag the elevator to Slide 1.
   i. Click the Slide Sorter View button, and examine your slides.
   j. Click the Slide Show button. The first slide of your presentation fills the screen. Advance through the slide show by clicking the left mouse button or by pressing [Enter].

3. **Save your presentation.**
   a. Change to the view in which you would like to save your presentation.
   b. Click File on the menu bar, and click Save As.
   c. Make sure your floppy disk is in the correct drive.
   d. Type "Practice Presentation" in the File name text box.
   e. Click Save.
   f. Click a different view button than the one you saved your presentation in.
   g. Click the Save button on the Standard toolbar.

4. **Explore PowerPoint Help.**
   a. If the Office Assistant is open, click it. If it is not on your screen, click the Office Assistant button on the Standard toolbar.
   b. Type "Tell me about Help" in the text box and click Search.
   c. Click the topic, "Get Help without the Office Assistant."
   d. After reading the information in the Help window, click the Help Topics button at the top of the window.
   e. Click the Contents tab in the Help Topics dialog box.
   f. Double-click any Help topics (identified by book icons) you wish to explore to display the Help subjects (identified by page icons).
   g. Double-click the page icons to review the Help information.
   h. Click the Help Topics button to return to the main Help Topics dialog box. Explore a number of topics that interest you.
   i. When you have finished exploring the Contents tab, click the Index tab.
   j. Type a word in the text box with the blinking insertion point.
   k. Click a word in the list box if the highlighted word is not the word you want to look up, then click Display.
   l. Click the Help Topics button to return to the main Help Topics dialog box. Explore a number of topics that interest you.
   m. When you have finished exploring the Index tab, click the Help window Close button.

5. **Print your presentation, close the file, and exit PowerPoint.**
   a. Click File on the menu bar, then click Print.
   b. Click the Print what list arrow, and click Handouts (3 slides per page).
   c. Make sure the Black & white check box is selected, and click OK.
   d. Click File on the menu bar, then click Print.
   e. Click the Print what list arrow, and click Outline View.
   f. Click OK.
   g. Click File on the menu bar, then click Close.
   h. Click No if you see a message asking if you want to save the changes.
   i. Click File on the menu bar, then click Exit.

► Independent Challenges

1. You have just gotten a job as a marketing assistant at Events, Inc., a catering firm specializing in clambakes and barbecues for large company events. John Hudspeth, the marketing manager, has some familiarity with PowerPoint. He has heard that you can print a presentation on a black-and-white printer, but he wants to know just what happens to the text, backgrounds, and so forth when they are converted to black and white.

To complete this independent challenge:

1. If PowerPoint is not already running, start it. When the startup dialog box appears, click Cancel. If PowerPoint is already running, go to Step 2.
2. Use PowerPoint Help to find the answer to John's question.
3. Write down which Help feature you used (Office Assistant, Index, etc.), and the steps you followed.
4. Print the Help window that shows the information you found. (*Hint*: Click the Options button at the top of the Help window, then click Print Topic and click OK in the Print dialog box that appears.)
5. Exit PowerPoint. Turn in the printed Help window and your notes.

2. You are in charge of marketing for ArtWorks, Inc, a medium-sized company that produces all types of art for corporations to enhance their work environment. The company has a regional sales area that includes three neighboring northeastern states. The president of ArtWorks is working on a proposal for American Digital, a national electronics firm, to supply artwork for all their 20 locations. You are given the responsibility of planning and creating the outline of the PowerPoint presentation the president will use to convey his proposal to American Digital.

Create an outline that reflects the major points ArtWorks needs to communicate to American Digital to secure this large contract. Assume the following: ArtWorks needs to promote their company and products to American Digital; ArtWorks supplies all types of artwork, from classic and contemporary posters and reproductions of old masters, to original artwork; and the ArtWorks proposal includes classic posters and art reproductions.

To complete this independent challenge:

1. Start PowerPoint if necessary and choose the AutoContent Wizard option button. (*Hint:* If PowerPoint is already running, click File on the menu bar, click New, click the Presentations tab and double-click AutoContent Wizard.)
2. Choose the Sales/Marketing category, then choose an appropriate presentation type from the list.
3. Scroll through the outline the AutoContent Wizard produced. Does it contain the type of information you thought it would?
4. Plan how you would change and add to the sample text created by the wizard. What information do you need to promote ArtWorks to a large company?
5. Take notes on how you might change the outline text.
6. Switch views. Run through the slide show at least once.
7. Save your presentation to your Student Disk with a meaningful name.
8. Print your presentation as Handouts (3 slides per page).
9. Close and exit PowerPoint. Hand in your notes for promoting ArtWorks along with your presentation.

3. You have recently been promoted to sales manager at Buconjic Industries. Part of your job is to train sales representatives to go to potential customers and give presentations describing your company's products. Your boss wants you to review the Dale Carnegie presentation techniques provided with PowerPoint 97 and describe some of the techniques at the next departmental meeting.

You decide to first review the Dale Carnegie information in PowerPoint Central. PowerPoint Central is a read-only slide show that provides you with extra clip art, templates, and other items available on the Office 97 CD-ROM and the World Wide Web (WWW). Then, you will review the Dale Carnegie information in the AutoContent Wizard.

To complete this independent challenge:

1. Start PowerPoint if necessary.
2. Click Tools on the menu bar, then click PowerPoint Central. Click the Magazine button at the top of the presentation window to open the Dale Carnegie mini-course. Click the right-arrow button at the bottom of the window to move through the slides. See Figure A-16. Take notes as you move through the slide show. When you reach the end of the slide show, click the Close button in the Presentation window.
3. Start the AutoContent Wizard (*Hint:* Click File on the menu bar, click New, click the presentations tab, then double-click AutoContent Wizard.) Choose Carnegie Coach in the Category list on the Presentation type screen, then choose Presentation Guidelines in the list box. Give the presentation an appropriate title, and add your name to the title slide.
4. View the presentation in any view you like, then run through the slide show. Read the guidelines offered and note the graphics on the slides.
5. Write a brief memo to your boss explaining the techniques you think will be most helpful. Print any screens from the presentation you created using the AutoContent Wizard that support your recommendations.
6. Exit PowerPoint without saving the presentation and submit your memo and any printouts.

FIGURE A-16

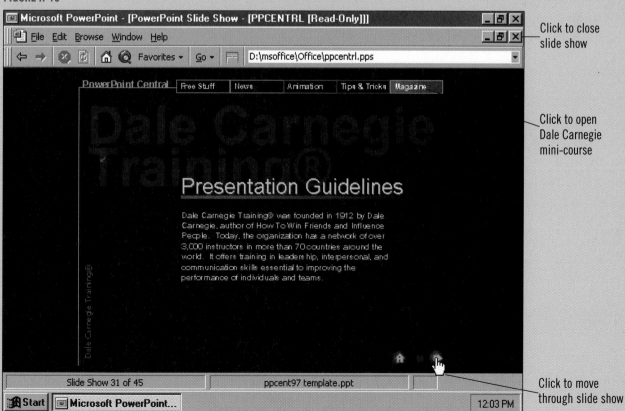

4. You are a marketing assistant for AllCare, a health maintenance organization (HMO) in Memphis, Tennessee. The management of AllCare is interested in expanding its service area to cover areas in the state that are currently underserved by existing health care organizations. The marketing director, Monica Spitz, has heard that you can use PowerPoint 97 to create presentations on the Internet and would like you to learn about it and give her a brief overview of the subject at the next departmental meeting.

You decide to learn the basics from the PowerPoint Office Assistant, then explore the Internet yourself to get a better feel for the subject. Then you will be better able to discuss the topic at the meeting.

To complete this independent challenge:

1. Start PowerPoint if necessary, and use the Office Assistant Search feature. Enter the word "Internet" in the Office Assistant dialog box.
2. When the Assistant displays a list of topics, select the topic, "Presentations on the Internet."
3. Read the information in the Help window that appears, noting how you can open a PowerPoint presentation on the Internet or an intranet, how you can use the Web toolbar and hyperlinks, and how you can publish a presentation on the World Wide Web (WWW).
4. Log on to the Internet and use your browser to go to http://www.course.com. From there, click the link Student On Line Companions, then click the Microsoft Office 97 Professional Edition—Illustrated: A First Course page, then click on the PowerPoint link for Unit A
5. Print the book Web page.
6. Click the Unit A link, and click any link to see what a presentation looks like on the Web. Click any links in the presentation that you want to follow.
7. Log off the Internet, and write a brief memo to Monica, explaining how presentations on the Web and the use of Web features can be useful to AllCare's marketing efforts. Describe the presentation that you saw on the links you followed. Attach any Web page printouts that support your recommendations.
9. Exit PowerPoint and submit your memo and attached printouts.

Creating
a Presentation

- ► **Plan an effective presentation**
- ► **Choose a look for a presentation**
- ► **Enter slide text**
- ► **Create a new slide**
- ► **Work in Outline view**
- ► **Enter text in Notes Page view**
- ► **Check spelling in the presentation**
- ► **Evaluate your presentation**

Now that you are familiar with PowerPoint basics, you are ready to plan and create your own presentation. To do this, you enter and edit text and choose a slide design. PowerPoint helps you accomplish these tasks with the AutoContent Wizard, which supplies sample text for a number of different presentation situations, and with a collection of professionally prepared slide designs, called **presentation design templates**, which can contribute to the look of your presentation. In this unit, you will create a presentation using a presentation design template. ✒ Carrie Armstrong's next assignment is to create the Annual Report the president will present at a shareholders' meeting later in the month. She begins by choosing a design template.

Planning an effective presentation

Before you create a presentation using PowerPoint, you need to plan and outline the message you want to communicate and consider how you want the presentation to look. When preparing the outline, you need to consider where you are giving the presentation and who your primary audience will be. It is also important to know what resources you might need, such as a computer or projection equipment. Using Figure B-1 and the planning guidelines below, follow Carrie as she outlines the presentation message.

Details

 Determine the purpose of the presentation and the location and audience
The company president needs to present the highlights of Nomad's Annual Report at a shareholders' meeting in a large hall at the Plaza Center Inn.

 Determine the type of output—black and white (B&W) or color overhead transparencies, on-screen slide show, or 35-mm slides—that best conveys your message, given time constraints and computer hardware availability
Since the president is speaking in a large hall and has access to a computer and projection equipment, an on-screen slide show is the best choice.

 Determine a look for your presentation that will help communicate your message
You can choose one of the professionally designed templates that come with PowerPoint, modify an existing PowerPoint template, or create one of your own. Your template should be appropriate for a corporate audience and should reinforce a message of confidence and accomplishment.

 Determine the message you want to communicate, then give the presentation a meaningful title and outline your message
The president wants to highlight the previous year's accomplishments and set the goals for the coming year. See Figure B-1.

 Determine what other materials will be useful in addition to the presentation
You need to prepare not only the slides themselves, but supplementary materials, including speaker's notes and handouts for the audience. Speaker's notes will allow the president to stay on track and deliver a concise message.

FIGURE B-1: Outline of the text in the presentation

1. Annual Report Executive Summary
   -Bill Davidson
   -June 18, 1998
2. Summary
   -1997 Accomplishments
   -1998 Goals
3. 1997 Accomplishments
   -Product sales up 23.9%
   -Expeditions up 10.4%
   -Environmental funding up 6.4%
4. 1998 Goals
   -Increase product sales 28%
   -Increase expeditions 15%
   -Increase environmental funding 8%

PowerPoint 97

Choosing a look for a presentation

To help you design your presentation, PowerPoint provides over 75 templates so you don't have to spend time creating the right presentation look. A **design template** has borders, colors, text attributes, and other elements arranged in a specific format that is applied to all the slides in your presentation. You can use a design template as is, or you can modify any element to suit your needs. Unless you know something about graphic arts, it is often easier and faster to use or modify one of the templates supplied with PowerPoint. No matter how you create your presentation, you can save it as a template for future use. ✒ Carrie doesn't have a lot of time but wants to create a good-looking presentation, so she uses an existing PowerPoint template.

Steps

1. Start PowerPoint, click the Template option button in the PowerPoint startup dialog box, then click OK

The New Presentation dialog box opens, containing four tabs. See Table B-1 for an overview of the tab contents.

2. Click the Presentation Designs tab

This displays 17 of the PowerPoint presentation design templates.

3. Click the Contemporary template icon once

A miniature version of the selected template appears in the Preview box on the right side of the dialog box, as shown in Figure B-2.

4. Click OK

The New Slide dialog box opens, displaying 24 AutoLayouts. An **AutoLayout** is a slide containing placeholders for text and graphics. The first layout is selected, and its name, Title Slide, appears on the right side of the dialog box. Since the first slide of the presentation is the **title slide**, this layout is appropriate.

5. Click OK

A blank title slide, containing placeholders for title and subtitle text, fills the Presentation window. The background of the slide is the Contemporary design template you chose. Notice that the name of the template is in the status bar. Now, restore your window so it will look like the figures in this book.

6. Click the Restore window button on the Presentation window, click the percentage number in the Zoom text box, type 36 and press [Enter], click Window on the menu bar, then click Fit to Page

If the Common Tasks toolbar is on top of the Presentation window, drag it to the right of the screen. Compare your screen with Figure B-3 and make any adjustments necessary, then save the presentation.

7. Click the Save button 🖫 on the Standard toolbar, then save your presentation as 97 Annual Report 1

Presentation templates versus presentation design templates

A **presentation design template** contains a background design, a color scheme, and text placeholders, like the box labeled "Click to add title" in Figure B-3. A **presentation template** contains a background design, a color scheme, and content, sample text for a particular type of presentation. You choose a presentation template when you use the AutoContent Wizard.

FIGURE B-2: Presentation Designs tab in the New Presentation dialog box

PowerPoint templates available to supply the look for your presentation

Contemporary template selected

Miniature version of selected template appears here

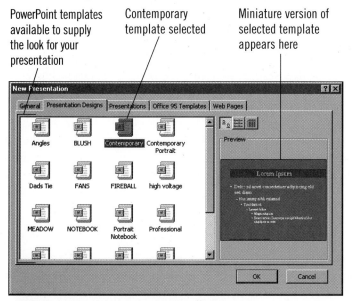

FIGURE B-3: Title slide with new template design

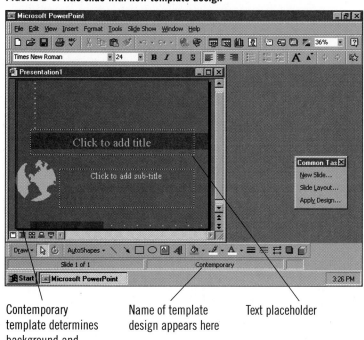

Contemporary template determines background and arrangement of text

Name of template design appears here

Text placeholder

TABLE B-1: New Presentation dialog box tabs

tab	contains	use
General	A blank presentation	When you want to create your own presentation, including backgrounds and text formats
Presentation Designs	17 design templates with backgrounds and text formats	When you want to use predesigned templates, so you know the text and graphic design will coordinate well with each other
Presentations	33 design templates that contain suggested content for specific uses. Some templates are available in both a standard version and an Internet version	When you want both a predesigned template design and content guidance
Web Pages	Two Web page banners	When you are designing your own Web page and want a professionally designed banner

Entering slide text

Now that you have applied a template to your presentation, you are ready to enter text into the title slide. The title slide has two **text placeholders**, boxes with dashed line borders where you enter text. Also, the title slide has a **title placeholder** labeled "Click to add title" and a **main text placeholder** labeled "Click to add sub-title" where you enter additional information, such as your company name or department. To enter text in a placeholder, simply click the placeholder and then type your text. After you enter text in a placeholder, the placeholder becomes a text object. An **object** is any item on a slide that can be manipulated. Objects are the building blocks that make up a presentation slide. ✎ Carrie begins working on the president's presentation by entering the title of the presentation in the title placeholder.

Steps

1. **Move the pointer over the title placeholder labeled "Click to add title"**
   The pointer changes to I when you move the pointer over the placeholder. The pointer changes shape, depending on the task you are trying to accomplish. Table B-2 describes the functions of the most common PowerPoint mouse pointer shapes.

2. **Click the title placeholder**
   The **insertion point**, a blinking vertical line, indicates where your text will appear in the title placeholder. A **selection box**, the slanted line border, appears around the title placeholder, indicating that it is selected and ready to accept text. See Figure B-4. Enter the presentation title.

3. **Type Annual Report, press [Enter], then type Executive Summary**
   PowerPoint centers the title text within the title placeholder, now called a text object. Pressing [Enter] in a text object moves the insertion point down to begin a new line of text.

4. **Click the main text placeholder**
   Enter the name and job title of Nomad's president and the meeting date in the main text placeholder.

5. **Type Bill Davidson, press [Enter], type President, press [Enter], then type June 18, 1998**
   Compare your title slide with Figure B-5.

6. **Click outside the main text object in a blank area of the slide**
   Clicking a blank area of the slide deselects all selected objects on the slide.

7. **Click the Save button 🖫 on the Standard toolbar to save your changes**

Trouble?

If you press a wrong key, press [Backspace] to erase the character, then continue to type. If you make a typing error and press [Spacebar] or [Enter], you may see a wavy, red line under the word. This simply means that the automatic spellchecking feature in PowerPoint is active.

TABLE B-2: PowerPoint mouse pointer shapes

shape	description
⬉	Appears when you select the Selection tool; use this pointer to select one or more PowerPoint objects
I	Appears when you move the pointer over a text object; use this pointer, called the I-beam, to place the insertion point where you want to begin typing or selecting text
✛	Appears when you move the pointer over a bullet, slide icon, or object; use this pointer to select title or paragraph text
+	Appears when you select a drawing tool; use this pointer, called the cross-hair cursor, to draw shapes

FIGURE B-4: Selected title placeholder

Title placeholder   Insertion point   Selection box

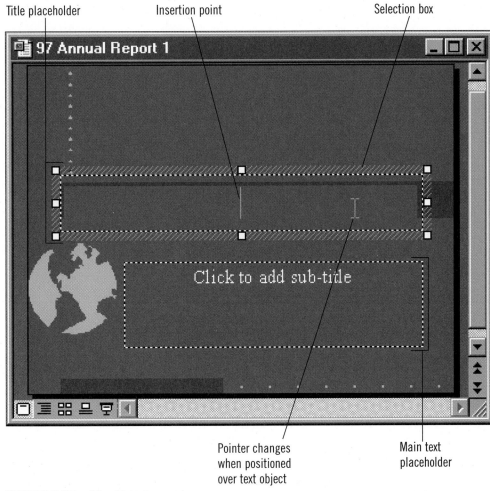

Pointer changes   Main text
when positioned   placeholder
over text object

FIGURE B-5: Title slide with text

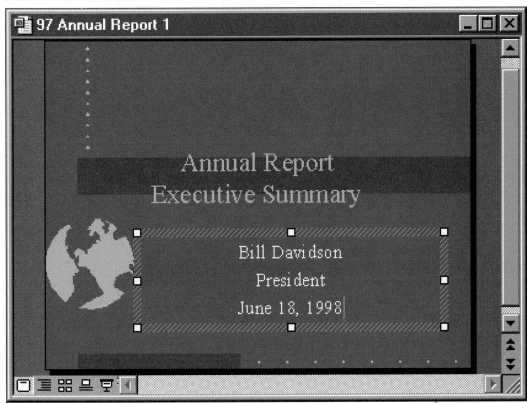

Creating a new slide

To help you create a new slide easily, PowerPoint offers 24 predesigned AutoLayouts, which include a variety of placeholder arrangements for objects including titles, main text, clip art, graphs, charts, and media clips. You have already used the title slide AutoLayout. See Table B-3 for an explanation of the different placeholders you'll find in the AutoLayouts. To continue developing the presentation, Carrie needs to create a slide that displays the topic headings for the president's presentation.

Steps

QuickTip

You also can click the Insert New Slide button 📋 on the Standard toolbar.

QuickTip

To add a new slide with the same layout as the current slide, press and hold [Shift], then click New Slide on the Common Tasks toolbar, or click 📋.

1. Click New Slide on the Common Tasks toolbar

The New Slide dialog box opens, displaying the different AutoLayouts. (Click the down scroll arrow to view more.) This is the same dialog box that appeared when you chose the title slide layout. The title for the selected AutoLayout appears in a Preview box to the right of the layouts, as shown in Figure B-6. You can choose the best layout by clicking it. Use the Bulleted List AutoLayout, which is already selected.

2. Click OK

A new slide appears after the current slide in your presentation, displaying a title placeholder and a main text placeholder for the bulleted list. Notice that the status bar displays Slide 2 of 2. Enter a title for this slide.

3. Click the title placeholder, then type Summary

4. Click the main text placeholder

This deselects the title text object. The insertion point appears next to a bullet in the main text placeholder. Enter the first two topic headings for the president's presentation.

5. Type 1997 Accomplishments, then press [Enter]

A new bullet automatically appears when you press [Enter].

6. Type 1998 Goals

7. Click outside the main text object in a blank area of the slide to deselect the main text object

Compare your slide to Figure B-7.

8. Click the Save button 🔲 on the Standard toolbar

Your changes are saved.

FIGURE B-6: **New Slide dialog box**

Default AutoLayout

Title of selected
AutoLayout

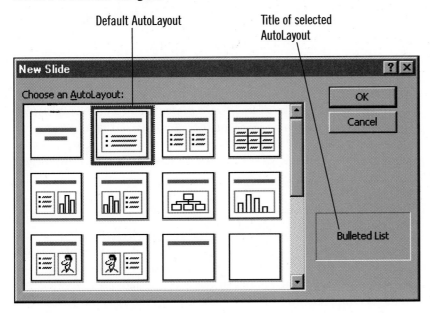

FIGURE B-7: **New slide with bulleted list**

Bulleted list

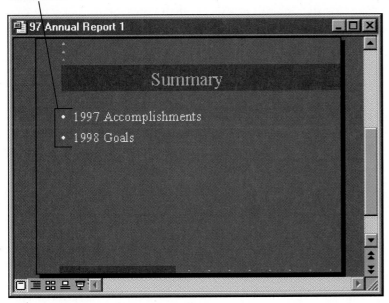

TABLE B-3: **AutoLayout placeholder types**

placeholder	symbol	description
Bulleted List		Displays a short list of related points
Clip Art		Inserts a picture, such as PowerPoint clip art
Chart		Inserts a chart that uses standard Microsoft chart techniques
Organization Chart		Inserts an organizational chart
Table		Inserts a table from Microsoft Word
Media clip		Inserts a music, sound, or video clip
Object		Inserts an external object such as WordArt, an equation, a spreadsheet, or a picture

Working in Outline view

In PowerPoint, you can enter your presentation text in Slide view or in Outline view. **Outline view** displays the titles and main text of all the slides in your presentation. As in a regular outline, the headings, or **titles**, appear first; then under them, the subpoints, or **main text**, appear. The main text appears as one or more lines of bulleted text under a title. Carrie entered the first two slides of her presentation in Slide view. Now, she switches to Outline view to enter text for two more slides.

Steps

1. **Click the Outline View button ▤ to the left of the horizontal scroll bar**
The outline fills the Presentation window with the title of Slide 2 selected (the slide you just created). The Outlining toolbar appears on the left side of the PowerPoint window, and the Drawing toolbar no longer appears at the bottom of the window. Table B-4 describes the buttons available on the Outlining toolbar. The slide miniature window appears to the right of the outline. Now, enter the text for the third slide. Since the third slide is a bulleted list like the second slide, insert a new slide with the same layout as Slide 2.

2. **Press [Shift] and click New Slide in the Common Task window**
Pressing [Shift] while clicking New Slide inserts a new slide with the same AutoLayout as the current slide. A symbol called a **slide icon** appears next to the slide number when you add a new slide to the outline. See Figure B-8. Text you enter next to a slide icon becomes the title for that slide.

3. **Type 1997 Accomplishments, then press [Enter]**
A new slide is inserted. You want to enter the main text for the Accomplishments slide; so you need to indent this line.

4. **Click the Demote button ➡ on the Outlining toolbar**
The slide icon changes to a bullet and indents one level to the right.

5. **Type Product sales up 23.9%, then press [Enter]; type Expeditions up 10.4%, then press [Enter]; type Environmental funding up 6.4%, then press [Ctrl][Enter]**
Pressing [Ctrl][Enter] while the cursor is in the main text creates a new slide with the same layout as the previous slide.

6. **Type 1998 Goals, then press [Ctrl][Enter]; type Increase product sales 28%, then press [Enter]; type Increase environmental funding 8% then press [Enter]; type Increase expeditions 15%**
Pressing [Ctrl][Enter] while the cursor is in title text creates a bullet. Two of the bulleted points you just typed for Slide 4 are out of order. Move them into the correct position.

7. **Position the pointer to the left of the last bullet in Slide 4, then click the mouse button**
The pointer changes from I to ✛. PowerPoint selects the entire line of text.

8. **Click the Move Up button ⬆ on the Outlining toolbar**
The third bullet point moves up one line and trades places with the second bullet point, as shown in Figure B-9. Now look at the slide you just created in Slide view.

9. **Double-click the slide icon for Slide 4, then click the Previous Slide button ⬆ below the vertical scroll bar three times to view each slide**
Double-clicking the slide icon in Outline view switches you to Slide view. When you are finished viewing all the slides, Slide 1 of 4 should appear in the status bar.

QuickTip
You can also press [Tab] to indent text one level.

Trouble?
If you accidentally pressed [Enter] after typing the last bullet, press [Backspace], then press [Ctrl][Enter].

QuickTip
You can also drag slide icons or bullets to a new location.

Time To
✔ Save

FIGURE B-8: Outline view

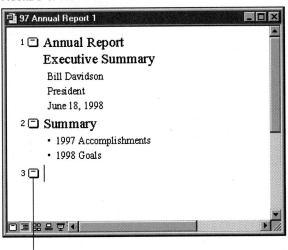

Slide icon

FIGURE B-9: Bulleted item moved up in Outline view

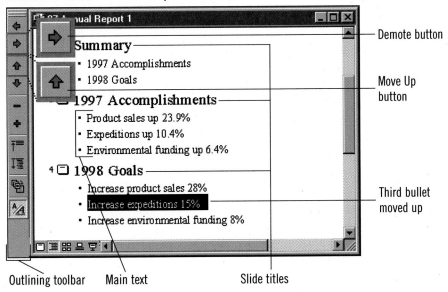

Demote button

Move Up button

Third bullet moved up

Outlining toolbar   Main text   Slide titles

TABLE B-4: Outlining toolbar commands

button	button name	description
⬅	**Promote**	Indents selected text one tab to the left
➡	**Demote**	Indents selected text one tab to the right
⬆	**Move Up**	Moves the selection above the previous line
⬇	**Move Down**	Moves the selection below the next line
−	**Collapse**	Displays only the titles of the selected slide
+	**Expand**	Displays all levels of the selected slide
⮝≡	**Collapse All**	Displays only the titles of all slides
⮟≣	**Expand All**	Displays all levels of all slides
▣	**Summary Slide**	Creates a new bulleted slide containing only the titles of selected slides. Good for creating an agenda slide
ᴬ⟋A	**Show Formatting**	Displays or hides all character formatting

Entering text in Notes Page view

To help you give your presentation in front of a group, you can create speaker's notes that accompany your slides so you don't have to rely on your memory. Notes Page view displays a reduced slide image and a text placeholder, where you enter the notes for each slide of your presentation. The notes you enter there do not appear on the slides themselves; they are private notes. You also can print these pages. To make sure the president doesn't forget key points of his presentation, Carrie enters notes for some of the slides.

Steps

QuickTip

If you want to provide pages on which your audience can take notes, print the Notes Pages, but leave the text placeholder blank.

1. Click the Notes Page View button

The view of your presentation changes from Slide view to Notes Page view, as shown in Figure B-10.

2. Click the text placeholder below the slide image

The insertion point appears, indicating the placeholder is ready to accept your text. The insertion point is small and difficult to see, so increase the view size.

3. Click the Zoom list arrow on the Standard toolbar, then click 66%

The text placeholder increases in size. Now that the text placeholder is larger and easier to see, enter the notes for Slide 1. In the next step, make sure you type "Welcome" without the "e" as shown.

4. Type Welcom to the 1997 Annual Report meeting for shareholders and employees.

The red, wavy line under the word "Welcom" means that this word is not in the Microsoft Office spellchecker dictionary. In the next step, make sure you misspell the word "Nomd," as shown.

Trouble?

If you don't see a red, wavy line under the word "Welcom," don't worry. Someone else may have turned this feature off on your machine.

5. Click the Next Slide button below the vertical scroll bar, click the text placeholder, then type The main purpose of this meeting is to share with you the exciting accomplishments Nomd Ltd has achieved in the last year, as well as our goals for 1998.

As you type, text automatically wraps to the next line.

6. Click to go to the third slide, click the text placeholder, then type Due to our record year in 1996, Nomad's 1997 goals were very aggressive. Let's see how we did. Our award-winning OutBack camping gear series has continued to do well and helped push overall product sales up almost 24%. New Directions, our travel subsidiary, has seen an increase in expeditions of over 10%, and we have increased our support for environmental causes over 6%.

7. Click , click the text placeholder, type, As a result of our accomplishments over the last year, we have set even higher goals for 1998. We are confident that we can achieve a sales increase of 28%, increase expeditions 15%, with the help of the incredible marketing and location development strategies of New Directions, and increase our environmental funding 8%.

8. Press [Enter], then type I would like to thank you all for your hard work and support, and I look forward to working with you all in 1998.

Slide 4 in Notes Page view is shown in Figure B-11.

Time To

✔ Save

FIGURE B-10: Notes Page view

Text placeholder

Reduced slide image

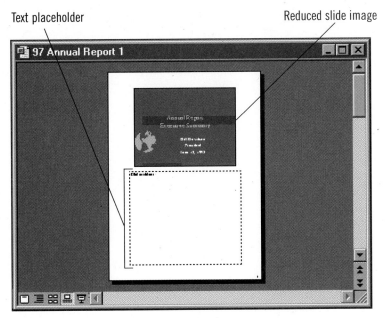

FIGURE B-11: Slide 4 in Notes Page view with text

Speaker's notes

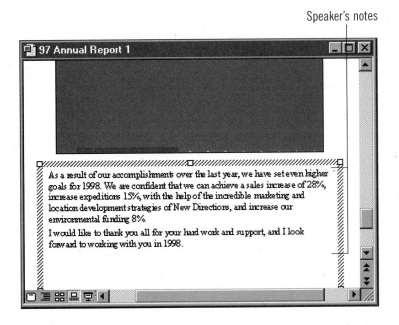

CLUES TO USE

Adding slide footers and headers

To customize your slides, notes pages, or handouts with information, such as your company or product name, the slide number, or the date, you can add headers and footers. To add a header or footer, click View on the menu bar, then click Header and Footer. Each element in the Header and Footer dialog box with a checkmark in the checkbox will be included as part of the header or footer. As you click the check-

boxes, watch the Preview box to see where the element will appear. On the Slide tab, you can add only footers. To have the footer appear on only the current slide, click Apply; to have footers appear on all the slides, click Apply to All. On the Notes and Handouts tab, you can choose to add headers and footers, and they will appear on all the pages.

PowerPoint 97

Checking spelling in the presentation

As your work nears completion, you need to review and proofread your presentation thoroughly for errors. You can use the spell-checking feature in PowerPoint to check for and correct spelling errors. The spell-checking feature compares the spelling of all the words in your presentation against the words contained in its electronic dictionary. You still must proofread your presentation for punctuation, grammar, and word-usage errors, however. The spell checker recognizes misspelled words, not misused words. For example, the spell checker would not identify "The Test" as an error even if you had intended to type "The Best." ✎ Carrie has finished adding and changing text in the presentation, so she checks her work.

1. **Click the Spelling button** ABC **on the Standard toolbar**
   PowerPoint begins to check the spelling in your presentation. It will check the spelling in the Notes Pages, even if you are in another view. When PowerPoint finds a misspelled word or a word it doesn't recognize, the Spelling dialog box opens, as shown in Figure B-12. In this case, PowerPoint does not recognize 'Welcom' in the speaker's notes for slide 1. (If you made a typing error, another word might appear in this dialog box.) Fix the spelling by choosing the correction offered by PowerPoint.

2. **Click Change**
   PowerPoint replaces the incorrect word, then continues checking the presentation. The next word the spell checker identifies as an error is the word "Nomd" in the second notes page. Choose the correct spelling from the list of suggestions.

Trouble?

If your spell checker doesn't find the word "Ltd," then a previous user probably added it to the custom dictionary. Skip Step 4 and continue with the lesson.

3. **Click Nomad in the Suggestions list box, then click Change**
   Next, the spell checker identifies "Ltd" as misspelled. This word is spelled correctly, so Carrie tells PowerPoint to ignore all instances of this word and continue through the presentation.

4. **Click Ignore All**
   The spell checker ignores all instances of the word "Ltd" throughout the presentation. Next, the spell checker finds the word "OutBack" in the Slide 4 speaker notes. Although the word is not misspelled, PowerPoint detects that the capital B in the middle of the word might be an error. This is the correct spelling, however, so tell PowerPoint to ignore all instances of this word.

5. **Click Ignore All**
   If PowerPoint finds any other words it does not recognize, either change them or ignore them. When the spell checker finishes checking your presentation, the spelling dialog closes and a PowerPoint alert box opens, indicating the spelling check is complete.

6. **Click OK**
   The alert box closes.

QuickTip

The spell checker does not check the text in pictures or embedded objects. You'll need to spell check text in imported objects, such as charts, Word documents or tables, using their original application.

7. **Click File on the menu bar, then click Print**

8. **Click the Print what list arrow, click Notes Pages, click the Black & white check box to select it, then click OK**

9. **Save your presentation, then return to Slide 1 in slide view**

FIGURE B-12: **Spelling dialog box**

Unrecognized word appears here

Suggested replacement appears here

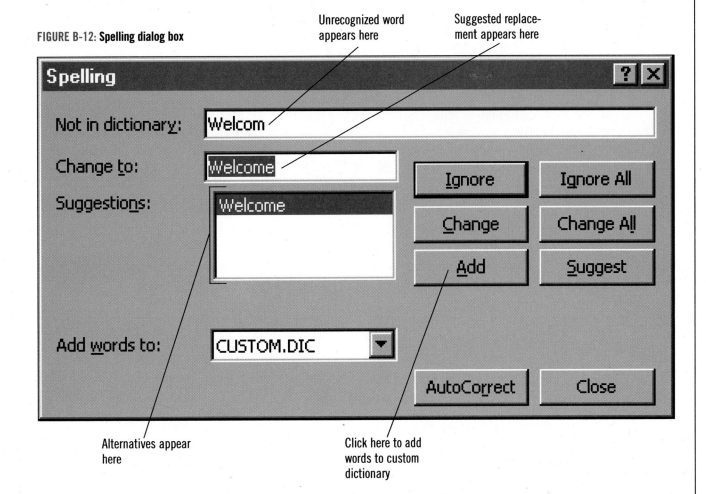

Alternatives appear here

Click here to add words to custom dictionary

Checking spelling as you type

PowerPoint checks your spelling as you type. If you type a word that is not in the electronic dictionary, a red, wavy line appears under it. To correct the error, right-click the misspelled word. A pop-up menu appears with one or more suggestions. You can select a suggestion, add the word you typed to your custom dictionary, or ignore it. To turn off automatic spell checking, click Tools on the menu bar, then click Options to open the Options dialog box. Click the Spelling tab, and in the section Check spelling as you type, click the Spelling check box to deselect it, then click OK. To temporarily hide the red, wavy lines, select the Hide spelling errors check box on the Spelling tab in the Options dialog box. See Figure B-13.

FIGURE B-13: **Spelling tab in the Options dialog box**

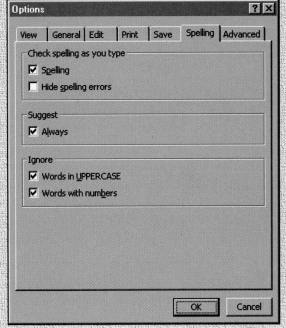

Evaluating your presentation

As you plan and create a presentation, keep in mind that good design involves preparation. An effective presentation is both focused and visually appealing. A planned presentation is easy for the speaker to present and easy for the audience to comprehend. The visual elements (colors, graphics and text) you choose can strongly influence audience attention and interest and can determine the success of your presentation. ✐ Carrie evaluates her presentation's effectiveness. Her final presentation is shown in Figure B-14. For contrast, Figure B-15 shows a poorly designed slide.

Time To

✔ **Save**

1. Click the Slide Show button ☐
2. Click the mouse button to move through the slide show
3. When you are finished viewing the slide show, click the Slide Sorter button ☐, click Window on the menu bar, then click Fit to Page
   See Figure B-14.

 Keep your message focused
Don't put everything you are going to say on your presentation slides. Keep the audience anticipating further explanations to the slides' key points. For example, the Annual Report presentation focuses the audience's attention on the sales numbers and projections because you included only the sales percentage increases and the goals for next year. You supplemented the slides with speaker's notes that explain the reasons for the increases.

 Keep the design simple, easy to read, and appropriate to the content
Usually, you will use a predesigned template that uses appropriate fonts, font sizes, and background colors. A design template also makes the presentation consistent. If you design your own layout or alter an existing one, do not add so many elements that the slides look cluttered. Use the same design elements consistently throughout the presentation; otherwise, your audience will get confused. The design template you used for the Annual Report presentation is simple; the horizontal bars on every slide give the presentation a clean, solid, and businesslike look that is appropriate to a Board of Directors meeting.

 Choose attractive colors that make the slide easy to read
Use contrasting colors for slide background and text, so that the slides are easy to read. If you are giving your presentation on a computer, you can use almost any combination of visually appealing colors.

 Keep your text concise
Limit each slide to six words per line and six lines per slide. Use lists and symbols to help prioritize your points visually. Your presentation text provides only the highlights; the president will use the speaker notes to give the background information.

 Choose fonts, typefaces, and styles that are easy to read and emphasize important text
Don't use the same typeface for all your text, and vary typeface weights. As a general rule, use no more than two fonts and three typefaces in a presentation. Use bold and italic selectively. Do not use text smaller than 18 point. In the design template you used, the titles are 44-point Arial and 32-point Times New Roman for the main text.

Use visuals to help communicate the message of your presentation
Commonly used visuals include clip art, photographs, charts, worksheets, tables, and movies. Whenever possible, replace text with a visual, but be careful not to overcrowd your slides. You will add some visuals in the next two units.

FIGURE B-14: **The final presentation**

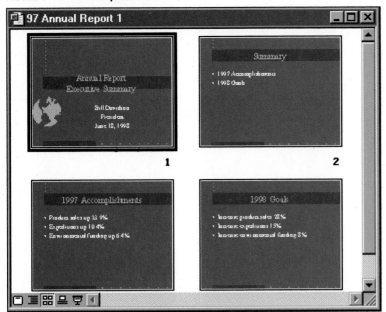

FIGURE B-15: **Poorly designed slide**

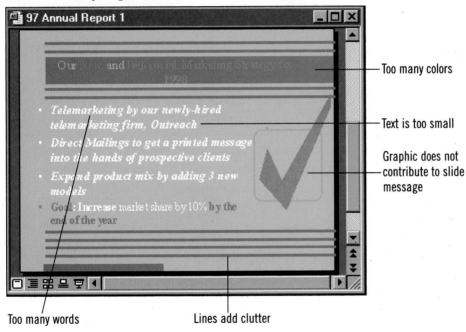

Too many colors

Text is too small

Graphic does not
contribute to slide
message

Too many words

Lines add clutter

Creating your own design templates

You are not limited to the templates in PowerPoint; you can either modify a PowerPoint template or create your own presentation template. For example, you might want to use your company's color as a slide background or incorporate your company's logo on every slide. If you modify an existing template, you can keep, change, or delete any color, graphic, or font. To create a new template, click File then click New, and on the General Tab double-click Blank Presentation, then click the Blank AutoLayout. Add the design elements you want, then use the Save As command on the File menu to name and save your customized design. Click the Save as type list arrow, and choose Presentation templates. PowerPoint will automatically add a .pot file extension to the filename. Then you can use your customized template as a basis for future presentations.

Practice

▶ Concepts Review

Label each of the elements of the PowerPoint window shown in Figure B-16.

FIGURE B-16

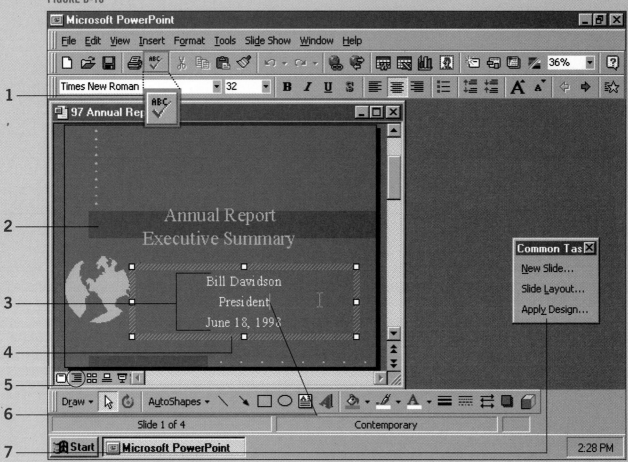

Match each of the terms with the statement that describes its function.

8. **Placeholder**
9. **Insertion point**
10. **Slide icon**
11. **template**

a. A specific design, format, and color scheme that is applied to all the slides in a presentation
b. A blinking vertical line that indicates where your text will appear in a text object
c. A dotted box containing prompt text in which you can enter text
d. In Outline view, the symbol that represents a slide

Select the best answer from the list of choices.

12. The ⊺ pointer shape appears for which one of the following tasks?
    a. Entering text
    b. Switching views
    c. Choosing a new layout
    d. Inserting a new slide

13. To move an item up one line in Outline view:
    a. Click ➡
    b. Click ⬆
    c. Press [Tab]
    d. Click ⬇

14. When the spell checker identifies a word as misspelled, which of the following is *not* a choice?
    a. To ignore this occurrence of the error
    b. To change the misspelled word to the correct spelling
    c. To have the spell checker automatically correct all the errors it finds
    d. To ignore all occurrences in the presentation of the error

15. When you evaluate your presentation, you should make sure it follows which of the following criteria?
    a. The slides should include every piece of information to be presented so the audience can read it.
    b. The slides should use as many colors as possible to hold the audience's attention.
    c. Lots of different typefaces will make the slides more interesting.
    d. The message should be clearly outlined without a lot of extra words.

16. According to the unit, which of the following is *not* a presentation planning guideline?
    a. Determine the purpose of the presentation
    b. Determine what you want to produce when the presentation is finished
    c. Determine which type of output you will need to best convey your message
    d. Determine who else can give the final presentation

17. Which of the following statements is *not* true?
    a. You can customize any PowerPoint template.
    b. The spell-checker will identify "there" as misspelled if the correct word for the context is "their."
    c. The speaker's notes do not appear during the slide show.
    d. PowerPoint has many colorful templates from which to choose.

18. What does a title text placeholder or a main text placeholder become when you type in it?
    a. A text object
    b. A title slide
    c. A text slide
    d. An insertion point

▶ Skills Review

1. **Choose a look for your presentation.**
   a. If PowerPoint is not running, start PowerPoint, click the Template option button, click OK, then go to Step c.
   b. If PowerPoint is already running, click File on the menu bar, then click New.
   c. Click the Presentation Designs tab.
   d. Review the PowerPoint design templates. Click each template icon to display a picture of the template in the Preview box.

e. When you have finished reviewing the PowerPoint design templates, find and click Contemporary Portrait then click OK. The New Slide dialog box opens.

f. Click OK to choose the Title Slide AutoLayout.

g. Save the presentation as "Weekly Goals" to your Student Disk.

2. **Enter slide text.**

a. Click the title placeholder.

b. Type "Product Marketing".

c. Click the main text placeholder.

d. Type "Les Bolinger".

e. Press [Enter], then type "Manager".

f. Press [Enter], then type "Aug. 2, 1998".

g. Display and examine the different pointer shapes in PowerPoint. Refer back to Table B-2 to help you display the pointer shapes.

h. Click in a blank area of the slide.

3. **Create new slides and enter text in Outline view.**

a. Click New Slide on the Common Tasks toolbar.

b. Click each of the AutoLayouts in the list. Identify each AutoLayout by its name in the Preview box.

c. Click the Bulleted List AutoLayout, then click OK.

d. Enter the text from Table B-5 into the new slide.

e. Switch to Outline view.

f. Press [Shift] and click New Slide on the Common Tasks toolbar.

g. Enter the text from Table B-6 into the new slide.

h. Press [Ctrl][Enter].

i. Enter the text from Table B-7 into the new slide.

4. **Enter text in Notes Page view.**

a. Switch to Notes Page view for Slide 2.

b. Click the notes placeholder.

c. Zoom in the view to 66%.

d. Enter the following speaker's notes:

— I am interviewing new candidates for the product marketing position.

— Each of you will interview the candidates who meet initial qualifications the following week.

— I need all reports for the weekly meeting by Fri.

— Reminder of the company Profit Sharing party next Fri. Work half day.

— Open agenda for new division items.

e. Click the Next Slide button.

TABLE B-5

(Slide title)	Goals for the Week
(Main text object, first indent level)	Les
(Main text object, second indent level)	Interview for new marketing rep
	Discuss new procedures with Pacific Rim marketing reps
	Finish marketing reports--see April by Thurs
	Prepare for weekly division meeting next Mon

TABLE B-6

(Slide title)	Goals for the Week
(Main text object, first indent level)	John
(Main text object, second indent level)	Revise product marketing report
	Set up plan for the annual sales meeting
	Discuss new procedures with U.S. marketing reps
	Thurs--fly to Phoenix for sales meeting planning session

TABLE B-7

(Slide title)	Goals for the Week
(Main text object, first indent level)	April
(Main text object, second indent level)	Complete division advertising plan for next year
	Establish preliminary advertising budget for division VP
	Complete monthly division report--due Fri
	Investigate new advertising agencies for company

f. Enter the following speaker's notes:
— I need the marketing report by Wed.
— John: Come by my office later this afternoon to review the sales meeting plan.
— Open agenda for new division items.

g. Click the Next Slide button.

h. Enter the following speaker's notes:
— I need to review the advertising company list by Fri.
— April: See me about weekly division report after this meeting.
— Status on the advertising budget and next year's advertising plan.
— Open agenda for new division items.

i. Switch back to Slide view.

5. Check the spelling in the presentation.

a. Click the Spelling button on the Standard toolbar.

b. Change any misspelled words. Ignore any words that are correctly spelled but that the spell checker doesn't recognize.

c. When the spell checker finishes, click OK to close the message box that tells you PowerPoint has finished spell checking.

d. Save the presentation.

6. Evaluate and print your presentation.

a. Move to Slide 1, click the Slide Show button, then click the mouse button to move through the slide show.

b. When the slide show is finished, click the Slide Sorter button.

c. Evaluate the presentation using the points described in the last lesson as criteria.

d. Click File on the menu bar, then click Print.

e. Click the Print what list arrow, then click Notes Pages.

f. Click the Black & white check box to select it.

g. Click OK.

▶ Independent Challenges

1. You have been asked to give a one-day course at a local adult education center. The course is called "Personal Computing for the Slightly Anxious Beginner" and is intended for adults who have never used a computer. One of your responsibilities is to create presentation slides and an outline of the course materials.

Plan and create presentation slides that outline the course material for the students. Create slides for the course introduction, course description, course text and grading, and a detailed syllabus. For each slide, include speaker's notes to help you stay on track during the presentation.

Create your own course material, but assume the following: the school has a computer lab with IBM-compatible computers and Microsoft Windows software; each student has a computer on his or her desk; the prospective students are intimidated by computers but want to learn; and the course is on a Saturday from 9 to 5, with a one-hour lunch.

To complete this independent challenge:

1. Think about the results you want to see, the information you need, and the type of message you want to communicate.

2. Write an outline of your presentation. What content should go on the slides? On the notes pages?

3. Create the presentation by choosing a presentation look, entering the title slide text and the outline text. Remember, you are creating and entering your own presentation material.

4. Create an ending slide that summarizes your presentation.

5. Add speaker's notes to the slides.
6. Check the spelling in the presentation.
7. Save the presentation as Class 1 on your Student Disk.
8. View the slide show, then view the slides in Slide Sorter view. Evaluate your presentation, and adjust it as necessary so that it is focused, clear, concise, and readable.
9. Print the slides and notes pages.
10. Submit your presentation plan, your preliminary sketches, and the final worksheet printout.

2. You are the training director for Events, Inc., which coordinates special events, including corporate functions, weddings, and private parties. Events, Inc. regularly trains groups of temporary employees that they can call on as coordinators, kitchen and wait staff, and coat checkers for specific events. One of your responsibilities is to introduce the monthly training class for new temporary employees. Events, Inc. trains 10 to 15 new workers a month for the peak season between May and September.

Plan and create presentation slides that outline your part of the new employee training. Create slides for the introduction, agenda, company history, dress requirements, principles for interacting successfully with guests, and safety requirements. For each slide, include speaker's notes that you can hand out to the employees.

Create your own presentation and company material, but assume the following: the new employee training class lasts for four hours; the training director's presentation lasts for 15 minutes; and the dress code requires uniforms, supplied by Events, Inc. (white for daytime events, black and white for evening events).

To complete this independent challenge:

1. Think about the results you want to see, the information you need, and the type of message you want to communicate for this presentation.
2. Write a presentation outline. What content should go on the slides? On the notes pages?
3. Create the presentation by choosing a presentation look, entering the title slide text, and the outline text. Remember, you are creating and entering your own presentation material.
4. Create an ending slide that summarizes your presentation.
5. Add speaker's notes to the slides.
6. Check the spelling in the presentation.
7. Save the presentation as Orientation Class on your Student Disk.
8. View the slide show, then view the slides in Slide Sorter view. Evaluate your presentation, and make any changes necessary so that the final version is focused, clear, concise, and readable. Adjust any items as needed.
9. Print the slides and notes pages.
10. Submit your presentation plan and the final worksheet printout.

3. You are an independent distributor of natural foods in Tucson, Arizona. Your business, Harvest Natural Foods, has grown progressively since its inception eight years ago, but sales and profits have plateaued over the last nine months. In an effort to turn your business around, you decide to acquire two major natural food dealers, which would allow Harvest Natural Foods to expand its territory into surrounding states. Use PowerPoint to develop a presentation that you can use to gain more business.

In this independent challenge, you will complete an outline and choose a look for the presentation. Create your own material to complete the slides of the presentation. To begin, open the presentation provided for you on your Student Disk.

To complete this independent challenge:

1. Open a new presentation. Choose the Meadow Presentation design. Add the title "Harvest Natural Foods" as the main title on the title slide.
2. Add five more slides with the following titles: Slide 2—Background; Slide 3—Current Situation; Slide 4—Acquisition Goals; Slide 5—Our Management Team; Slide 6—Funding Required.
3. Think about the results you want, the information you need, and the way you want to communicate your message.

4. Change the sample text in the title and main text placeholders of the slides. Use both Slide and Outline views to enter text.

5. Create a new slide at the end of the presentation. Enter concluding text on the slide, summarizing the presentation's main points.

6. Add speaker's notes to the slides.

7. Check the spelling in the presentation.

8. Save the presentation as Crystal Clear Presentation to your Student Disk.

9. Click the Slide Show button and view the slide show. Evaluate your presentation. If you make any changes, click the Save button to save them.

10. Print the slides as Handouts, 6 per page and including the outline of the presentation.

11. Submit your final printouts.

4. You are an employee at the Literacy Project of Massachusetts, a nonprofit organization that provides free reading and English-language tutoring for adults across the state. Traditionally, the state government has provided most of the funding for the project. However, due to recent state budget cuts, it has become necessary to solicit private corporations and private trusts for grants. It is your responsibility to develop the outline and basic look for a standard presentation that the president of the Literacy Project can present to various corporate officers and trust fund boards. You want your presentation to emphasize that the English-language tutoring for people from other countries (English as a Second Language, or ESL) is becoming a larger part of the Literacy Project mission.

In this independent challenge, you will complete the outline and choose a look for the funding presentation. Create your own material to complete the slides of the presentation. At least one fact in your presentation should be based on your research on the Internet. To begin, open the presentation provided on your Student Disk.

To complete this independent challenge:

1. Open a new presentation. Choose the Notebook Presentation Design. Add the title "Literary Project on Massachusetts" as the main title on the Title Slide.

2. Add five more slides with the following titles: Slide 2–History of the Literacy Project; Slide 3–Our Accomplishments; Slide 4–Our Mission; Slide 5–Our Goals; Slide 6–Past Funding Sources.

3. Think about the results you want, the information you need, and the way you want to communicate the message. Remember that this presentation should be standardized so the president of the Literacy Project can use it for different audiences.

4. Enter text into the main text placeholders of the slides. Use both Slide and Outline views to enter text.

5. You want to support your argument that there is increased need for funding, based especially on the percentage of people who have limited English language skills. Log on to the Internet and use your browser to go to http://www.course.com. From there, click the link Student On Line Companions, then click Microsoft Office 97 Professional Edition – Illustrated: A First Course page, then click the PowerPoint link for Unit B.

6. Use the Internet to find additional information. Use a search engine (such as http://excite.com or http://www.yahoo.com) to look for information on the 1990 U.S. Census of Population and Housing for the State of Massachusetts. Use the language-skill information you find there (or from any other site) and incorporate it into your presentation.

7. Create a new slide at the end of the presentation. Enter concluding text on the slide, summarizing the financial needs of the Literacy Project.

8. Add speaker's notes to the slides.

9. Spell-check the presentation.

10. Save the presentation as Funding Presentation to your Student Disk.

11. Click the Slide Show button and view the slide show. Evaluate your presentation. If you make any changes, click the Save button to save them.

12. Print the slides and outline of the presentation.

13. Submit your final printouts.

▶ Visual Workshop

Create the marketing presentation shown in Figures B-17 and B-18. Save the presentation as Sales Project 1 on your Student Disk. Review your slides in Slide view, then print your presentation in Slide view and in Outline view.

FIGURE B-17

FIGURE B-18

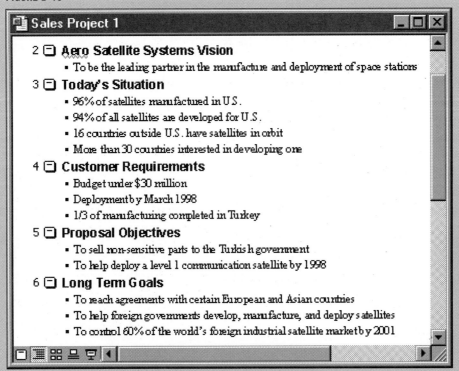

Modifying
a Presentation

Objectives

- ▶ **Open an existing presentation**
- ▶ **Draw and modify objects**
- ▶ **Edit drawing objects**
- ▶ **Align and group objects**
- ▶ **Add and arrange text**
- ▶ **Format text**
- ▶ **Change the color scheme and background**
- ▶ **Correct text automatically**

After you create the basic outline of your presentation and enter text, you need to add visuals to your slides to communicate your message in the most effective way possible. In this unit, you will open an existing presentation; then draw and modify objects; add, arrange, and format text; change a presentation color scheme; and automatically correct text. ✐ After Carrie Armstrong reviews her presentation with her supervisor, Lynn Shaw, Carrie continues to work on the Annual Report Executive Summary presentation for the president of Nomad Ltd. Carrie uses the PowerPoint drawing and text-editing features to bring the presentation closer to a finished look.

Opening an Existing Presentation

PowerPoint 97

Sometimes the easiest way to create a new presentation is by changing an existing one. Revising a presentation saves you from typing duplicate information. You simply open the file you want to change, then use the Save As command to save a copy of the file with a new name. Whenever you open an existing presentation in this book, you will save a copy of it with a new name to your Student Disk, which keeps the original file intact. Saving a copy does not affect the original file. To add visuals to her presentation, Carrie opens the presentation she has been working on.

1. Start PowerPoint and insert your Student Disk in the appropriate disk drive

Trouble?

If PowerPoint is already running, click the Open button 📂 on the Standard toolbar.

2. Click the **Open an existing presentation radio button** in the PowerPoint startup dialog box, then click **OK**
   The Open dialog box opens. See Figure C-1.

3. Click the **Look in list arrow**, then locate the drive that contains your Student Disk
   A list of drives opens.

4. Click the drive that contains your Student Disk
   A list of the files on your Student Disk appears in the Look in list box.

Trouble?

If the Open dialog box on your screen does not show a preview box, click the Preview button 🖼 in the toolbar at the top of the dialog box.

5. In the Look in list box, click **PPT C-1**
   The first slide of the selected presentation appears in the preview box on the right side of the dialog box.

6. Click **Open**
   The file named PPT C-1 opens. Now save a copy of this file with a new name to your Student Disk, using the Save As command.

7. Click **File** on the menu bar, then click **Save As**
   The Save As dialog box opens. See Figure C-2. The Save As dialog box works just like the Open dialog box.

QuickTip

Ordinarily, when you save copies of files, you may want to use a naming system. Many people use the name of the original file followed by consecutive numbers (1, 2, 3...) or letters (a, b, c...) to designate revisions of the same document or presentation.

8. Make sure the Save in list box displays the drive containing your Student Disk and the current filename in the File name text box is selected, then type **97 Annual Report 2**
   Compare your screen to the Save As dialog box in Figure C-2.

9. Click **Save** to close the Save As dialog box
   PowerPoint creates a copy of PPT C-1 with the name 97 Annual Report 2 and closes PPT C-1.

10. Make sure the percentage in the Zoom text box is 36, click the **Restore button** on the Presentation window, click **Window** on the menu bar, then click **Fit to page**

FIGURE C-1: Open dialog box

The list of files in your Look in list box might be different

Step 3

Step 6

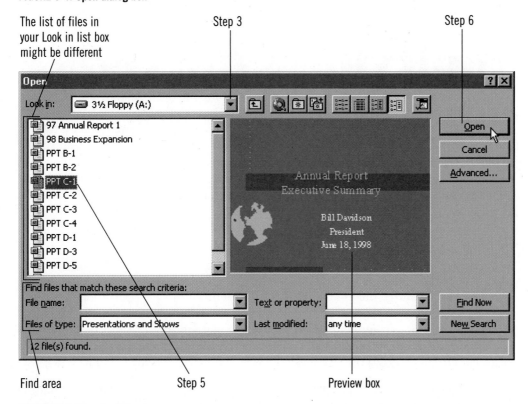

Find area   Step 5   Preview box

FIGURE C-2: Save As dialog box

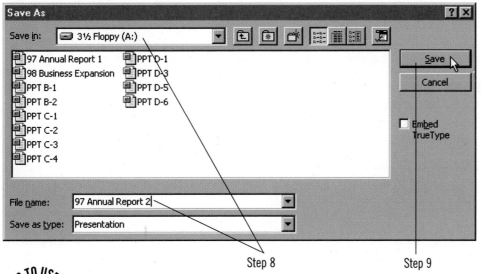

Step 8   Step 9

Searching for a file by properties

If you can't find a file, you can search for it using the Find area of the Open dialog box. (See Figure C-1.) To search for a file, click the Open an existing presentation radio button in the PowerPoint startup dialog box or click the Open button on the Standard toolbar to display the Open dialog box. Type the name of the presentation file in the File name text box at the bottom of the dialog box, then click Find Now. PowerPoint searches for the file in the current drive and directory.

If the file (or a related file) is found, it is displayed in the Look in list box. You also can type information into the Text or property text box to help PowerPoint find a file. For example, if you want to find a presentation that contains the word "investment," type "investment" in the Text or property text box. Then, the Look in list box lists presentations containing that word (not just with that word in the title).

Drawing and Modifying Objects

The drawing capabilities of PowerPoint allow you to draw and modify lines, shapes, and pictures to enhance your presentation. Lines and shapes that you create with the PowerPoint drawing tools are objects that you can change and manipulate at any time. These objects have graphic attributes that you can change, such as fill color, line color, line style, shadow, and 3-D effects. To add drawing objects to your slides, you use the buttons on the Drawing toolbar at the bottom of the screen above the status bar. Table C-1 describes some of the Drawing toolbar buttons. ✎ Carrie decides to draw an object on Slide 4 of the president of Nomad Ltd's presentation to add impact to her message.

1. Click the Next Slide button [⚡] three times to move to Slide 4
The 1997 Accomplishments slide appears.

2. Press and hold [Shift], then click the main text object
A dotted selection box with small boxes called **sizing handles** appears around the text object. If you click a text object without pressing [Shift], you make the object active, but you do not select the entire object. When an object is selected, you can adjust the size and shape of it or change its attributes. Resize the text object to make room for a drawing object next to it.

3. Position the pointer over the right, middle sizing handle, then drag the sizing handle to the left until the text object is about half its original size
When you position the pointer over a sizing handle, it changes to ↔ or ✛. It points in different directions depending on which sizing handle it is positioned over. When you drag a text object's sizing handle, the pointer changes to ✛, and a dotted outline representing the size of the text object appears. See Figure C-3. Now, add a shape to the slide.

4. Click the AutoShapes menu button on the Drawing toolbar, point to Stars and Banners, then click the Up Ribbon button [🎀] (third row, first item)
After you select a shape in the Stars and Banners menu and move the pointer off the menu, the pointer changes to ✛ again.

5. Position ✛ in the blank area of the slide to the right of the text object, press [Shift], drag down and to the right to create a ribbon object, then release the mouse button and release [Shift]
When you release the mouse button, a ribbon object appears on the slide, filled with the default color and outlined with the default line style, as shown in Figure C-4. Pressing [Shift] while you create the object keeps the object's proportions as you change its size.

6. If your ribbon object is not approximately the same size as the one shown in Figure C-4, press [Shift] and drag one of the sizing handles to resize the object
Now change the color of the outline of the ribbon object using the Line Color button.

7. Click the Line Color list arrow [✏️▾] on the Drawing toolbar, then click the black square
PowerPoint applies the color black to the selected object's outline. Next, change the color of the ribbon.

8. Click the Fill Color list arrow [🪣▾] on the Drawing toolbar, then click the royal blue square (the second square from the right)
PowerPoint fills the ribbon with the royal blue color.

Trouble?

If you are not satisfied with the size of the text object, resize it again.

QuickTip

Position the pointer on top of a button to see its name.

QuickTip

To create a circle or square, click the Oval or Rectangle button on the Drawing toolbar and either press [Shift] while dragging the pointer to create a proportional object from the edge of the object or press [Ctrl] while dragging the pointer to create a proportional object from the center of the object.

Time To

✔ Save

FIGURE C-3: Resizing the text object

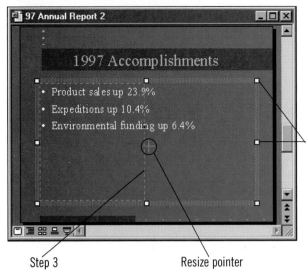

Sizing handles

Step 3

Resize pointer

FIGURE C-4: Slide showing ribbon object

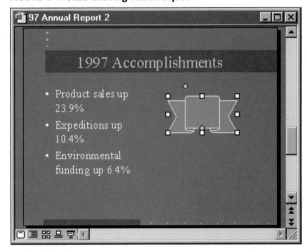

TABLE C-1: Drawing toolbar buttons

button	name	use it to
Draw ▾	**Draw menu button**	Choose commands from the Draw menu
AutoShapes ▾	**AutoShapes menu button**	Add one of over 150 shapes
＼	**Line button**	Add lines
↘	**Arrow button**	Add arrows
▢	**Rectangle button**	Add rectangles and squares
◯	**Oval button**	Add ovals and circles
▤	**Text Box button**	Add word-processing boxes
◢	**Insert Word Art button**	Open WordArt Galley to apply special text formatting
◌	**Fill Color button**	Add colored fill to any selected object
◢	**Line Color button**	Change the color of any selected line
A	**Font Color button**	Change the color of any selected text
≡	**Line Style button**	Change the thickness of any selected line
▤	**Shadow button**	Apply shadow styles to selected objects
▱	**3-D button**	Apply 3-D styles to selected objects

Editing Drawing Objects

Often, a drawing object does not match the slide or presentation "look" you are trying to achieve. PowerPoint allows you to manipulate the size and shape of objects on your slide. You can change the appearance of all objects by resizing their shape, as you did when you resized the text object in the previous lesson, or by adjusting the objects' dimensions. You also can cut, copy, and paste objects and add text to most PowerPoint shapes. Carrie changes the shape of the ribbon object, then makes two copies of it to help emphasize each point on the slide.

1. **If the ribbon object is not selected, click it to make the sizing handles appear around the edge of the ribbon object**
   In addition to sizing handles, small diamonds called **adjustment handles** appear above and below the selected object. You drag the adjustment handles to change the appearance of an object, usually its most prominent feature, like the size of an arrow head, or the proportion of a ribbon's center to its "tails." Now, resize the ribbon object.

2. **Drag the bottom right sizing handle up and to the right about ¼" in both directions**
   Next, move the ribbon next to the first bulleted item on the slide.

3. **Position the pointer over the middle of the selected ribbon object**
   The pointer changes to ⊹.

Trouble?

If you have trouble aligning the objects with the text, press and hold down [Alt] while dragging the object to turn off the automatic grid.

4. **Drag the ribbon so that the top of the ribbon is aligned with the top of the first bullet**
   A dotted outline appears as you move the ribbon object to help you position it. Compare your screen to Figure C-5, and make any adjustments necessary. Now, make two copies of the ribbon object and place them below the first object.

5. **Position ⊹ over the ribbon object, then press and hold [Ctrl]**
   The pointer changes to ⊹, indicating that PowerPoint will make a copy of the ribbon object when you drag the mouse.

QuickTip

You can use PowerPoint rulers to help you align objects. To display rulers, position the pointer in a blank area of the slide, right-click, then click Ruler in the pop-up menu or click View on the menu bar and click Ruler.

6. **Drag a copy of the ribbon object down the slide until the dotted lines indicating the position of the copy are aligned with the second bullet, then release the mouse button**
   An exact copy of the first ribbon object appears. Compare your screen to Figure C-6. Next, make a copy of the second ribbon object.

7. **Position the pointer over the second ribbon object, press [Ctrl], then drag a copy of the ribbon object down the slide until it is aligned with the third bullet**
   Compare your screen to Figure C-6. Now add text to the ribbon objects.

8. **Click the top ribbon object, then type 23.9%**
   The text appears in white in the center of the object. The text is now part of the object, so if you move the object, the text will move with it. Now add text to the other two ribbon objects.

Time To

✔ Save

9. **Click the middle ribbon object, type 10.4%; click the bottom ribbon object, type 6.4%, then click a blank area of the slide to deselect the object**
   The graphics you have added reinforce the slide text. The ribbon shape suggests achievement, and the numbers, which are the focus of this slide, are more prominent.

FIGURE C-5: Slide showing resized ribbon object

Adjustment handle

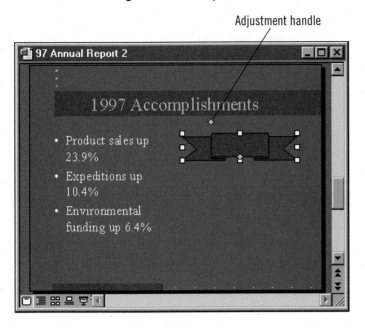

FIGURE C-6: Slide showing duplicated ribbon objects

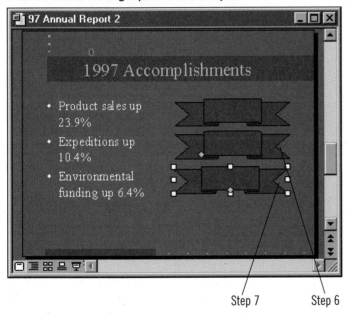

Step 7   Step 6

More ways to change objects

You can change the appearance of an object by rotating or flipping it, or by making it three-dimensional. To rotate or flip an object, select it, click the Draw menu button on the Drawing toolbar, point to Rotate or Flip, then click one of the available menu commands, as shown in Figure C-7. To make an object three-dimensional, select it, click the 3-D button, and click one of the options shown on the 3-D menu in Figure C-8.

FIGURE C-7: Rotate or Flip submenu

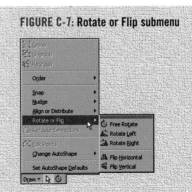

FIGURE C-8: 3-D menu

Aligning and Grouping Objects

After you create objects, modify their appearance, edit their size and shape, and position them on the slide, you can align and group them. The Align command aligns objects relative to each other by snapping the selected objects to an invisible grid of evenly spaced vertical and horizontal lines. The Group command groups objects into one object to make editing and moving them much easier. ✐ Carrie aligns, groups, and positions the ribbon objects. Then she copies and pastes the grouped ribbon object to the next slide.

1. **Press and hold [Shift], then click each ribbon object to select all three objects**
Next, align the ribbon objects vertically and then group them together.

2. **Click the Draw menu button on the Drawing toolbar, then point to Align or Distribute**
A menu of alignment and distribution options appears. The top three options align objects horizontally, whereas the next three options align objects vertically.

3. **Click Align Center**
The ribbon objects align on their centers, as shown in Figure C-9. Now group the objects together to maintain their exact spacing and position relative to each other.

4. **Click the Draw menu button on the Drawing toolbar, then click Group**
The ribbon objects group to form one object without losing their individual attributes. Notice the sizing handles now appear around the outer edge of the grouped object, not around each individual object. You can ungroup objects to restore each individual object. Now, move the grouped ribbon object to a specific position on the slide.

5. **Right-click a blank area of the slide, then click Guides in the pop-up menu**
The PowerPoint guides appear as white dotted lines on the slide. (The dotted lines might be very faint on your screen.) The guides intersect at the center of the slide. Use the guides to position the ribbon object on the slide.

6. **Position the pointer over the vertical guide in a blank area of the slide and press and hold the mouse button until the pointer changes to a guide measurement box, then drag the guide to the right until the guide measurement displays approximately 1.75**
Now move the grouped ribbon object over the vertical guide until it is centered on the guide.

7. **Press [Shift], drag the grouped ribbon object over the vertical guide until the center sizing handles are approximately centered over the vertical guide**
Pressing [Shift] while you drag an object constrains the movement to either vertical or horizontal. Next, copy the grouped object to Slide 5.

8. **Right-click the ribbon object, click Copy on the pop-up menu, click the Next Slide button ⬇, then click the Paste button 🖺 on the Standard toolbar**
Slide 5 appears and the ribbon object from Slide 4 is pasted onto Slide 5. Notice that the position of the pasted ribbon object on Slide 5 is the same as it was on Slide 4. Now, hide the guides and ungroup the ribbons so you can change the text in the ribbon objects to match the slide text.

9. **Click the Draw menu button on the Drawing toolbar, click Ungroup, click View on the menu bar, then click Guides**

10. **Triple-click the top ribbon object, then type 28%; triple-click the middle ribbon object, then type 15%; triple-click the bottom ribbon object, type 8%, then click outside the object to deselect it**
Compare your screen to Figure C-10.

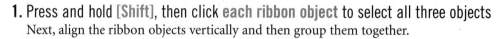

FIGURE C-9: Slide 4 showing aligned ribbon objects

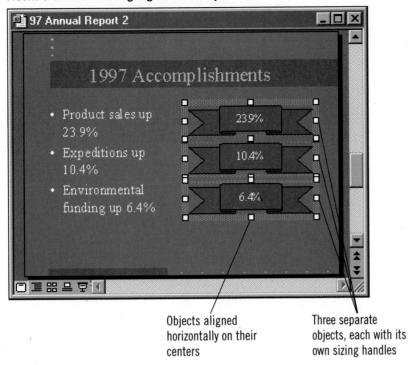

Objects aligned horizontally on their centers

Three separate objects, each with its own sizing handles

FIGURE C-10: Slide 5 showing pasted ribbon objects

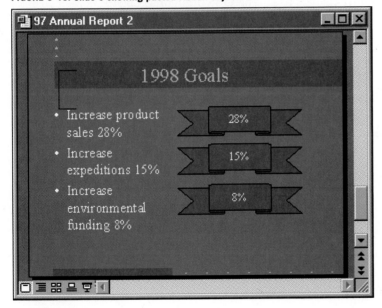

Object stacking order

Stacking order refers to how objects are placed, or layered, on top of one another. The first object you draw is on the bottom of the stack. The last object you draw is on the top of the stack. You can change the order of the stack by right-clicking an object and then clicking Order, or by clicking the Draw menu button on the Drawing toolbar and clicking Order, then choosing the Bring to Front, Send to Back, Bring Forward, or Send Backward command. For example, if you drew a colored box on top of a text object, but you wanted the text to appear on top of the box, you would change the stacking order to bring the text object to the front or send the box object to the back.

Adding and Arranging Text

Using the advanced text editing capabilities of PowerPoint, you can easily add, insert, or rearrange text. On a PowerPoint slide, you either enter text in prearranged text placeholders or use the Text Box button on the Drawing toolbar to create your own text objects when the text placeholders don't provide the flexibility you need. With the Text Box button, you can create two types of text objects: a text label, used for a small phrase inside a box where text doesn't automatically wrap to the next line, and a word processing box, used for a sentence or paragraph where the text wraps inside the boundaries of a box. Carrie already added a slide to contain Nomad Ltd's Mission Statement. Now, she uses the Text Box button to create a word-processing box on Slide 3 to enter the Nomad Ltd mission statement.

1. **Drag the scroll box up the vertical scroll bar until the Slide Indicator box displays Slide 3**
   Now create a word processing box and enter the company mission statement next to the balloon graphic.

2. **Click the Text Box button 🔲 on the Drawing toolbar**

3. **Position the pointer about ½" from the left edge of the slide and about even with the top of the balloon graphic already on the slide, then drag the word processing box toward the balloon graphic so that your screen looks like Figure C-11**
   After you click 🔲, the pointer changes to ↓. When you begin dragging, the pointer changes to ✛ and an outline of the box appears, indicating how wide a text object you are drawing. After you release the mouse button, an insertion point appears inside the text object, ready to accept text.

4. **Type Nomad Ltd is a national sporting goods retailer dedicated to delivering high-quality adventure sporting gear and travel.**
   Notice that the word processing box increases in size as your text wraps inside the object. There is a mistake in the mission statement. It should be "adventure travel" not "adventure sporting gear." Correct the error by moving "adventure" to its correct position.

5. **Double-click I on the word adventure to select it**
   When you select a word, the pointer changes from I to ⬧.

6. **Position the pointer on top of the selected word and press and hold the mouse button**
   The pointer changes to ⬧. The dotted insertion line indicates where PowerPoint will place the word when you release the mouse button.

7. **Drag the word "adventure" to the left of the word "travel" in the mission statement, then release the mouse button**

8. **Click a blank area of the slide outside the text object, then save your changes**
   The text object is deselected. Your screen should look similar to Figure C-12.

FIGURE C-11: **Slide showing word processing box ready to accept text**

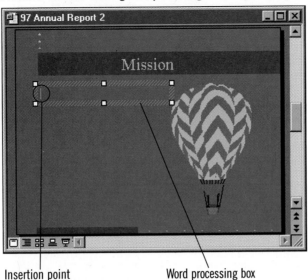

Insertion point

Word processing box

FIGURE C-12: **Slide after adding text to a word processing box**

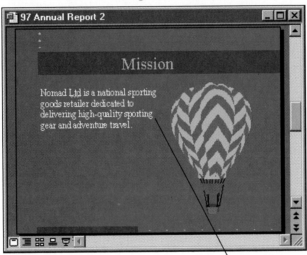

Your text might wrap differently, depending on the size of your word processing box

CLUES TO USE

Adding comments

The comment feature in PowerPoint allows you to insert comments on a presentation. To insert a comment, click Insert on the menu bar, click Comment, then type your notes. The comment appears in a yellow box in the upper-left corner of the slide, as shown in Figure C-13. Your name as it appears on the General tab of the Options dialog box (on the Tools menu) appears as the first line of the comment. The Reviewing toolbar also appears. To hide or show comments, click View on the menu bar, then click Comments. You also can insert or show a comment by clicking the appropriate button on the Reviewing toolbar .

FIGURE C-13: **Comment on a slide**

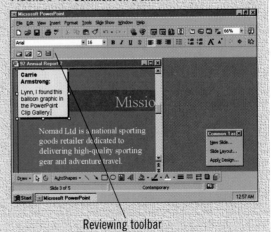

Reviewing toolbar

Formatting Text

Once you have entered and arranged the text in your presentation, you can change and modify the way the text looks to emphasize your message. Important text needs to be highlighted in some way to distinguish it from other text or objects on the slide. For example, if you have two text objects on the same slide, you could draw attention to one text object by changing its color or size. To change the way text looks, you need to select it, and then choose one of the Formatting commands. ◀━━━ Carrie uses some of the commands on the Formatting and Drawing toolbars to change the way the company mission statement looks.

Steps

1. **On Slide 3, press [Shift], then click the main text box**
   The entire text box is selected. Any changes you make will affect all the text in the selected text box. Change the size and appearance of the text to emphasize it on the slide.

2. **Click the Increase Font Size button A on the Formatting toolbar twice**
   The text increases in size to 32 points.

3. **Click the Italic button I on the Formatting toolbar**
   The text changes from normal to italic text. The Italic button, like the Bold button, is a toggle button, which you click to turn the attribute on or off. Next, change the color of the mission statement text.

4. **Click the Font Color list arrow A ▾ on the Drawing toolbar**
   The Font Color menu appears, displaying the eight colors used in the current presentation.

5. **Click the gold box**
   The text in the word-processing box changes to the gold color. Now, put the finishing touch on the mission statement by changing the font.

6. **Click the Font list arrow on the Formatting toolbar**
   A list of available fonts opens, as shown in Figure C-14. The double line at the top of the font list separates the most recent fonts you used from the complete list of available fonts. Choose the Arial font to replace the current font in the text object.

7. **Click the scroll arrows if necessary, then click Arial**
   The Arial font replaces the original font in the text object. Compare your screen to Figure C-15.

8. **Click a blank area of the slide outside the text object to deselect the text object**

Time To

✔ Save

FIGURE C-14: Font list open

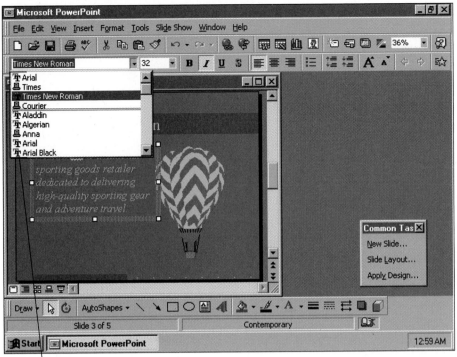

Your list of fonts
may be different

FIGURE C-15: Slide showing formatted text box

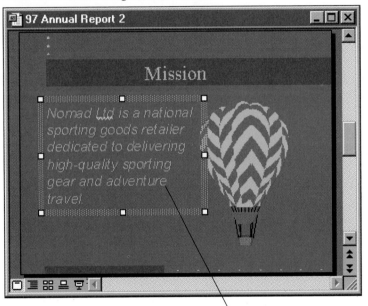

Arial, 32-point,
italic type

Replacing Text and Attributes

As you review your presentation, you may decide to replace certain words or fonts throughout the entire presentation. You can automatically modify words, sentences, fonts, text case, and periods. To replace specific words or sentences, use the Replace command on the Edit menu. To change a font, use the Replace

Fonts command on the Format menu. To automatically add or remove periods from title or body text and to automatically change the case of title or body text, select Style Checker on the Tools menu and click the Options button.

PowerPoint 97

Changing the Color Scheme and Background

Every PowerPoint presentation has a set of eight coordinated colors, called a **color scheme**, that determines the main colors in your presentation for the slide elements: slide background, text and lines, title text, shadows, fills, and accents. See Table C-2 for a description of the slide color scheme elements. The **background** is the area behind the text and graphics. Every design template has a default color scheme and background that you can use, or you can create your own. 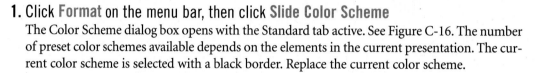 Carrie decides she doesn't like the solid blue color of the presentation background, so she decides to change it.

1. **Click Format on the menu bar, then click Slide Color Scheme**
   The Color Scheme dialog box opens with the Standard tab active. See Figure C-16. The number of preset color schemes available depends on the elements in the current presentation. The current color scheme is selected with a black border. Replace the current color scheme.

QuickTip

To apply a new color scheme to only selected slides, switch to Slide Sorter view, select the slides you want to change, then click Apply instead of Apply to All in the dialog box.

2. **Click the bottom-left color scheme with the teal background, then click Apply to All**
   The dialog box closes, and the new color scheme is applied to all the slides in the presentation. Now, change the background shading to emphasize the presentation's message.

3. **Click Format on the menu bar, then click Background**
   The Background dialog box opens.

4. **In the Background fill section, click the list arrow below the preview of the slide, click Fill Effects, then click the Gradient tab**
   See Figure C-17. Change the background colors to a combination of teal and black.

5. **In the Colors section, click the Two colors option button, click the Color 2 list arrow, then click the black box**
   The horizontal shading style is selected, as is the first of the four variants, showing that the background is shaded from color 1 (teal) on the top to color 2 (black) on the bottom.

6. **In the Shading Styles section, click the Diagonal up option button, click OK, then click Apply to all**
   The background is now shaded from teal (upper-left) to black (lower-right), and the text stands out because it is on the lighter color. Next, make the title color brighter.

QuickTip

To see which colors are used in the current color scheme, click a color button on the Drawing toolbar, such as the Font Color button, then move the pointer over each of the eight colors below the Automatic box.

7. **Click Format on the menu bar, click Slide Color Scheme and click the Custom tab**
   The eight colors for the selected color scheme appear.

8. **In the Scheme colors section, click the Title text color box, then click Change Color**
   The Title Text Color dialog box opens with the current Title text color selected.

9. **Click the yellow color cell just above and to the left of the current color, as shown in Figure C-18**
   The Current color and the New color appear in the box in the lower-right of the dialog box. Now, apply this scheme to the presentation, and save it as a standard scheme for future use.

Time To

✔ Save

10. **Click OK, click Add As Standard Scheme, then click Apply to All**
    PowerPoint updates the color scheme in all your slides, and the title text is changed to the lighter yellow. The next time you open the Color Scheme dialog box in this presentation, your new scheme will appear, along with the existing schemes.

FIGURE C-16: Color Scheme dialog box

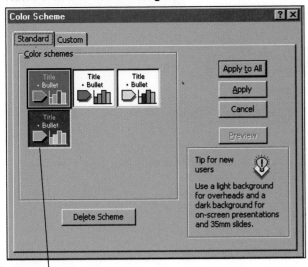

Choose this color scheme

FIGURE C-17: Gradient tab of Fill Effects dialog box

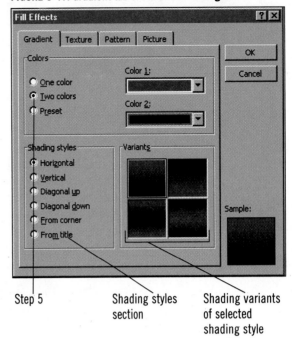

Step 5   Shading styles section   Shading variants of selected shading style

FIGURE C-18: Standard tab in the Title Text Color dialog box

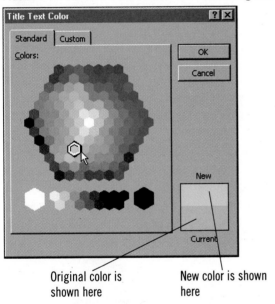

Original color is shown here   New color is shown here

TABLE C-2: Color scheme elements

scheme element	description
Background color	Color of the slide's canvas, or background
Text and lines color	Used for text and drawn lines; contrasts with the background color
Shadows color	Color of the text's shadow or other object; generally a darker shade of the background color
Title text color	Used for slide title; like the text and line colors, contrasts with the background color
Fills color	Contrasts with both the background and the text and line colors
Accent color	Colors used for other objects on slides, such as bullets
Accent and hyperlink colors	Colors used for accent objects and for hyperlinks you insert
Accent and followed hyperlink	Color used for accent objects and for hyperlinks after they have been clicked

Correcting Text Automatically

As you enter text into your presentation, the AutoCorrect feature in PowerPoint automatically replaces misspelled words and corrects some word-capitalization mistakes, whether on slides or in speaker notes, without bringing up a dialog box or a menu; for example, if you type "THursday" instead of "Thursday," PowerPoint corrects it as soon as you type it. If there is a word you often type incorrectly, for example, if you type "tehm" instead of "them," you can create an AutoCorrect entry that corrects that misspelled word whenever you type it in a presentation. After reviewing the presentation, Lynn asks Carrie to add one more slide, thanking the employees and stockholders for their support.

Steps 1234

1. Click the Next Slide button 🔻 as necessary to move to Slide 5, hold down [Shift] and click New Slide on the Common Tasks toolbar

A new bulleted list on Slide 6 appears. First, check the AutoCorrect dialog box to see which options are selected and to have PowerPoint automatically correct a particular word.

2. Click Tools on the menu bar, then click AutoCorrect

The AutoCorrect dialog box opens, as shown in Figure C-19. The top part of the dialog box contains check boxes that have PowerPoint automatically change two capital letters at the beginning of a word to a single capital letter, capitalize the first letter of a sentence and the names of days, and correct capitalization errors caused by accidental use of the Caps Lock key. The fifth check box, Replace text as you type, tells PowerPoint to change any of the mistyped words on the left in the scroll box in the lower part of the dialog box with the correct word on the right. The scroll box contains customized entries. For example, if you type (c), PowerPoint will automatically change it to ©, the copyright symbol. See Table C-3 for a summary of AutoCorrect options.

3. Click any check boxes that are not selected

4. In the Replace text as you type section, click the down scroll arrow to view all the current text replacement entries, then click OK

To test the AutoCorrect feature, you decide to enter incorrect text on the fifth slide. First, you'll type text using two capital letters in the word "Thank." Watch what happens to that word when you press [Spacebar].

5. Click the title placeholder, then type THank You

As soon as you pressed [Spacebar] after typing the word "THank," PowerPoint automatically corrected it to read "Thank." Now enter the word "adn," which is currently in the Replace text as you type list.

6. Click the main text placeholder, type Sales adn Marketing staff, and press [Enter]

As soon as you pressed [spacebar] after typing the word "adn," PowerPoint automatically corrected it to read "and." Now, enter the trademark symbol ™ after a product name.

7. Type OutBack(tm) promotional team, then click outside the main text object

As soon as you pressed the spacebar after OutBack(tm), PowerPoint automatically changed the (tm) to the trademark symbol ™.

8. Click the Slide Sorter View button 🖥, click the Maximize button in the Presentation window

Compare your screen to Figure C-20. (The Common Tasks toolbar does not appear in the figure.)

9. Save your presentation, print the slides, then exit PowerPoint

QuickTip

In order for an automatic correction to take effect, you must first press [spacebar], [Enter], or [Tab] after the word.

FIGURE C-19: **AutoCorrect dialog box**

Automatic
correction options

Type your own
custom AutoCorrect
entries here

Default AutoCorrect
entries

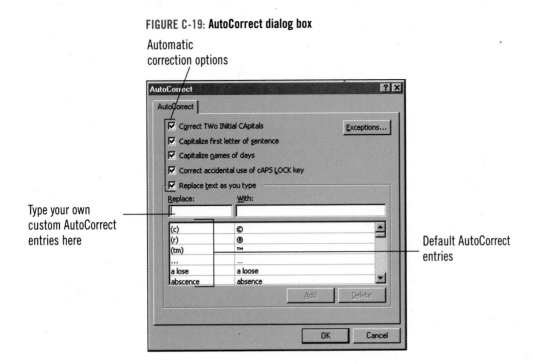

FIGURE C-20: **The final presentation**

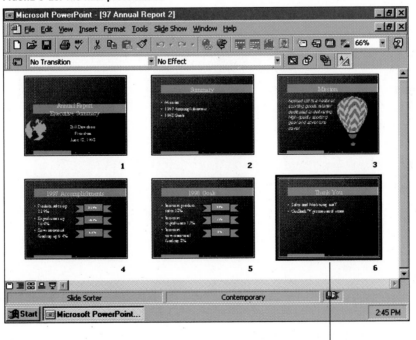

New slide with
corrected text

TABLE C-3: **AutoCorrect Options**

option	action
Turn off AutoCorrect	Click to remove all the check marks in the AutoCorrect dialog box
Edit an AutoCorrect entry	Select the entry in the list, click in the With text box, correct the entry, and click Replace
Delete an AutoCorrect entry	Highlight the entry in the scroll box and click Delete
Rename an AutoCorrect entry	Select the entry in the list, click in the Replace text box, click Delete, type a new name in the Replace box, and click Add

Practice

▶ Concepts Review

Label each of the elements of the PowerPoint window shown in Figure C-21.

FIGURE C-21

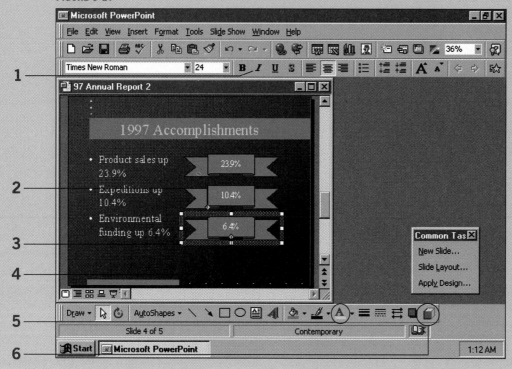

Match each of the terms with the statement that describes its function.

7. Word processing box
8. Text label
9. 📇
10. 🅰
11. Sizing handles

a. Button that changes the text color
b. Use this to create a text object on a slide
c. Small boxes that surround an object when it is selected
d. A text object that does not word wrap
e. A text object you create by dragging to create a box after clicking the Text Box button

Select the best answer from the list of choices.

12. How do you draw or resize an object proportionally?
   a. Press and hold the spacebar while you draw or resize the object.
   b. Press and hold [Shift] or [Ctrl] while you draw or resize the object.
   c. Very carefully drag sizing handles on each side of the object so the proportions stay the same.
   d. Double-click, then draw or resize the object.

13. What is the best way to align objects?
   a. Drag each object to the center of the slide.
   b. Align each object using a reference point on the PowerPoint window.
   c. Select all the objects, then click Group on the Draw menu.
   d. Select all the objects, click Align or Distribute on the Draw menu, then click an alignment option.

14. How do you change the size of a PowerPoint object?

   a. Move a sizing handle.

   b. Click the Resize button.

   c. Move the adjustment handle.

   d. You can't change the size of a PowerPoint object.

15. What would you use to position objects at a specific place on a slide?

   a. PowerPoint placeholders

   b. PowerPoint guides and rulers

   c. PowerPoint grid lines

   d. PowerPoint anchor lines

▶ Skills Review

1. Open an existing presentation.

   a. Start PowerPoint, click the Open an existing presentation radio button in the PowerPoint startup dialog box, then click OK. If PowerPoint is already open, click the Open button on the Standard toolbar.

   b. Make sure the drive containing your Student Disk is listed in the Look in list box, type "ppt" in the File name text box at the bottom of the dialog box, then click Find Now to find all the files on your Student Disk that have ppt in the filename and that are presentation or show files.

   c. Click PPT C-2 in the Look in list box to select it.

   d. Click Open.

   e. Click File on the menu bar, then click Save As.

   f. Make sure the text in the File name text box is highlighted, type "Series Report", then click Save.

2. Draw and modify an object.

   a. Move to Slide 3, then Click the AutoShapes menu button on the Drawing toolbar.

   b. Point to Stars and Banners, and click the Explosion 1 button.

   c. Position the pointer in the lower-right corner of the slide, press [Shift], then drag up to create an explosion shape about 1½" in diameter, so that it partially covers the text.

   d. Click the Line Color button on the Drawing toolbar, then click No Line.

   e. Click the Shadow button on the Drawing toolbar, then click the Shadow Style 1 button in the upper left.

   f. Click the Draw menu button, point to Order, then click Send to Back, then deselect the object.

   g. Click the Save button on the Standard toolbar.

3. Edit drawing objects.

   a. Move to Slide 4, and click the arrow object to select it.

   b. Drag the right, middle, sizing handle to the left about 1".

   c. Make two copies of the arrow object by holding down [Ctrl] and dragging the arrow object. Position the copies approximately as shown in Figure C-22.

   d. Click the left arrow object, then type "Teams"; click the middle arrow object, then type "Goals"; click the right arrow object, then type "Resources"; click the cube, type "OutBack," press [Enter], then type "Product."

   e. Drag to select the OutBack Product text on the cube, click the Font Color button, and click the black square.

   f. Click the Save button on the Standard toolbar.

4. Align and group objects.

   a. Select the four objects on Slide 4.

   b. Click the Draw menu button, point to Align or Distribute, and click Align Bottom.

c. Click the Font list arrow and click Arial, then click the Italic button on the Standard toolbar.

d. Select only the three arrow objects, click the Draw menu button on the Drawing toolbar, then point to Align or Distribute, and click Distribute Horizontally.

e. Click the Draw menu button on the Drawing toolbar, then click Group.

f. Click the right mouse button in a blank area of the slide, then click Guides on the pop-up menu.

g. Move the vertical guide to the left and stop when you reach the approximate measurement 4.15.

h. Move the horizontal guide down and stop when you reach the measurement 3.00.

i. Click the grouped object, then move the object until the bottom-left corner of the object snaps to the corner where the guides intersect. If your object does not snap to the guides, click the Draw menu button, point to Snap, and make sure the "To Grid" command on the Snap menu is selected (it should look indented).

j. Right-click in an empty area of the slide, then click Guides to hide the guides. Compare your screen to Figure C-22 and make any adjustments necessary.

FIGURE C-22

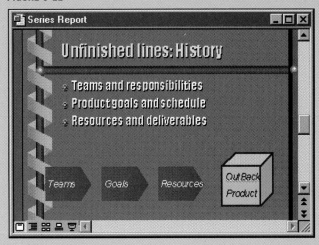

5. Add and arrange text.

a. Move to Slide 2, click the I-beam cursor to place the blinking insertion point at the end of the word "developed" in the main text object.

b. Press [Enter], then type "Consumer response to the series".

c. Click the Text Box button on the Drawing toolbar, position the pointer near the bottom of the slide, below the tree graphic, then drag to create a box about 3" wide.

d. Type "Department product managers have 20 minutes for line reports."

e. Double-click the word "product," then drag it in front of the word "line."

6. Format text.

a. Click in the Presentation window to deselect the word processing box, press [Shift], then click the word processing box you just created again to select it.

b. Click the Font Color list arrow on the Drawing toolbar, then click the black box.

c. Click the Increase Font Size button on the Formatting toolbar.

d. Move the text object so the text is inside the slide border, then deselect the text.

e. Press [Shift], then click the main text object.

f. Click the Bullets button on the Formatting toolbar to add bullets to the list.

g. Click on a blank area of the slide to deselect the text object then save your changes.

7. **Change a presentation color scheme and background.**
   a. Click Format on the menu bar, then click Slide Color Scheme.
   b. Click the lower-left color scheme, with the white background and green arrow, then click Apply to All.
   c. Click Format on the menu bar, then click Background.
   d. Click the list arrow below the slide miniature, click Fill Effects, then click the Gradient tab.
   e. Click the Two colors option button, click the Color 2 list arrow, then click the light green square on the far right.
   f. In the Shading Styles section, click the Diagonal up option button, click OK, and click Apply to all.
   g. Click Format on the menu bar, click Slide Color Scheme, and click the Custom tab.
   h. Click the Title text color square, then click Change Color.
   i. Click the third gray cell from the left in the bottom row, then click OK.
   j. Click Add As Standard Scheme.
   k. Click the Standard tab. The new color scheme is added to the available color scheme list.
   l. Click Apply to All, then save your changes.

8. **Correct text automatically.**
   a. Go to Slide 5 and press the Caps Lock key.
   b. Click the I-beam pointer after the word "report," press [Enter] to add a fourth bullet, and type "Schedules" (it will come out sCHEDULES), but do not press [Enter].
   c. Press [Enter] and notice how PowerPoint reverses the capitalization as soon as you press [Enter].
   d. Type "All by next thursday" and press [Spacebar]. Notice that PowerPoint automatically capitalizes the word "Thursday" for you.
   e. Check the spelling in the presentation and make any changes necessary.
   f. Go to Slide 1, view the final slide show, and evaluate your presentation.
   g. Save your changes, print the slides and then close the presentation.

▶ Independent Challenges

1. You work for Chicago Language Systems (CLS), a major producer of computer-based language training materials sold in bookstores and computer stores. CLS products include CD-ROMs with accompanying instructional books. Twice a year, the Acquisitions and Product Development departments hold a series of meetings, called Title Meetings, to determine the new title list for the following production term. The meetings, which last an entire day, are also used to decide which current CD titles need to be revised. As the director of acquisitions, you chair the September Title Meeting and present the basic material for discussion. You decide to create a presentation that describes the basic points to be addressed.

To complete this independent challenge:

1. Open the file PPT C-3 on your Student Disk and save it as "Title Meeting 9-98".
2. After you open the presentation, look through it in Slide view and consider the results you want to see on each slide. What slides could you add or delete? Look at the organization of the presentation; you may need to make some adjustments in Outline view. If you reorganize the presentation, be able to support your decision.
3. Add a design template to the presentation.
4. Evaluate the fonts used throughout the presentation. Format the text so that the most important information is the most prominent.
5. Use the drawing tools to add appropriate shapes that amplify the most important parts of the slide content. Format the objects using color and shading. Use the Align and Group commands to organize your shapes.
6. Evaluate the color scheme and the background colors. Make any changes you feel will enhance the presentation.
7. Spell check the presentation, view the final slide show and evaluate your presentation. Make any changes necessary.
8. Save the presentation, print the slides, and submit your final printouts.

2. The Software Learning Company is a Silicon Valley-based corporation dedicated to the design and development of instructional software that helps college students learn software applications. As the company's main graphics designer, you have been asked by the marketing manager to design and develop a standardized set of graphics for the company that all the employees can use for their business presentations. To help promote the company, the marketing group unveiled a new company slogan: "Software is a snap!"

Plan and create standard text and graphical objects for the Software Learning Company that employees can copy and paste into their business presentations. Create five different slides with a company logo, using the AutoShapes toolbar, and a company slogan, using the Text tool. The marketing group will decide which of the five designs looks best. Create your own presentation slides, but assume that: the company colors are blue and green.

To complete this independent challenge:

1. Think about the results you want to see and the information you need to create this presentation.
2. Sketch your logos and slogan designs on a piece of paper. What text and graphics do you need for the slides?
3. Create a new presentation using a design template, and save it as "Software Learning" on your Student Disk. Remember, you are creating and entering your own presentation material. The logo and the marketing slogan should match each other in tone, size, and color, and the logo objects should be grouped together to make it easier for other employees to copy and paste.
4. Change the color scheme and background as necessary.
5. Spell check the presentation, View the final slide show, and evaluate your presentation. Make any changes necessary.
6. Save the presentation and print the slides and notes pages (if any).
7. Submit your presentation plan, preliminary sketches, and the final presentation printout.

3. You work for Scenes, Inc., a firm that designs and builds sets for television shows, and theater, opera, and ballet companies in California. One of your responsibilities is to create a process flow diagram for the new apprentice construction team to follow during the building of a theater set. The process flow diagram describes the construction process from start to finish. Plan and create a construction process flow diagram using PowerPoint text and drawing tools. The diagram should include shapes, lines, and text labels to indicate the flow of information. Assume that the process includes filling out materials requisition forms, getting the requisitions signed by the director, ordering materials, setting the construction schedule, hiring contract workers, building backdrops, platforms and set pieces (statues, pillars, etc.), installation, and finishing work.

To complete this independent challenge:

1. Think about the desired results, the information you need to create this presentation, and the type of message you want to communicate. What text and graphics are needed for the slides?
2. Create a new presentation using a design template. Save it as Construction Process to your Student Disk. Remember, you are creating and entering your own presentation material. Group the diagram objects together to make it easier for other employees to change.
3. You can add explanatory notes using Speaker's notes if this will help the viewer understand your decisions.
4. Evaluate your color scheme and background. Make changes to make the flow diagram the central focus of each slide.
5. Spell check the presentation, view the final slide show and evaluate your presentation. Make any changes necessary.
6. Save your changes and print the slides and notes pages (if any).
7. Submit your presentation plan, preliminary sketches, and the final presentation printout.

4. You are the customer service manager for State Bank, a full-service bank with its home office located in San Diego, California, and six branches located throughout the state. To keep tellers and customer service personnel up to date with new services, procedures, and general bank policy information, State Bank conducts a three-day update seminar once every six months for the entire customer service department at each branch office. It is your job to travel around the state to each of State Bank's regional offices and give the first day of the three-day seminar. Your portion of the seminar covers new services and procedures.

To complete this independent challenge:

1. Open the file PPT C-4 on your Student Disk and save it as "State Training Sept 98".
2. After you open the presentation, look through it in Slide Show view and think about the results you want to see on each slide. What information is provided, and what could you add? How do you want to communicate the message? Look at the organization of the presentation; you may need to make some adjustments. If you decide to reorganize the presentation, be able to support your decision.
3. Apply an appropriate design template to the presentation.
4. Customers have been asking if State Bank will be starting a page on the World Wide Web (WWW). In fact, the vice president asked you to look into the issue and to do some research to help you make suggestions on what the Web page should contain. Create two new slides in your presentation that outline some of the major elements you think the State Bank Web page will have. To get ideas for content, go to the following WWW sites:
   - Log on to the Internet and use your browser to go to http://www.course.com. From there, click the link Student On Line Companions, then click the Microsoft Office 97 Professional Edition—Illustrated: A First Course page, then click the PowerPoint link for Unit C.
   Circle the links there then choose several elements from these web pages that you think would be useful for a State Bank web page, and create a slide that outlines your ideas.
5. Make sure the AutoCorrect options are all selected, then create a new slide titled "Training Seminar Agenda" with the information provided in Table C-4. Put the slide in the proper place so it flows in the presentation.

TABLE C-4

bullet	information
First bullet point	Sept 23rd (morning session) — Bank Policy on minority hiring
Second bullet point	Sept 23rd (afternoon session) — Bank Role in Community Development
Third bullet point	Sept 24th (morning session) — Federal Regulations on FHA loans
Fourth bullet point	Sept 24th (afternoon session) — Federal Regulations on Retirement Allocation advice

6. Add a word-processing box to Slide 3, and add text that describes a two-day turnaround time that anxious first-time buyers will appreciate.
7. Use the drawing tools to add shapes to your slides that help reflect the presentation message and environment. Add text to any shapes you feel would help communicate the message more clearly. Format the objects using color and shading. Use the Align and Group commands to organize your shapes.
8. Change the color scheme and background.
9. Add speaker's notes (at least one sentence) to each slide.
10. Spell check the presentation, view the final slide show and evaluate your presentation.
11. Save your changes and print the Notes Pages and Handouts (6 slides per page) of the presentation.

▶ Visual Workshop

Create a three-slide presentation that looks like the examples shown in Figures C-25, C-26, and C-27. Save the presentation as Bowman Logos to your Student Disk. Spell check the presentation, then save and print the slides in Slide view. (*Hint:* Design 8 uses the 3-D Settings option on the 3-D menu. You can find other effects using the Object command on the Format menu on the menu bar.)

FIGURE C-25

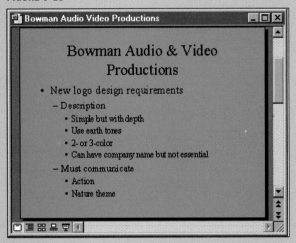

FIGURE C-26

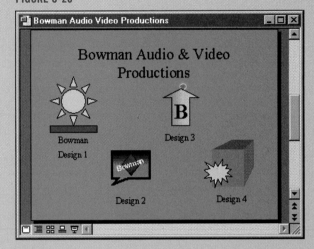

FIGURE C-27

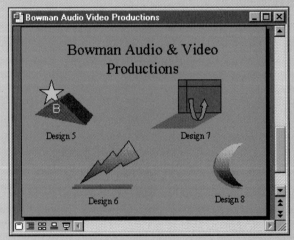

PowerPoint 97

Enhancing
a Presentation

Objectives

► **Insert clip art**
► **Insert and crop a picture**
► **Embed a chart**
► **Enter and edit data in the datasheet**
► **Format a chart**
► **Use slide show commands**
► **Set slide show timings and transitions**
► **Set slide animation effects**

After completing the content of your presentation, you can enhance it to make it more visually interesting. When you prepare a presentation, it's important to supplement your slide text with clip art or graphics, charts, and other visuals that help communicate your content and keep your slide show interesting. In this unit, you will learn how to insert three of the most common visual enhancements: a clip art image, a picture, and a chart. These objects are created in other programs. After you add the visuals, you will rehearse the slide show and add special effects. Carrie Armstrong has changed the presentation based on feedback from Lynn and the president of Nomad Ltd. Now, she wants to revise the Annual Report Executive Summary presentation to make it easier to understand and more interesting to watch.

Inserting Clip Art

PowerPoint has over 1000 professionally designed images, called **clip art**, that you can place in your presentation. Using clip art is the easiest and fastest way to enhance your presentations. Clip art is stored in a file index system called a **gallery** that sorts the clip art into categories. You can open the Clip Gallery in one of three ways: by double-clicking a clip art placeholder from an AutoLayout; using the Insert Clip Art button ⬚ on the Standard toolbar; or choosing Picture, then Clip Art on the Insert menu. As with drawing objects, you can modify clip art images by changing their shape, size, fill, or shading. Clip art is the most widely used method of enhancing presentations, and it is available from many sources outside Clip Gallery, including the World Wide Web (WWW) and collections on CD-ROMs. ✎ Carrie wants to add a picture from the Clip Gallery to one of the slides and then adjust its size and placement.

1. Open the presentation **PPT D-1** from your Student Disk, save it as **97 Annual Report Final** to your Student Disk, make sure it is at 36% zoom, click the **Restore Window** button on the presentation window, click **Window** on the menu bar, then click **Fit to Page**

2. Drag the vertical scroll box to the last slide in the presentation, Slide 9 of 9
   The Thank You slide appears. Change the AutoLayout to a layout that contains a clip art placeholder, so you'll be able to easily add a piece of clip art to the slide.

3. Click **Slide Layout** on the Common Tasks toolbar
   The Slide Layout dialog box opens with the Bulleted List AutoLayout selected. Choose the layout with bulleted text on the left and clip art on the right.

4. Click the **Text & Clip Art AutoLayout** (third row, first column), then click **Apply**
   PowerPoint applies the Text and Clip Art AutoLayout to the slide, which makes the existing text object narrower, and then inserts a clip art placeholder, where the clip art object will be placed on the slide.

5. Double-click the **clip art placeholder**
   The Microsoft Clip Gallery 3.0 dialog box opens, similar to Figure D-1.

6. Make sure the **Clip Art tab** is selected and in the category list on the left, drag the scroll box to the bottom, then click **Transportation**
   If the Transportation category doesn't appear, select a different category. The preview box to the right of the categories displays small previews of the clip art in the Transportation category. Now, select a graphic and import it to Slide 9.

7. In the preview box, click the **down scroll arrow** twice, click the **sailboat** shown in Figure D-1, then click **Insert**
   The picture of the sailboat appears on the right side of the slide, and the Picture toolbar automatically opens. If you don't have a picture of a sailboat in your Clip Gallery, select a similar picture. Now, resize the sailboat picture.

8. Place the pointer over the lower-right sizing handle, hold down [Shift], and drag the handle slightly up and to the left, until the image height is approximately the same as the height of the text box
   Remember, pressing [Shift] while resizing an object causes the object to be resized proportionately. Now, adjust the placement of the clip art and text blocks.

9. With the sailboat object still selected, press the keyboard arrow keys until the sailboat is centered between the text block and the right edge of the slide as shown in Figure D-2, then deselect the picture
   Compare your screen with Figure D-2, and make any necessary corrections.

Trouble?
If this is the first time the Clip Gallery is opened, PowerPoint needs to build the clip art visual index. Click OK to build the index, then click OK when you get a message telling you that the index is complete. If a dialog box appears telling you that additional clips are available on the Microsoft Office 97 CD-ROM disc, click OK to close the dialog box.

Time To
✔Save

FIGURE D-1: Microsoft Clip Gallery 3.0 dialog box

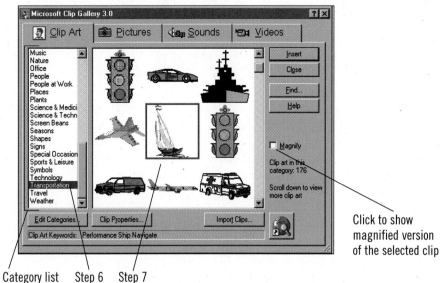

Category list   Step 6   Step 7

Click to show
magnified version
of the selected clip

FIGURE D-2: Last slide with sailboat resized and repositioned

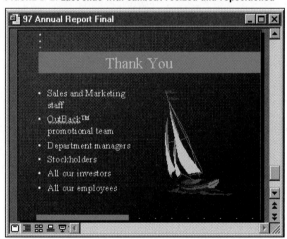

More about Clip Gallery

To add other clip art (or pictures, sounds, or videos) to the Clip Gallery, you must first import them into the Clip Gallery using the Import Clips command button. When you import a clip, Clip Gallery asks you to assign keywords to each one. **Keywords** are words you use to quickly find the object in the future. Notice in Figure D-1 the keywords Performance, Ship, and Navigate below the preview box have already been assigned to the selected sailboat graphic. To use keywords to find an image, click the Find button in the Clip Gallery dialog box to open the Find Clip dialog box shown in Figure D-3. Type a keyword in the Keyword text box or click the Keyword list arrow and click a keyword, then click Find Now. Clip Gallery places images of all objects that have that keyword assigned to them in the Clip Gallery window and assigns a new category to them called [Results of Last Find].

FIGURE D-3: Find Clip dialog box

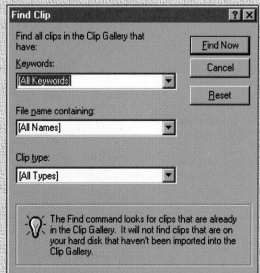

Inserting and Cropping a Picture

A picture in PowerPoint is a scanned photograph, a piece of line art, clip art, or other artwork that is created in another program and inserted into a PowerPoint presentation. You can insert over 20 types of pictures using the Insert Picture command. As with other PowerPoint objects, you can move or crop an inserted picture. **Cropping** a picture means to hide a portion of the picture in cases where you don't want to include all of the original. Carrie inserts a picture, crops it, and adjusts its background.

1. Go to **Slide 7**, titled "1997 Environmental Funding," click **Slide Layout** on the Common Tasks toolbar, click the **Text & Object AutoLayout** (fourth row, first column), then click **Apply**

2. Double-click the object placeholder
The Insert Object dialog box appears. You will insert a picture that has already been saved in a file.

3. Click the **Create from file option button**
The dialog box changes to a text box that lists the filename of the object you will insert.

4. Click **Browse**, click the **Look in list arrow**, click the drive containing your Student Disk, click **PPT D-2** in the Look in list, click **OK**, then click **OK** in the Insert Object dialog box
The picture appears on the slide, and the Picture toolbar automatically opens. See Figure D-4. Now that the picture is in place, crop out the sun from the top to give the picture more impact.

5. Click the **Crop button** on the Picture toolbar, then place the cursor over the **top middle handle** of the tree picture
The pointer changes to .

6. Drag the **top edge** downward until the dotted line indicating the top edge of the picture is below the sun image, as shown in Figure D-5
As you drag with the cropping tool, the pointer changes to . Now, increase the size of the text and the picture to make better use of the space on the slide.

7. Click twice on a blank area of the slide to deselect the cropping tool and the picture, press [Shift] and click on the main text box, then click the **Increase Font Size button** on the Formatting toolbar

8. Click on the picture to select it, press [Shift], drag the **upper-right sizing handle** until the right border of the picture is touching the edge of the slide, then release [Shift] and drag the selected picture up and to the left to center it in the space
The tree would look better without its white background. Make the background transparent.

9. With the image still selected, click the **Set Transparent Color button** on the Picture toolbar, click the white background, and click on a blank area of the slide to deselect the picture
The white background is no longer visible, and the tree contrasts well with the teal background, as shown in Figure D-6.

10. Save your changes

Trouble?

If the Picture toolbar does not appear, right-click on the picture, then click Show Picture Toolbar on the pop-up menu.

Trouble?

If the Microsoft Paint program becomes active when you click on the picture, click anywhere in the window outside of the picture to return to PowerPoint.

FIGURE D-4: Inserted picture object and Picture toolbar

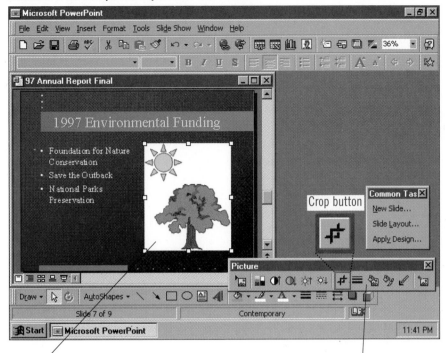

Crop button

Inserted picture
object

Picture toolbar may
appear in a
different position
on your screen

FIGURE D-5: Using the
cropping pointer to
crop out the sun image

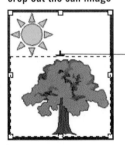

Cropping pointer
changes shape as
you drag

FIGURE D-6: Completed slide with the cropped and resized graphic

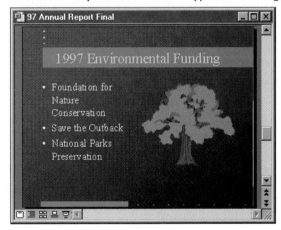

Graphics in PowerPoint

You can insert many different types of pictures with a variety of graphics **formats**, or file types, in PowerPoint. By looking at its file extension, you can see what format a graphic is in. The clip art that comes with PowerPoint is in **.wmf**, or **Windows metafile**, format. A graphic in .wmf format can be ungrouped (using the Ungroup command on the Draw menu) into its separate PowerPoint objects and then edited with PowerPoint drawing tools. **Bitmap** pictures, which have the file extension **.bmp**, cannot be ungrouped. Although you cannot ungroup .bmp files, you can still modify some of their characteristics with PowerPoint drawing tools. The clip art sailboat you inserted in the last lesson is in .wmf format, and the tree picture you inserted in this lesson is in .bmp format.

Embedding a Chart

Often, the best way to communicate information is with a visual aid such as a chart. PowerPoint comes with a program called **Microsoft Graph** (often called **Graph**) that you use to create graph charts for your slides. A **graph object** is made up of two components: a **datasheet**, containing the numbers you want to chart, and a **chart**, which is the graphical representation of the datasheet. Table D-1 lists the Graph chart types. When you insert a graph into PowerPoint, you are actually embedding it. **Embedding** an object means that the object copy becomes part of the PowerPoint file, but you can double-click on the embedded object to display the tools of the program in which the object was created. You can use these tools to modify the object. If you modify the embedded object, the original object file does not change. ✎ Carrie wants to embed a Graph object in the slide containing the 1997 Sales Analysis.

Steps¹²³⁴

1. **Go to Slide 5, titled "1997 Sales Analysis"**
   Because you are going to place a chart on this slide, change the slide layout to accommodate a chart.

2. **Click Slide Layout on the Common Tasks toolbar**
   The Slide Layout dialog box opens with the Bulleted List AutoLayout selected. Select the Chart AutoLayout to replace the current layout.

3. **Click Chart AutoLayout (second row, far right), then click Apply**
   The Chart AutoLayout, which contains a chart placeholder, appears on the slide. Double-click the chart placeholder to open Microsoft Graph.

4. **Double-click the chart placeholder**
   Microsoft Graph opens and embeds a default datasheet and chart into the slide, as shown in Figure D-7. The Graph datasheet is composed of rows and columns. The intersection of a row and a column is called a **cell**. Cells are referred to by their row and column location; for example, the cell at the intersection of column A and row 1 is called cell A1. Cells along the left column and top row of the datasheet typically display **data labels** that identify the data in a column or row; for example, "East" and "1st Qtr" are data labels. Cells below and to the right of the data labels display the data values that are represented in the Graph chart. Each column and row of data in the datasheet is called a **data series**. Each data series has corresponding **data series markers** in the chart, which are graphical representations such as bars, columns, or pie wedges. The PowerPoint Standard and Formatting toolbars have been replaced with the Microsoft Graph Standard and Formatting toolbars, and the menu bar has changed to include Microsoft Graph commands.

5. **Move the pointer over the datasheet**
   The pointer changes to ✛ . Cell A1 is the **active cell**, which means that it is selected. The active cell has a heavy black border around it.

6. **Click cell B3**
   Cell B3 is now the current cell.

7. **Click a blank area of the Presentation window to exit Graph and deselect the chart object**
   Compare your slide to Figure D-8. In the next lesson, you will replace the default information in the chart with Nomad's sales information for 1997.

FIGURE D-7: Datasheet and chart open in the PowerPoint window

Graph toolbars   Data labels   Active cell

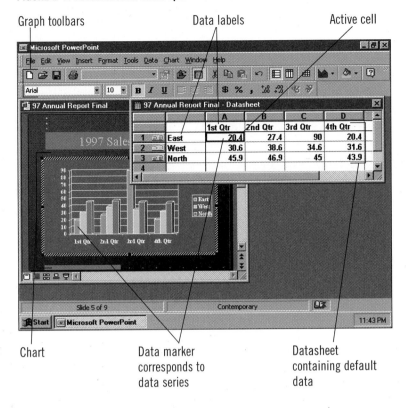

Chart   Data marker corresponds to data series   Datasheet containing default data

FIGURE D-8: Chart object on a slide

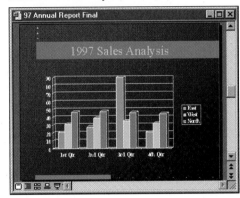

TABLE D-1: Microsoft Graph Chart Types

chart type	use to
Column	Track values over time or across categories
Bar	Compare values in categories or over time
Line	Track values over time
Pie	Compare individual values to the whole
XY (Scatter)	Compare pairs of values
Area	Show contribution of each data series to the total over time
Doughnut	Compare individual values to the whole with multiple series
Radar	Show changes in values in relation to a center point
Surface	Show value trends across two dimensions
Bubble	Indicate relative size of data points
Stock	Show stock market information or scientific data
Cylinder, cone, pyramid	Track values over time or across categories

Entering and Editing Data in the Datasheet

After you embed the default datasheet and chart into your presentation, you need to change the data label and cell information in the sample datasheet to create the chart you need. While you can import information from a spreadsheet, it is often easier to use Graph and type in the information. As you enter data or make changes to the datasheet, the chart automatically changes to reflect your alterations. ◄▬▬ Carrie enters the 1997 quarterly sales figures by product type that Nomad Ltd's president wants to show to the stockholders and employees. She first changes the data labels and then the series information in the cells.

Steps 1 2 3 4

1. **Double-click the chart**
   The graph is selected and the datasheet appears.

2. **Click the East data label, type Expeditions and press [Enter]**
   After you press [Enter], the first data label changes from East to Expeditions and the data label in row 2, the cell directly below the active cell, becomes selected. Don't worry if the column is not quite wide enough to accommodate the label; you'll fix that after you enter all the column labels.

3. **Type Sporting Gear, press [Enter], type Clothing, and press [Enter]**
   Notice that row 1 has scrolled up behind the column data labels, and there is no automatic label text in row 4.

4. **Type Supplies, press [Tab], then press [↑] three times to display all the rows**
   Pressing [Tab] moves the active cell one column to the right. Notice that in the chart itself, below the datasheet, the data labels you typed are now in the legend to the right of the chart. Now that you have entered all the column data labels, widen the data label column.

5. **Position the pointer on top of the column divider to the left of the letter A so that ✛ changes to ↔ and double-click**
   The data label column automatically widens to display all the column label text. Now, enter the data series information for each product type by quarter.

6. **With cell A1 selected, type 98, press [Enter], type 50, press [Enter], type 45, press [Enter], type 30 and press [Tab], then press the [↑] three times to move to the top of the second data series column**
   Notice that the heights of the bar chart columns changed to reflect the numbers you typed.

7. **Enter the rest of the numbers shown in Figure D-9 to complete the datasheet, then navigate using the arrow keys to make cell A1 the active cell**
   The chart bars adjust to reflect the new information. The chart currently shows the bars grouped by quarter (the legend represents the columns in the datasheet). It would be more effective if the bars were grouped by product type (with the legend representing the rows in the datasheet). Change this by using the Series in Columns command on the Data menu.

8. **Click Data on the menu bar, then click Series in Columns**
   The horizontal axis labels now displays Expeditions, Sporting Gear, and so on, instead of the quarters. The groups of data markers (the bars) now represent product types and show sales for each quarter.

9. **Click in the Presentation window outside the chart area and compare your chart to Figure D-10**
   The datasheet closes, allowing you to see your entire chart. This chart layout clearly shows that Expeditions are Nomad's largest revenue source.

Trouble?

The datasheet window can be manipulated in the same ways other windows are. If you can't see a column or a row, use the scroll bars to move another part of the datasheet into view or resize the datasheet window so you can see all the data.

Time To

✓ Save

FIGURE D-9: Datasheet showing Nomad Ltd's revenue for each quarter

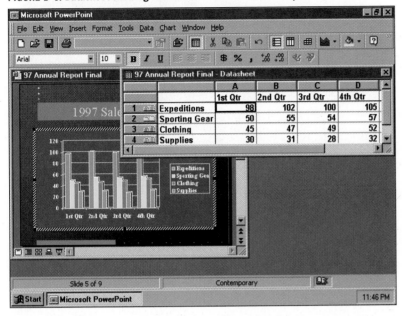

FIGURE D-10: Chart showing data grouped by product type

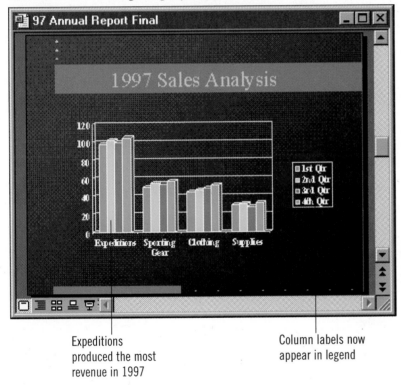

Expeditions
produced the most
revenue in 1997

Column labels now
appear in legend

Series in Rows vs. Series in Columns

If you have difficulty visualizing the difference between the Series in Rows and the Series in Columns commands on the Data menu, think about the legend. **Series in rows** means that the information in the *rows* will become the legend in the chart (and the col-umn labels will be on the horizontal axis). **Series in Columns** means that the information in the *columns* will become the legend in the chart (and the row labels will be on the horizontal axis).

Formatting a Chart

Graph lets you change the appearance of the chart to emphasize certain aspects of the information you are presenting. You can change the chart type, create titles, format the chart labels, move the legend, or add arrows. ◀──── Carrie wants to improve the appearance of her chart by formatting the vertical and horizontal axes and by inserting a title.

1. **Double-click the chart to reopen Microsoft Graph, then click the Close button in the Datasheet window to close the datasheet**
   Display the vertical axis numbers in currency format with dollar signs ($).

2. **Click the sales numbers on the vertical axis to select them, then click the Currency Style button $ on the Chart Formatting toolbar**
   The numbers on the vertical axis appear with dollar signs and two decimal places. You don't need to display the two decimal places, since all the values are whole numbers.

3. **Click the Decrease Decimal button ⌗ on the Chart Formatting toolbar twice**
   The numbers on the vertical axis now have dollar signs and show only whole numbers. The product type names on the horizontal axis take up a lot of space, and actually reduce the size of the chart itself. Decrease the font size to improve the fit.

4. **Click any of the product type names on the horizontal axis, click the Font Size list arrow on the Chart Formatting toolbar, and click 14**
   The font size changes from 18 points to 14 points for all the labels on the horizontal axis, and the labels now fit horizontally under each column group. Now, add a title to the chart and labels to the vertical and horizontal axes.

5. **Click Chart on the menu bar, click Chart Options, and click the Titles tab**
   The Chart Options dialog box opens, in which you can change the chart title, axes, gridlines, legend, data labels, and the table. First, add a title to the chart.

6. **Click the Chart title text box, then type Revenue by Product Type**
   The preview box changes to show you the chart with the title.

7. **Press [Tab] to move the cursor to the Category (X) axis text box, type Product Type, press [Tab] to move the cursor to the Value (Z) axis text box, then type Sales in 000s**
   In the 3-D chart, the vertical axis is called the Z axis and the depth axis, which you don't typically work with, is the Y axis. See Figure D-11 for the completed Titles tab. Now, place the legend below the chart, so the chart itself can be as wide as possible allowing the audience to see the bars clearly.

8. **Click the Legend tab, click the bottom option button, and click OK**
   Now, turn the vertical axis label 90 degrees to the left, so it takes up less room.

9. **Make sure the Value Axis title "Sales in 000s" label is selected, click Format on the menu bar, click Selected Axis Title to open the Format Axis Title dialog box, click the Alignment tab, drag the red diamond in the Orientation section up to a vertical position so the spin box reads 90 degrees, click OK, then click a blank area of the Presentation window**
   Graph closes and the PowerPoint toolbars and menu bar appear. The completed chart displays as shown in Figure D-12.

FIGURE D-11: Titles tab in the Chart Options dialog box

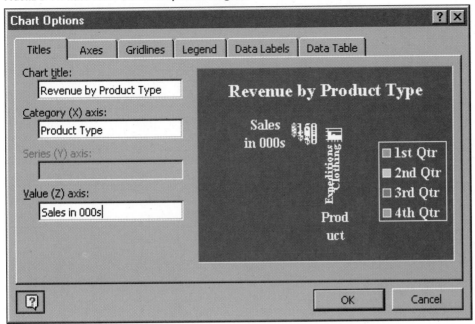

FIGURE D-12: Slide showing formatted chart

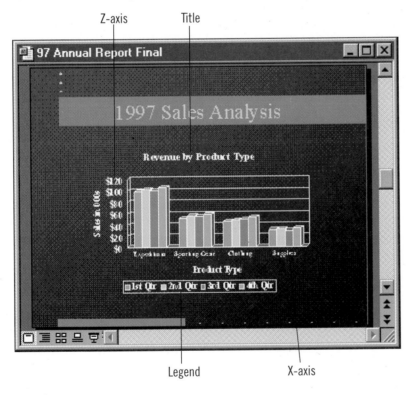

CLUES TO USE

Customizing Charts

You can easily customize the look of any chart in Microsoft Graph. Click the chart to select it, then double-click any data series element (a column, for example) to display the Format Data Series dialog box. Use the tabs to change the element's fill color, border, shape, or data label. You can even use the same fill effects you apply to a presentation background. In 3-D charts, you can change the chart depth as well as the distances between series.

Using Slide Show Commands

With PowerPoint, you can show a presentation on any compatible computer using Slide Show view. As you've seen, Slide Show view fills your computer screen with the slides of your presentation, displaying them one at a time—similar to how a slide projector displays slides. Once your presentation is in Slide Show view, you can use a number of slide show options to tailor the show. For example, you can draw on, or **annotate**, slides or jump to a specific slide. Carrie runs a slide show of the president's presentation and practices using some of the custom slide show options. Then she can suggest them to Nomad Ltd's president to help make his presentation more effective.

Steps 1 2 3 4

1. Go to Slide 1, then click the **Slide Show button**

The first slide of the presentation fills the screen. Advance to the next slide.

2. Press [Spacebar]

Slide 2 appears on the screen. Pressing the spacebar or clicking the left mouse button is the easiest way to move through a slide show. You can also use the keys listed in Table D-2.

3. Move the mouse

When you move the mouse, the Slide Show menu icon appears in the lower-left corner of the screen. Clicking the Slide Show menu icon or right-clicking anywhere on the screen displays a pop-up menu, which offers several choices for working with an electronic slide show. Sometimes, you will want to use the pop-up menu to go to a specific slide or to make annotations. You can emphasize major points in your presentation by annotating the slide during a slide show using the Pen.

4. Click the **Slide Show menu icon**, then click **Pen**

The pointer changes to.

5. Press and hold [Shift] and drag to draw a line under each of the bulleted points on the slide

Holding down [Shift] constrains the Pen tool to straight horizontal or vertical lines. Compare your screen to Figure D-13. While the annotation pen is visible, mouse clicks do not advance the slide show. However, you can still move to the next slide by pressing the spacebar or [Enter]. Next, erase your annotations.

6. Right-click to display the Slide Show pop-up menu, point to **Screen**, then click **Erase Pen**

The annotations on Slide 2 are erased. Now, jump to Slide 5.

7. Right-click anywhere on the screen to display the Slide Show pop-up menu, point to **Go**, then click **Slide Navigator**

8. Click **5. 1997 Sales Analysis** in the Slide titles list box, then click **Go To**

Slide 5 appears. Examine it, then return to Slide 1 and go through the entire presentation in Slide view.

9. Press [Home], then click the mouse, press [Spacebar], or press [Enter] to advance through the slide show

After Slide 9 appears, the next click ends the slide show and returns you to Slide view.

FIGURE D-13: Slide 2 in Slide Show view with annotations

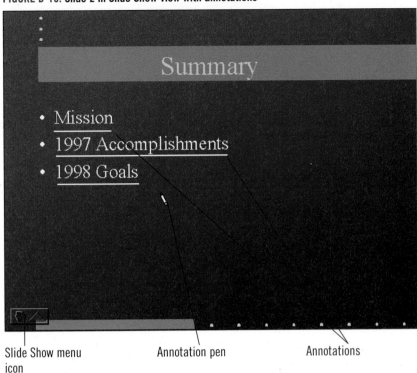

Slide Show menu icon   Annotation pen   Annotations

TABLE D-2: Slide show keyboard controls

control	description
[E]	Erases the annotation drawing
[Enter], [Spacebar], [→] or [N]	Advances to the next slide
[H]	Displays a hidden slide
[←] or [PgUp]	Returns to the previous slide
[W]	Changes the screen to white; press again to return
[S]	Pauses the slide show; press again to continue
[B]	Changes the screen to black; press again to return
[Ctrl][P]	Changes pointer to
[CTRL][A]	Changes pointer to
[Esc]	Stops the slide show

Showing slide shows on other computers

You can show a PowerPoint presentation on any compatible computer, even if PowerPoint is not installed on it. To do this, you use a special program called PowerPoint Viewer, which comes with PowerPoint. Put the Viewer on the same disk as your presentation by using the Pack and Go Wizard on the File menu. Then, unpack the Viewer and the presentation together to run the slide show on another computer. You can freely install the PowerPoint Viewer program on any compatible system. If you have access to the World Wide Web (WWW), you can download PowerPoint Viewer by pointing to Microsoft on the Web on the Help menu, and then clicking Free Stuff.

Setting Slide Show Timings and Transitions

In a slide show, you can preset when and how each slide appears on the screen. You can set the **slide timing**, which is the amount of time a slide is visible on the screen. Each slide can have the same or different timing. Setting the right slide timing is important because it determines the amount of time you have to discuss the material on each slide. Also, you can set **slide transitions**, special visual and audio effects you apply to a slide that determine how it moves in and out of view during the slide show. For example, during a slide show you might have one slide fade out while the next one fades in or have another slide uncover slowly across the screen. You make most timing and transition changes in Slide Sorter view. Carrie decides to set her slide timings for 15 seconds per slide and to set the transitions for all slides but the last one to fade to black before the next slide appears.

Steps

1. Click the Slide Sorter View button

Slide Sorter view displays a miniature image of the slides in your presentation. The number of slides you see on your screen depends on the current zoom setting. Notice that the Slide Sorter toolbar appears below the Formatting toolbar.

2. Right-click one of the slides, then click Slide Transition

The Slide Transition dialog box, shown in Figure D-14, opens. You want to set the timing between slides to 15 seconds, but you also want to be able to advance to the next slide manually, in case the president finishes talking in less time than that.

3. In the Advance section, make sure the On mouse click check box is selected, click the Automatically after check box to select it, type 15 in the seconds text box, then click Apply to All

The duration you set appears under each slide. When you run the slide show again, each slide will remain on the screen for 15 seconds. If you want to advance more quickly, press [Spacebar] or click the mouse button. Now, set the slide transitions.

4. Right-click one of the slides, click Slide Transition on the pop-up menu, then click the Effect list arrow in the top section

A drop-down menu appears, showing all the transition effects.

5. Scroll down the list, click Fade through black, click Apply to All, then click in a blank area of the Presentation window to deselect the slide

In Slide Sorter view, each slide now has a small transition icon under it, as shown in Figure D-15, indicating there is a transition effect set for the slides. Now, preview the effect.

6. Click the transition icon under any slide

The slide fades and reappears. Apply a different effect to the last slide.

7. Scroll down the Presentation window, right-click the last slide, click Slide Transition, click the Effect list arrow, and click Split Vertical Out

The last slide will now appear with a split from the center of the screen.

8. Click the Sound list arrow, scroll down the list and click Drum Roll or choose another sound effect, then click Apply

Make sure you did not click Apply to All this time. The last slide now has a different visual effect and a drum roll transition applied to it.

9. Press [Home], click the Slide Show View button and watch as the slide show advances with its special effects

To move more quickly, press the spacebar or [Enter].

QuickTip

You also can click Slide Show on the menu bar, then click Slide Transition.

QuickTip

You also can click Edit on the menu bar, click Select All, then click the Transition list arrow on the Slide Sorter toolbar to apply a transition effect to all the slides.

Time To

✔Save

FIGURE D-14: Slide Transition dialog box

Click to set
transition effects

Click to apply
selections to all slides
in the presentation

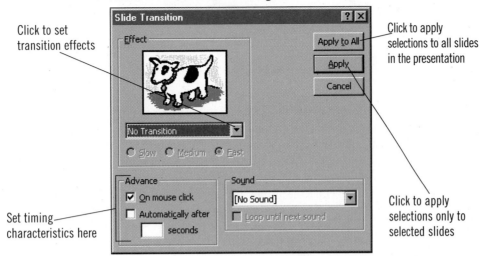

Set timing
characteristics here

Click to apply
selections only to
selected slides

FIGURE D-15: Slide Sorter view showing transition effects and timing

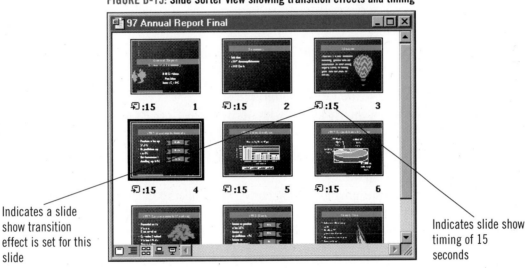

Indicates a slide
show transition
effect is set for this
slide

Indicates slide show
timing of 15
seconds

CLUES TO USE

Rehearsing slide show timing

You can set different slide timings for each slide. For example, you can have the title slide appear for 20 seconds, the second slide for 3 minutes, and so on. You also can set timings by clicking the Rehearse Timings button on the Slide Sorter toolbar or by choosing the Rehearse Timings command on the Slide Show menu. The Rehearsal dialog box shown in Figure D-16 appears. It contains buttons to pause between slides and to advance to the next slide. Practice giving your presentation while the slide show is running. PowerPoint keeps track of how long each slide appears and sets the timing accordingly. You can view your rehearsed timings in Slide Sorter view. The next time you run the slide show, you can use the timings you rehearsed.

FIGURE D-16: Rehearsal dialog box

Total time elapsed

Time elapsed while
viewing this slide

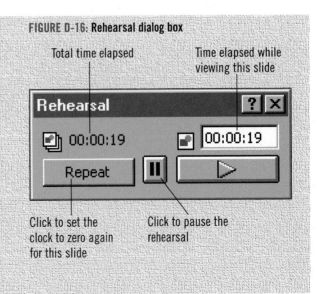

Click to set the
clock to zero again
for this slide

Click to pause the
rehearsal

Setting Slide Animation Effects

Animation effects let you control how the graphics and main points in your presentation appear on the screen during a slide show. For example, you might want to set the individual slide bullets to "fly in" from the left. You can animate text, images, or even individual chart elements, or you can add sound effects. Keep in mind that the animation effects you choose give a certain "flavor" to your presentation. They can be serious and businesslike or humorous. Choose appropriate effects for your presentation content and audience. ✐ Carrie wants to animate the text and graphics of several slides in her presentation.

Steps

1. **In Slide Sorter view, click Slide 2, press [Shift], and click Slides 4, 7, 8, and 9**
   The selected slides have bullets on them, and you will animate the bullets so they appear on the slide individually when you click the mouse during the slide show.

2. **On the Slide Sorter toolbar, click the Text Preset Animation list arrow and click Fly From Left**
   When you run the slide show, the bullets of the selected slides, instead of appearing all at once, will appear one at a time, "flying" in from the left, each time you click the mouse button.

   > **QuickTip**
   > Use the ToolTips to see the names of the toolbar buttons.

3. **Click Slide 1, then run through the slide show**
   The bullets fly in from the left, but the tree and the sailboat do not fly in. To set custom animation effects, the target slide must be in Slide view.

   > **QuickTip**
   > If you want a grouped object, like the ribbons on Slides 4 and 8, to fly in individually, then you must ungroup them first.

4. **Double-click Slide 9 to view it in Slide view, click Slide Show on the menu bar, and click Custom Animation**
   The Custom Animation dialog box opens, similar to the one shown in Figure D-17. Objects that are already animated appear in the Animation Order section in the order in which they will be animated. Set the object (the sailboat) to materialize gradually.

5. **On the Timing tab, click Object 3 in the text box at the top, then click the Animate option button on the right**

6. **Click the Effects tab, click the top list arrow in the Entry animation and sound section, scroll down and click Dissolve, click Preview in the upper-right corner of the dialog box to see the new animation effect, then click OK**

7. **Go to Slide 7 and repeat steps 5 and 6 to change the animation effect for the tree**

8. **Run the Slide Show again**
   The special effects have helped make the presentation easier to understand and more interesting to view.

9. **Click the Zoom list arrow, click 33, click Window on the menu bar, then click Fit to Page**
   Figure D-18 shows the completed presentation in Slide Sorter view at 33% zoom.

10. **Save your presentation, then exit PowerPoint**

Text will be
animated first   Text and Object have
been animated   Preview box   Click to preview
special effects

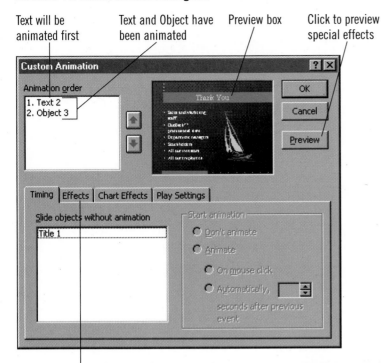

Click here to change
animation effects

FIGURE D-18: **Completed presentation in Slide Sorter view**

Presentation Checklist

You should always rehearse your slide show. If possible, rehearse your presentation in the room and with the computer that you will use. Use the following checklist to prepare for the slide show.

✔ Is **PowerPoint** or **PowerPoint Viewer** installed on the computer?

✔ Is your **presentation file** on the hard drive of the computer you will be using? Try putting a shortcut for the file on the desktop. Do you have a backup copy of your presentation file on a floppy disk?

✔ Is the **projection device** working correctly? Can the slides be seen from the back of the room?

✔ Do you know how to control **room lighting** so that the audience can both see your slides as well as their handouts and notes? You may want to designate someone to control the lights if the controls are not close to you.

✔ Will the **computer** be situated so you can advance and annotate the slides yourself? If not, designate someone to advance them for you.

✔ Do you have enough copies of your **handouts**? Bring extras. Decide when to hand them out, or whether you prefer to have them waiting at the audience members' places when they enter.

Practice

▶ Concepts Review

Label each of the elements of the PowerPoint window shown in Figure D-19.

FIGURE D-19

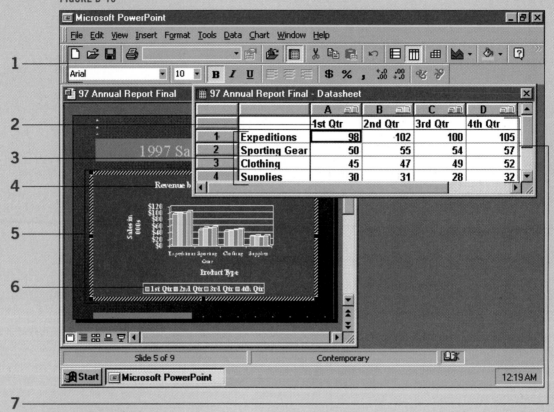

Match each of the terms with the statement that describes it.

8. Chart
9. Embedded object
10. Animation effect
11. Data series markers
12. Clip Gallery or Clip art gallery
13. Active cell

a. The selected cell in a datasheet.
b. A graphical representation of a datasheet.
c. Graphical representations of data series.
d. The way bulleted items and images appear on a slide.
e. A copy of an object from which you can access another program's tools.
f. A file index system that organizes images.

Select the best answer from the list of choices.

14. The PowerPoint clip art is stored in a:
   a. Folder
   b. Gallery
   c. Card Catalogue
   d. Floppy disk

15. **PowerPoint animation effects let you control:**
    a. the order in which text and objects are animated.
    b. the direction from which animated objects appear.
    c. which text and images are animated.
    d. all of the above.

16. **Which of the following is *not* true of a Microsoft Graph chart?**
    a. A graph is made up of a datasheet and chart.
    b. You can double-click a chart to view its corresponding datasheet.
    c. An active cell has a black selection rectangle around it.
    d. You cannot import data from other programs into a datasheet.

17. **If you annotate in Slide Show view, what are you doing?**
    a. Speaking
    b. Answering questions
    c. Drawing on the slide
    d. Changing the content of the slides

▶ Skills Review

1. **Insert clip art.**
    a. Open the presentation PPT D-3 on your Student Disk, save it as "OutBack Report" on your Student Disk.
    b. Click the Next Slide button, then double-click the clip art placeholder on Slide 2.
    c. Click the Clip Art tab, scroll down the category list, then click Maps. If the Maps category doesn't appear, select a different category.
    d. In the preview box, click the 3-D U.S. Map with State Boundaries clip art, then click Insert.
    e. Press and hold [Shift], then drag the lower-right sizing handle to enlarge the map slightly.
    f. Press and hold [Shift] and click to select both the main text block and the map, click the Draw menu button on the Drawing toolbar, point to Align and Distribute, and click Align Top to align the tops of the two objects.

2. **Insert and crop a picture.**
    a. Go to Slide 6, which is the last slide.
    b. Click the Slide Layout button on the Common Tasks toolbar and select the Text & Object layout.
    c. Double-click the Object placeholder, click Create from file, click Browse, and locate the drive containing your Student Disk. Click PPT D-4, then click OK.
    d. Click the Crop button on the Picture toolbar and position the cursor over the left-middle handle of the shuttle image.
    e. Drag the left edge to the right to crop off about ¾" of the steam, then click on a blank area of the slide twice to deselect the cropping pointer and deselect the image.
    f. Press [Shift], click the main text box, click the Increase Font Size button on the Formatting toolbar, then click on a blank area of the slide to deselect the text box.
    g. Press [Shift], then drag the upper-left sizing handle so the image is approximately as large as the main text box.

3. Embed a chart.
   a. Go to Slide 3, OutBack Division Sales.
   b. Click Slide Layout on the Common Tasks toolbar and select the Chart AutoLayout.
   c. Double-click the chart placeholder to start Graph.

4. Enter and edit data in the datasheet.
   a. Click the row 1 label in the datasheet, and type North.
   b. Enter the chart information shown in Table D-3 into the datasheet. Use [Tab], [Return], and the keyboard arrow keys to navigate through the datasheet as you enter data.
   c. Click Data on the menu bar, and click Series in Columns.
   d. Click a blank area of the Presentation window twice to exit Graph.
   e. Click the Save button on the Standard toolbar.

TABLE D-3

	1st Qtr	2nd Qtr	3rd Qtr	4th Qtr
North	36	40	45	43
East	44	50	52	53
South	31	36	40	38
West	54	44	57	59

5. Format a chart.
   a. Double-click the chart object, then click the Close button in the datasheet window.
   b. Click the region names on the X-axis, click the Font Size list arrow on the Formatting toolbar, then click 24.
   c. Click the vertical axis, and click the Currency Style button on the Formatting toolbar.
   d. Click the Decrease Decimal button twice on the Formatting toolbar.
   e. Click Chart on the menu bar, click Chart Options, click the Title tab, click the Chart title text box, and type "1997 OutBack Sales."
   f. Press [Tab] twice to place the insertion point in the Value (Z) Axis text box, type "in 000s," and click OK.
   g. Click Format on the menu bar, click Selected Axis Title, then click the Alignment tab.
   h. In the orientation pane, drag the red diamond up to the 90-degree position, and click OK.
   i. Click the Legend to select it, click Format on the menu bar, and click Selected Legend.
   j. Click the Placement tab, click the Left option button, and click OK.
   k. Click a blank area of the Presentation window to exit Graph.

6. Use slide show commands.
   a. Go to Slide 1, and click the Slide Show button.
   b. Click the mouse button to move to the next slide.
   c. Press [Enter] to advance to Slide 3.
   d. Click the Slide Show menu icon, then click Pen.
   e. Hold down [Shift] and draw two annotation lines under the West axis label on the chart.
   f. Right-click to display the Slide Show pop-up menu, point to Screen, then click Erase Pen.
   g. Open the Slide Show pop-up menu again, point to Go, then click Slide Navigator.
   h. Click 2. OutBack Sales Regions.
   i. Return to Slide 1 by typing the number 1 and pressing [Enter].
   j. Press [End] to move to the last slide, and press [Enter] to return to Slide view.

7. Set slide show timings and transitions.
   a. Click the Slide Sorter View button, and enter 66% in the Zoom text box so all six slides fit on the screen.
   b. Right-click one of the slides, and click Slide Transition from the pop-up menu.

c. In the Advance section of the dialog box, make sure the On Mouse Click is selected, click the Automatically after check box to select it, and type 15 in the seconds text box.

d. In the Effect list box, select Box Out, and click Apply to All.

e. In Slide Sorter view, click the small transition icon under any slide and view the transition effect.

f. Right-click the last slide in the presentation, and click Slide Transition from the pop-up menu.

g. In the Effect List box, select Cover Down, and click Apply.

h. Click View on the menu bar, then click Slide Show to view the transitions.

8. Set slide animation effects.

a. In Slide Sorter view, press [Shift] and click Slides 2, 5, and 6.

b. On the Slide Sorter Toolbar click the Text Preset Animation list box and click Peek From Right.

c. Deselect the slides, then double-click Slide 2 to open it in Slide view.

d. Click Slide Show on the menu bar, and click Custom Animation.

e. In the Animation Order list box, click Object 3, and click the Effects tab.

f. In the Entry animation and sound list box, choose Dissolve, then click Preview.

g. In the Animation Order list box click Text 2.

h. In the After animation list box, click More Colors, click the Standard tab, choose any red color, then click OK.

i. Click Preview, then click OK.

j. Press [Home], then run the slide show.

k. Save, print, and then close the presentation.

▶ Independent Challenges

1. You are a financial management consultant for "Pacific Coast Investments", located in San Jose, California. One of your primary responsibilities is to give financial seminars on different financial investments and how to determine which fund to invest in. In this challenge, you'll need to enhance the look of the slides by adding and formatting objects and adding animations effects and transitions. To begin, open the presentation provided on your Student Disk.

   To complete this independent challenge:

1. Open the file PPT D-5 on your Student Disk, and save it as "Fund Seminar" on your Student Disk.

2. Look through the presentation in Slide view and think about how you want each slide to look. What information is provided, and what could you add? How do you want to communicate the message? Look at the presentation organization; you may need to make some adjustments. Is it well done? If you reorganize the presentation, be able to support your decisions.

3. Create a Graph chart, and embed it on Slide 6. Enter the data in Table D-4 into the datasheet.

4. Format the chart. Add titles as necessary.

5. Add clip art to the presentation.

6. Format the objects in the presentation. Use the align and group commands to organize your shapes.

7. Spell check the presentation, then save it.

8. View the slide show and evaluate your presentation. Make changes if necessary.

TABLE D-4

	1 Yr	3 Yr	5 Yr	10 Yr
Bonds	4.2%	5.2%	7.9%	9.4%
Stocks	7.5%	8.3%	10.8%	12.6%
Mutual Funds	6.1%	6.3%	6.4%	6.1%

9. Set animation effects, slide transitions, and slide timings. Your audience includes potential investors who need the information you are presenting to make decisions about where to put their hard-earned money. View the slide show again.

10. Print the slides of the presentation, then show the presentation in Slide Show view. Close the presentation.

2. You are the communications director at Heridia Design, Inc, an international advertising agency. One of your responsibilities is to create an on-screen presentation for a presentation contest at the National Association of Advertising Agencies (NAAA) convention.

Create a presentation using any type of company. The presentation can be aimed to either convince or educate your audience.

To complete this independent challenge:

1. Think about the results you want to see, the information you need to create the slide show presentation, and the message you want to communicate.
2. Plan and create the slide show presentation. Add interesting visuals, and use a color scheme appropriate to the type of business you choose. Use a chart to show how well the company has performed. Evaluate your presentation content.
3. Use slide transitions, animation effects, and slide timings. Remember, your audience consists of a group of advertising executives who create eye-catching ads every day. View the slide show to evaluate the effects you added.
4. Spell-check and save the presentation as "NAAA Presentation" on your Student Disk.
5. Submit your presentation plan and the final slide show presentation.

3. You are the manager of the Markland University Student Employment Office. The office is staffed by work-study students; new, untrained students start work every semester. Create a presentation that you can use to make the training easier. You can create your own content, or use the following: the work-study staff needs to learn about the main features of the office, including its employment database, library of company directories, seminars on employment search strategies, interviewing techniques, and résumé development, as well as its student consulting and bulk mailing services.

To complete this independent challenge:

1. Think about the results you want to see, the information you need to create the slide show presentation, and the message you want to communicate.
2. Plan and create the color slide presentation using Microsoft Clip Gallery. (Check the Business and People categories.)
3. Save the presentation as "Student Employment" on your Student Disk. Before printing, evaluate the contents of your presentation. Preview the file so you know what the presentation will look like. Adjust any items, and then print the slides.
4. Add transitions, build effects and timings to the presentation. Remember, your audience is university students who need to assimilate a lot of information in order to perform well in their new jobs. View the slide show again.
5. Submit your presentation plan and the final slide show presentation.

4. You work for Asset Advisors, a successful investment service company in South Carolina. The company provides a full set of investment opportunities, including stocks, bonds, and mutual funds. Most of the company's clients are individuals who have large estates or who are retired. To generate more business, you've decided that the company needs a standardized presentation promoting the company and its investment principles. John Ricci, president of the company, liked your idea and asked you to develop the presentation.

To complete this independent challenge:

1. Open the file "PPT D-6" from your Student Disk, and save it as Investment Presentation on your Student Disk.
2. After you open the presentation, look through it in Slide view and think about the results you want to see on each slide. What information is provided, and what could you add? How do you want to communicate the message? Look at how the presentation is organized; you may need to make some adjustments. Is it well done? If you reorganize the presentation, be able to support your decision.
3. Create a Graph chart and embed it on Slide 7. Enter the data in Table D-5 into the Graph datasheet.
4. Format the chart, then title the chart "Investment Risk Over Time."
5. Make changes to the color scheme. Add the new color scheme to the available color scheme list.
6. Add clip art to the presentation wherever you think it would enhance, but not clutter, the message. Try the Currency, People, and Shapes categories.

TABLE D-5

	1 Year	3 Year	5 Year	10 Year
Bonds	8.2	7.5	5.6	2.9
Stocks	17.3	8.9	6.1	3.2
Mutual Funds	15.4	6.1	5.2	4.7

7. Format the objects in the presentation. Use the align and group commands to organize your shapes.
8. The president has also asked you to add information about socially responsible investing, a topic many clients have been asking about. You can find information on this topic on the World Wide Web (WWW). Create two new slides in your presentation, one about organizations that promote socially responsible investing, and another about investment funds that invest only in socially responsible organizations. To get ideas for content, log on to the Internet and use your browser to go to http://www.course.com. From there, click the link Student On Line Companions, then click the link to go to the Microsoft Office 97 Professional Edition—Illustrated: A First Course page, then click on the PowerPoint link for Unit D. http://www.yahoo.com/Business_and_Economy/Markets_and_Investments:Socially_Responsible_Investments(SRI).
9. Fill in the appropriate information on the last two slides in the presentation.
10. Change the slide background to a 2-color background with the gradient of your choice.
11. Spell check the presentation.
12. View the slide show, and evaluate the presentation. Set animations, slide transitions, and slide timings. Keep in mind that your audience is comprised of serious investors, so you'll want to keep any animations or transitions simple, serious, and businesslike, to build trust in your company and keep the audience focused on the presentation content, not the form.
13. View the slide show again to see the animations and transitions you added.
14. Save the presentation.
15. Print the slides of the presentation, then show the presentation in Slide Show view. Close the presentation.

► Visual Workshop

Create two slides that look like the examples in Figures D-20 and D-21. Save the presentation as Sales Presentation to your Student Disk. Save the presentation and print the slides. Submit the final presentation output.

FIGURE D-20

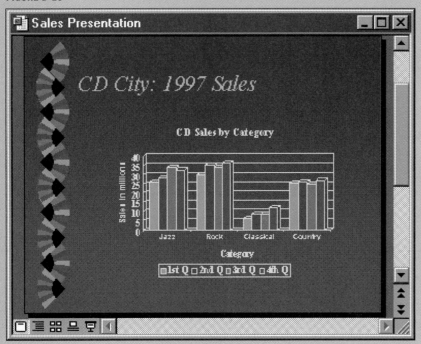

FIGURE D-21

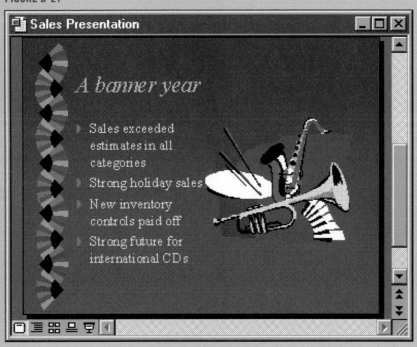

Customizing
Your Presentation

- ► **Understand PowerPoint masters**
- ► **Format master text**
- ► **Change master text indents**
- ► **Add footers to slides**
- ► **Adjust text objects**
- ► **Use advanced drawing tools**
- ► **Use advanced formatting tools**
- ► **Use the Style Checker**

Design features such as text spacing and color are some of the most important qualities of a professional-looking presentation. When preparing a presentation, however, it is also important to make design elements consistent throughout a presentation to hold the reader's attention and to avoid confusing the reader. PowerPoint helps you achieve the look you want by providing ways to customize and enhance your slides, notes pages, and handouts. ✎ Carrie Armstrong, the new executive assistant to the president of Nomad Ltd, is working on a presentation that the president will give to the company as part of the annual report. After receiving feedback from the president, she revises her presentation by customizing the format of her slides and by enhancing her graphics.

Understanding PowerPoint Masters

Presentations in PowerPoint uses slide **masters**, templates for all of the slides in the presentation. Three of the PowerPoint views have a corresponding master view—Slide Master view for Slide view, Notes Master view for Notes Pages view, and Handout Master view for Slide Sorter view. Slide view actually has two master views; the second view, called the Title Master, allows you to customize just the title slide of your presentation. Formatting changes and design elements that you place on the slide master appear on every slide in the presentation (except for the title slide). When you insert an object, or change a text attribute in one of the text placeholders on the master slide, the change appears in all the slides of the corresponding view. For example, you could insert a company e-mail address in the upper right corner of the Slide Master and that address would then appear on every slide in your presentation. ✎ Carrie wants to make a few changes to the presentation design, so she opens her presentation and examines the Slide Master.

Steps

1. Start PowerPoint, open the presentation **PPT E-1**, save it as **97 Annual Report Revised Version**, then to make sure your screen matches the figures in this book, make sure the Zoom text box is **36%**, click the **Restore Window button** in the Presentation window, click **Window** on the menu bar, then click **Fit to Page**
   The title slide of the presentation appears. Switch to the Title Master to view the master elements.

2. Press [Shift], then click the **Slide View button** ▣
   The presentation's Title Master and the Master toolbar appear. Examine the placeholder elements of the Title Master and then switch to the Slide Master view.

3. Drag the **vertical scroll box** to the top of the scroll bar
   The Slide Master appears. Notice that the Slide Master displays a **Master title placeholder**, and a **Master text placeholder** as shown in Figure E-1. These placeholders control the format for each title text object and main text object for each slide in the presentation after Slide 1. Figure E-2 shows Slide 2 of the presentation. Examine Figures E-1 and E-2 to better understand the relationship between Slide Master view and Slide view.

Details

 The Master title placeholder, labeled "Title Area for AutoLayouts," in Figure E-1 indicates the title text object's position, font size, style, and color as shown in Figure E-2.

 The Master text placeholder, labeled "Object Area for AutoLayouts" determines the characteristics for the main text objects on all the slides in the presentation as shown in Figure E-2. Notice how the bullet levels in the main text object of Figure E-2 compare with the corresponding bullet levels of the Master text placeholder in Figure E-1.

FIGURE E-1: Slide Master view

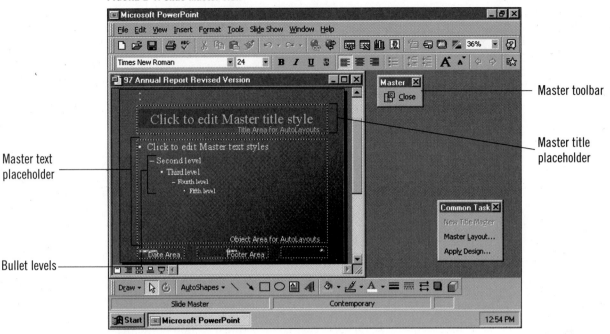

Master text placeholder

Bullet levels

Master toolbar

Master title placeholder

FIGURE E-2: Slide view

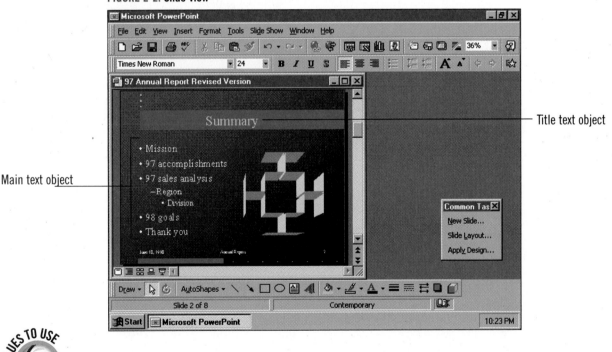

Main text object

Title text object

Clues to Use

Changing the Master Layout

When you are in Slide Master view, the Slide Layout command on the Common Tasks toolbar changes to Master Layout. Clicking Master Layout opens the Master Layout dialog box as shown in Figure E-3. If you happen to delete a master placeholder or if one doesn't appear in a master view, use the Master Layout dialog box to reapply a master placeholder. Each master view has its own Master Layout dialog box.

FIGURE E-3: Master Layout dialog box

Formatting Master Text

Formatting text in a master view works the same as it does in a normal view, but remember that PowerPoint applies the changes you make in the master view to the whole presentation. This is a convenient way to change a feature of your entire presentation without having to change each slide. It also ensures that you don't use a mixture of fonts throughout the presentation. For example, if your presentation is part of a marketing campaign for a travel tour to the Middle East, you may decide to switch the title text font of the entire presentation from the standard Times New Roman font to a scripted font. You can change text color, style, size, and bullet type in the master view. Carrie decides to make a few formatting changes to the text of her Slide Master.

1. Make sure the Slide Master is still visible

2. Move I anywhere in the first line of text in the Master text placeholder, then click
   The insertion point appears. To make the formatting changes to the whole line of text, you don't have to select the line; just click to insert the insertion point. Make the first line of text stand out by making it bold and adding a shadow.

Trouble?

Make sure you check the shadow button on the formatting toolbar, not on the Drawing toolbar.

3. Click the Bold button **B** on the Formatting toolbar, then click the Shadow button on the Formatting toolbar
   The first line of text becomes bold with a shadow. Now, change the bullet symbol in the second line of text of the master text placeholder.

4. Right-click anywhere in the second line of text in the Master text placeholder, then click Bullet on the pop-up menu
   The Bullet dialog box opens displaying the current bullet symbol. Choose a different bullet symbol for this line of text.

QuickTip

The size of a bullet looks best if it is the same size or smaller than the text it is identifying.

5. Click the Bullets from list arrow, then click Monotype Sorts
   The available bullet choices change.

6. Click the "X" in the first row as shown in Figure E-4, click the Color list arrow, then click the dark yellow square
   You can now apply the new bullet to the line of text.

7. Click OK, then click in a blank area of the Presentation window
   Compare your screen to Figure E-5. Switch to Slide view to see how the changes you've made look on the slide.

Time To

✔ Save

8. Click the Slide View button ▢, then click the Next Slide button ⬇
   Slide 2 appears.

FIGURE E-4: Bullet dialog box

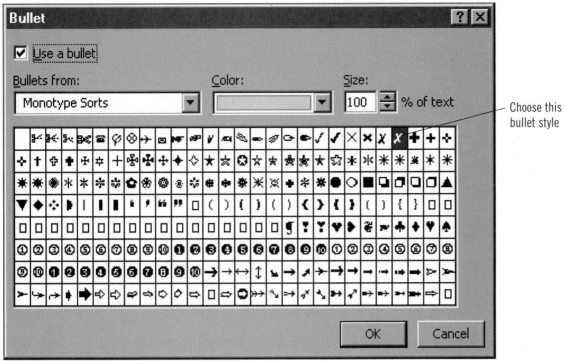

Choose this bullet style

FIGURE E-5: Slide Master showing formatted text

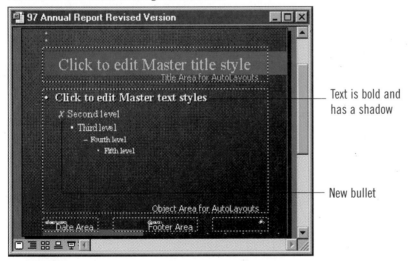

Text is bold and has a shadow

New bullet

Exceptions to the Slide Master

If you change the format of text on a slide and then apply a template to the presentation, the slide that you formatted retains the text formatting changes you made. These format changes that differ from the Slide Master are known as **exceptions**. Exceptions can only be changed on the individual slides where they occur. For example, you might change the font and size of a particular piece of text on a slide to make it stand out and then you decide later to add a different template to your presentation. The piece of text you formatted before you applied the template is unaffected by the new template. This text formatting is an exception.

Changing Master Text Indents

The master text placeholder in every presentation has five levels of text, called **indent levels**. You can use the horizontal slide ruler to control the space between the bullets and the text or to change the position of the whole indent level. Each indent level is represented by two small triangles called **indent markers** that identify the position of each indent level in the master text placeholder. Table E-1 gives a brief description of the symbols on the horizontal ruler. Carrie decides to change the distance between the bullet symbols and the text in the first two indent levels of her presentation to emphasize the bullets.

Steps 1 2 3 4

1. **Click View on the menu bar, point to Master, then click Slide Master**
   Slide Master view appears. Now, display the rulers for the Master text placeholder to change the first two indent levels.

2. **Click anywhere in the master text placeholder to place the insertion point, click View on the menu bar, then click Ruler**
   PowerPoint displays the rulers and indent markers for the Master text placeholder. Notice that the indent markers for each indent level are set so that the first line of text, in this case the bullet, begins to the left of subsequent lines of text. This is a **hanging indent** and is commonly used for bulleted text. Figure E-6 illustrates how a hanging indent looks in a main text object. Change the distance between the bullet symbol and the text in the first indent level.

Trouble?

If you accidentally drag an indent marker into another marker, the second indent marker moves along with the first until you release the mouse. Click the Undo button 🔄 to restore the indent levels to their original position.

3. **Position the pointer over the bottom indent marker (triangle) of the first indent level, then drag to the right to the ½" mark**
   Compare your screen to Figure E-7. Now, move the bottom indent marker of the second indent level to change the distance between the bullet symbol and the second level of text.

4. **Position the pointer over the bottom indent marker of the second indent level, then drag to the right until the ruler looks like Figure E-8**
   Compare your screen to Figure E-8. Now, hide the rulers and check your work.

5. **Click the right mouse button in a blank area of the Presentation window, then click Ruler**
   Switch to Slide view and check your work.

6. **Click Close on the Master toolbar**
   Slide 2 appears, showing the results of changing the indent markers in the master text placeholder. Save your work.

7. **Click the Save button 💾 on the Standard toolbar**

TABLE E-1: Indent Markers

symbol	name	function
▽	Top indent marker	Controls the position of the first line of text in an indent level
△	Bottom indent marker	Controls the position of subsequent lines of text in an indent level
▢	Margin marker	Moves both indent markers of an indent level at the same time

FIGURE E-6: Example of hanging indent

First line of text (in this example, the bullet) aligns with the top indent marker

Subsequent lines of text align with the bottom indent marker

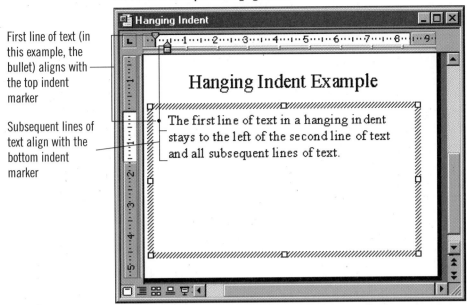

FIGURE E-7: Slide Master with first level bottom indent marker moved

Horizontal slide ruler

First indent level bottom indent marker

Margin marker

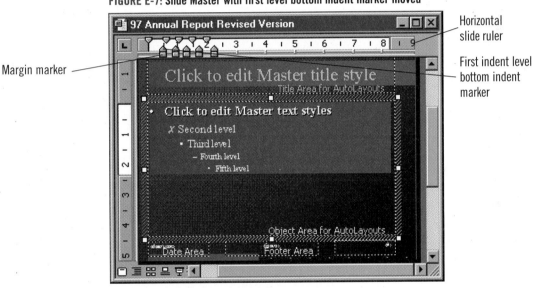

FIGURE E-8: Slide Master with changed indent markers

Second indent level bottom indent marker

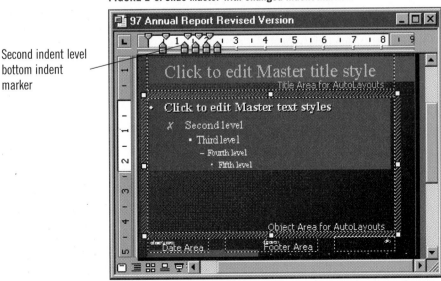

Adding Footers to Slides

Each Slide Master and Title Master has preset placeholders for footer text, the date and time, and the slide number. To place text in the placeholders, you use the Header and Footer dialog box. You can also add the page number to the Handouts and Speaker's Notes. ◀——— Carrie uses the preset placeholders to identify her slides and make them easier to navigate through during the presentation.

Steps 1234

QuickTip

To add other background items such as lines, shapes, or pictures to a master view, display the master view and then add the background item directly to the master slide.

1. **Click View on the menu bar, then click Header and Footer**
   The Header and Footer dialog box opens with the Slide tab on top. You can use this dialog box to insert the date and time, slide number, and footer text into a presentation. Notice that the left and middle placeholders in the Preview box are shaded. The left placeholder will contain the date. The middle placeholder contains footer text.

2. **In the Include on slide section, make sure the Date and time check box and the Fixed option button are selected, click in the Fixed text box, then type June 18, 1998**
   Now add a slide number to the presentation.

3. **In the Include on slide section, click the Slide number check box**
   This places a slide number in the bottom right corner of each slide in the presentation. The right placeholder is now shaded in the Preview box.

4. **In the Include on slide section, click the Footer check box to select it, click in the Footer text box, if necessary, then type Annual Report**

5. **Click the Don't show on title slide check box**
   Because the title slide is the first slide in the presentation, there is no reason to include the footer information on it. Compare your dialog box to Figure E-9.

6. **Click Apply to All**
   Notice that the footer information appears on the slide, as shown in Figure E-10. Now review the presentation in Slide Show view to make sure the footer information looks good.

7. **Click the Slide Show button 🖳, then click the mouse button to advance through each slide in the presentation**
   Slide Show view opens to Slide 2. The footer information you added looks good on all slides. Save your presentation.

8. **Click the Save button 🖫 on the Standard toolbar**

FIGURE E-9: Header and Footer dialog box

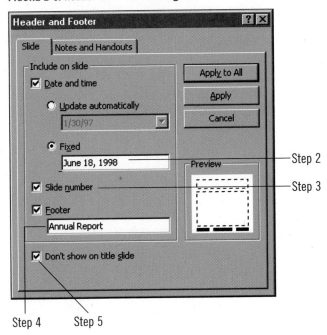

Step 2
Step 3
Step 4   Step 5

FIGURE E-10: Slide showing completed footer information

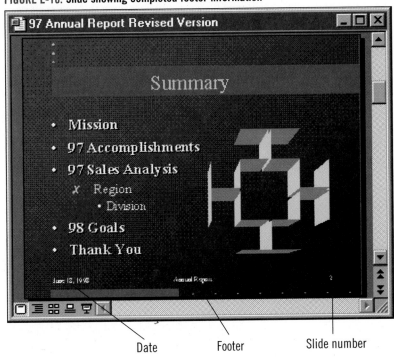

Date   Footer   Slide number

CLUES TO USE

Objects on the Slide Master

The text placeholders on the Slide Master and Title Master can be manipulated the same way text placeholders on slides are manipulated; you can resize and move them. You can also add additional background objects to the Slide Master. If you add an object to the Slide Master, it will appear on every slide in the presentation behind the text and objects you place on the slides. To add an object to the Slide Master, simply add the AutoShape, clip art, picture, or other object the same way you add objects to other slides in a presentation.

Adjusting Text Objects

You have complete control over the placement of your text in PowerPoint. With the **text anchor** feature, you can adjust text position within text objects or adjust shapes to achieve the best look. If you want your text to fill more or less of the slide, you can adjust the spacing between lines of text. Carrie decides that the sailboat image clutters the last slide in her presentation. She will delete it, then adjust the text position and line spacing to give the slide a more open and polished look.

Steps

1. Drag the vertical scroll box to the last slide in the presentation, click the sailboat image, press [Delete], click Slide Layout on the Common Tasks toolbar, select the Bulleted List AutoLayout, then click Apply

   Give this slide a cleaner look by moving the text anchor to the center.

2. Press [Shift], right-click the main text object, click Format AutoShape on the pop-up menu, then click the Text Box tab

   The Format AutoShape dialog box opens, similar to Figure E-11. To center the text at the top of the text box, change the text anchor point to top centered.

3. Click the Text anchor point list arrow, click Top Centered, click Preview, then drag the dialog box title bar to the bottom portion of the screen

   The text moves to the center of the text object. Now, adjust the size of the text box to fit the text.

4. Drag the dialog box back up the screen, click the Resize autoshape to fit text check box, then click OK

   The shape of the text box resizes to fit the size of the text object. Now, adjust the spacing between the lines of text and between each paragraph in the main text object so that there is less empty space on the slide.

5. Click Format on the menu bar, then click Line Spacing

   The Line Spacing dialog box opens, similar to Figure E-12. First, to emphasize the paragraphs in the text object, change the space after each paragraph.

6. In the After paragraph section, click the up arrow until 0.15 appears, click Preview, then drag the dialog box out of the way, if necessary

   The space, or leading, after each paragraph increases. **Leading** is the vertical space between lines of text. Decrease the leading between the text lines.

7. In the Line spacing section, click the down arrow until 0.7 appears, then click Preview

   The line spacing between the text lines decreases.

Time To

✔ Save

8. Click OK, then click in a blank area of the presentation window to deselect the main text object

   Compare your screen to Figure E-13.

FIGURE E-11: Format AutoShape dialog box

Step 3

Text anchor point
list arrow

Step 4

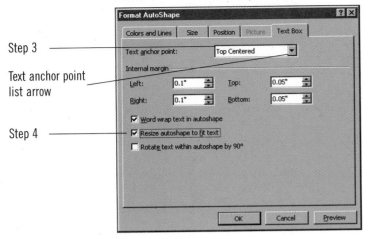

FIGURE E-12: Line Spacing dialog box

Step 7

Step 6

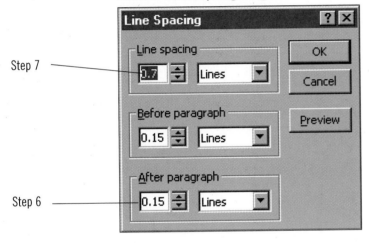

FIGURE E-13: Slide showing formatted text object

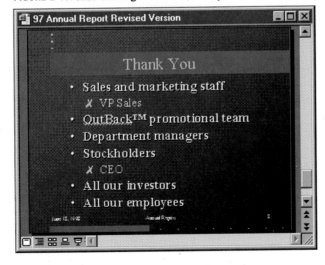

Changing margins around text in shapes

You can also use the Text anchor point command to change the margins around a text object to form a shape that suits the text better. Right-click the shape, click Format AutoShape, click the Text Box tab, then adjust the Internal margin settings. Click Preview to see your changes before you apply them to the shape.

Using Advanced Drawing Tools

PowerPoint has a number of powerful drawing tools on the AutoShapes menu to help you draw all types of shapes. For example, the Curve drawing tool allows you to create a freeform curved line, the Arc tool helps you draw smooth curved lines and pie-shaped wedges, and the Connector line tools allow you to connect objects on your slide with a line. Once you have drawn a shape, you can format and rearrange it to create the effect you want. Carrie uses the Arc tool and a Connector line tool to complete the diagram on the slide.

1. Click the **Previous Slide button** to move to Slide 7
   Slide 7 appears. Select the Arc tool to draw an arrow between the objects in the diagram.

2. Click the **AutoShapes menu button** on the Drawing toolbar, point to **Basic Shapes**, then click the **Arc button**

3. Position ✛ on the left center edge of the object labeled "Objectives," and then drag down to the top center of the object labeled "Planning," as shown in Figure E-14
   The direction in which you drag the arc determines whether the arc opens up or down and the distance you drag the arc determines its size. To constrain the arc to a proportional size, press [Shift]. Next, extend the arc.

4. Drag the bottom adjustment handle to the right so it becomes a half circle, then drag the lower middle sizing handle down so that the end of the arc touches the middle of the object labeled "Engineering"
   The adjustment handle determines the length of the arc; the sizing handle changes its size. Now, format the arc to match the other arc on the slide.

5. Click the **Line Style button** on the Drawing toolbar, then click the 4½ pt line style
   The line style of the arc changes to a thicker weight.

QuickTip

To change the default attributes of a particular AutoShape, format the AutoShape, select it, click Draw on the Drawing toolbar, then click Set AutoShape Defaults.

6. Click the **Arrow Style button** on the Drawing toolbar, then click **Arrow Style 5**
   An arrowhead appears on the arc. The direction in which you drag the arc determines the direction of the arrowhead. Now, send the arc behind the cube.

7. Click the **Draw menu button** on the Drawing toolbar, point to **Order**, click **Send to Back**, then click a blank area of the slide
   Draw a connector line between two of the objects.

8. Click the **AutoShapes menu button** on the Drawing toolbar, point to **Connectors**, then click the **Straight Double-Arrow Connector button**
   The pointer changes to ✛.

9. Move ✛ to the right side of the "Planning" object until it changes to ⬦, click to place the left side of the connector line, position ⬦ on the left side of the "Manufacturing" object, then click to place the right side of the connector line
   Format the connector line so it looks similar to the other lines on the slide.

10. Click ▦, click 4½ pt, then click in a blank area of the Presentation window
    Compare your screen to Figure E-15.

Time To

✔ Save

FIGURE E-14: Slide showing drawn arc object

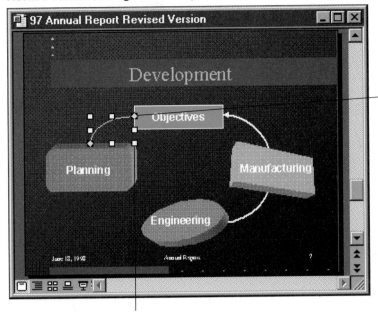

Adjustment handle

Sizing handle

FIGURE E-15: Slide showing formatted arc and connector line

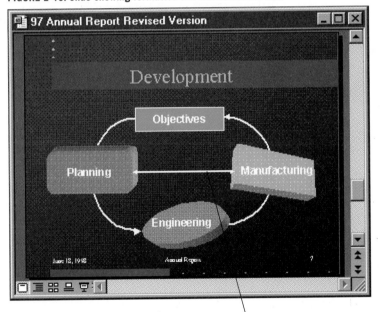

Connector line

Drawing a freeform shape

A **freeform** shape can consist of straight lines, free-hand (or curved) lines, or a combination of the two. To draw a freeform shape, click the AutoShapes menu button, point to Lines, then click the Freeform button. Drag the mouse to draw the desired shape (the cursor changes to a pencil), then double-click when you are done. To draw a straight line with the Freeform tool, click where you want to begin the line, move the mouse and click again to end the line, then double-click to deactivate the Freeform tool. To edit a freeform object, right-click the object, then click Edit Points on the pop-up menu.

Using Advanced Formatting Tools

With PowerPoint's advanced formatting tools, you can change formatting attributes such as fill texture, 3-D effects, and shadow for text and shapes. If you like the attributes of an object, you can use the Format Painter feature to pick up the attributes and apply them to another object. Carrie wants to use the advanced formatting tools to enhance the diagram on the slide.

Steps

1. Click the rectangle labeled "Planning"
   Make sure the rectangle is selected and not the word "Planning."

2. Right-click the object, click **Format AutoShape** on the pop-up menu, click the **Colors and Lines tab**, click the **Color list arrow** in the Fill section, then click **Fill Effects**
   The Fill Effects dialog box opens.

3. Click the **Texture tab**, click the **White marble square**, then click **OK** twice
   Now, change the 3-D settings for the object.

4. Click the **3-D button** on the Drawing toolbar, then click **3-D Settings**
   The 3-D Settings toolbar opens.

5. Click the **Depth button** on the 3-D Settings toolbar, then click **72 pt**.
   The depth of the 3-D effect lengthens. Now, change the direction of the 3-D effect.

6. Click the **Direction button** on the 3-D Settings toolbar, then click the left effect in the top row
   The 3-D effect changes to the bottom of the object. Now, change the direction of the lighting on the object.

7. Click the **Lighting button** on the 3-D Settings toolbar, click the middle effect in the right column, then click the 3-D Settings toolbar **Close button**
   Now, copy the formatting attributes of the selected rectangle to the other three objects on the slide.

8. Double-click the **Format Painter button** on the Standard toolbar, click the other three objects, click again, then click in a blank area of the slide
   When you use the Format Painter tool, it picks up the attributes of the object that is selected and copies them to the next object that you click. Now, all the objects on the slide have the same fill effect. Compare your screen to Figure E-16. Next, run through the slide show, then switch to Slide Sorter view and evaluate your presentation.

9. Press [Ctrl][Home] to move to Slide 1, click the **Slide Show button**, press [Spacebar] or click the left mouse button to run through the presentation, click the **Slide Sorter View button**, then maximize the Presentation window
   Compare your screen to figure E-17.

10. Save your changes, then print the presentation as **Handouts (2 per page)**

FIGURE E-16: Slide showing formatted objects

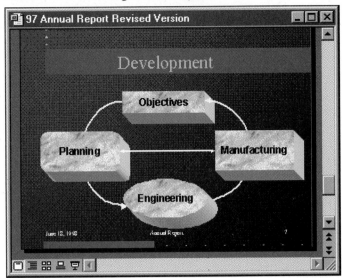

FIGURE E-17: Final presentation in Slide Sorter view

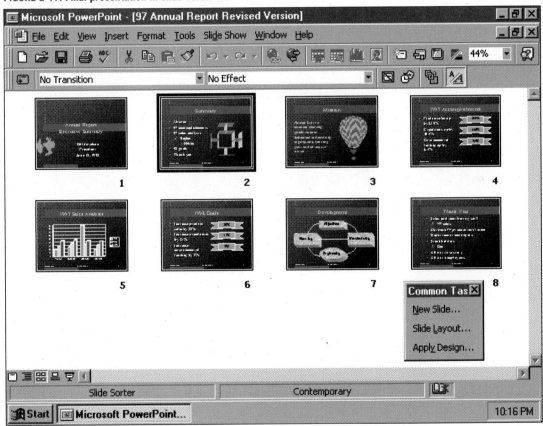

CLUES TO USE

Applying a color scheme to another presentation

If you develop a custom color scheme that you like, you can use the Format Painter tool to apply it to another presentation. To apply a color scheme from one presentation to another, open each presentation in Slide Sorter view. Select a slide in the presentation with the color scheme, click the Format Painter button on the Standard toolbar, then click each slide that you want to change in the other presentation.

Using the Style Checker

To help you correct common design mistakes, the Style Checker feature in PowerPoint reviews your presentation for typical errors such as incorrect font sizes, use of too many fonts, excess words, errors in punctuation, and other readability problems. The Style Checker then suggests ways to improve your presentation. ✒ Carrie knows it's easy to overlook mistakes while preparing a presentation, so she uses the Style Checker to look for errors she may have missed.

Steps 1234

1. **Click Tools on the menu bar, then click Style Checker**
   The Style Checker dialog box opens. Review the options before you begin the Style Checker.

2. **Click Options, review the options on the Case and End Punctuation tab, then click the Visual Clarity tab**
   The Style Checker Options dialog box displays the current option settings for visual clarity. Change several of these options.

3. **Adjust the settings in the Style Checker Options dialog box so that your screen matches Figure E-18**
   When the Style Checker begins, it will ensure that the text style on the slides matches the descriptions in this dialog box.

4. **Click OK**
   To speed up the Style Checker, turn off the spelling.

5. **In the Check for section of the Style Checker dialog box, click the Spelling check box to clear it, then click Start**
   The Style Checker Summary dialog box opens, displaying progress information as PowerPoint checks the presentation style. The Style Checker finds four inconsistencies as shown in Figure E-19. Click OK to complete the style check, then review the slides that the Style Checker identified.

6. **Click OK, click the Slide View button ▣ then drag the verticle scroll box to Slide 2, Slide 4, Slide 6, and Slide 8 to review each slide**
   The Style Checker is helpful for identifying potential errors, but you are not required to make changes to your presentation based on the summary. The four slides with potential errors all look fine and are easy to read.

7. **Close your presentation without saving the changes**

FIGURE E-18: Style Checker Options dialog box

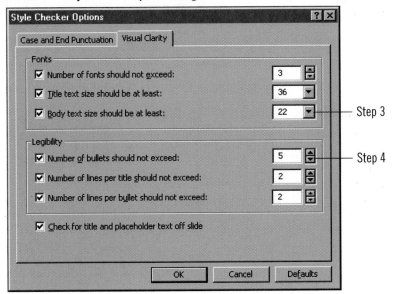

— Step 3

— Step 4

FIGURE E-19: Style Checker Summary dialog box

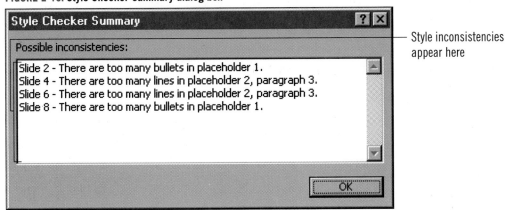

— Style inconsistencies
appear here

Understanding Style Checker Options

The Style Checker is helpful, however, it may make some changes that you don't expect. Figure E-20 shows the Case and End Punctuation tab in the Style Checker Options dialog box. For example, notice that the Body text style is set to Sentence case. This option treats each line of text as a sentence and therefore removes uppercase letters in the middle of a line. If you run Style Checker, be sure to review your slides for any unexpected changes.

FIGURE E-20: Case and End Punctuation tab in Style Checker Options dialog box

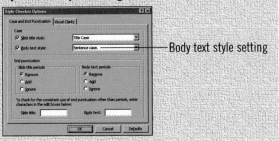

— Body text style setting

CUSTOMIZING YOUR PRESENTATION PP E-17

PowerPoint 97

Practice

▶ Concepts Review

Label each of the elements of the PowerPoint window shown in Figure E-21.

FIGURE E-21

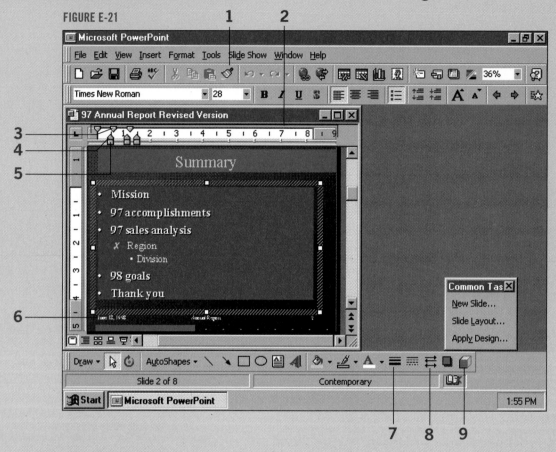

Match each of the terms with the statement that describes its function.

10. Each master text placeholder has five levels of text called
11. Moves the whole indent level
12. Controls subsequent lines of text in an indent level
13. A template for all the slides in a presentation
14. Adjusts the distance between text lines
15. Adjusts the position of text in a text object

a. Line spacing
b. Indent levels
c. Text anchor
d. Margin marker
e. Master
f. Bottom indent marker

Select the best answer from the list of choices.

16. Each line of text is identified on the ruler with
    a. Indent markers
    b. Indent levels
    c. Text levels
    d. Ruler markers

17. A hanging indent is an indent in which the
   a. First line of text is to the right of subsequent lines of text
   b. First line of text is to the left of subsequent lines of text
   c. The bullet symbol is to the left of the first line of text
   d. The bullet symbol is to the right of the first line of text

18. Inserting a background item on the Slide Master
   a. Changes all views of your presentation
   b. Is only seen on the title slide
   c. Is a simple way to place an object on every slide of your presentation
   d. Does not affect the slides of your presentation

19. Which of the following does the Style Checker not check for?
   a. Case and punctuation in the presentation
   b. A specified text font size
   c. Title text that is off the slide
   d. Incorrect color scheme colors

20. What is leading?
   a. Vertical space between text lines
   b. Horizontal space between lines of text
   c. Diagonal space between text characters
   d. Vertical space between text characters

 ## Skills Review

1. Format master text.
   a. Start PowerPoint and open the presentation PPT E-2, then save it as Apparel Presentation.
   b. Click the Next Slide button.
   c. Switch to Slide Master view, then click anywhere in the first line of text in the Master text placeholder.
   d. Click the Bold button on the Formatting toolbar.
   e. Click Format on the menu bar, then click Bullet.
   f. Use bullets from Monotype Sorts, click the second bullet from the left in the fourth row, then click the Size up arrow until 75 appears.
   g. Click the Color list arrow, click the second color cell from the right, then click OK.
   h. Click anywhere in the second line of text.
   i. Click the Italic button on the Formatting toolbar.
   j. Click the Font list arrow on the Formatting toolbar, then click Arial.
   k. Click the Save button on the Standard toolbar.

2. Change master text indents.

a. With the insertion point still in the Master text placeholder, click View on the menu bar, then click Ruler.

b. Move the indent markers and margin markers of all the indent levels to match Figure E-22.

FIGURE E-22

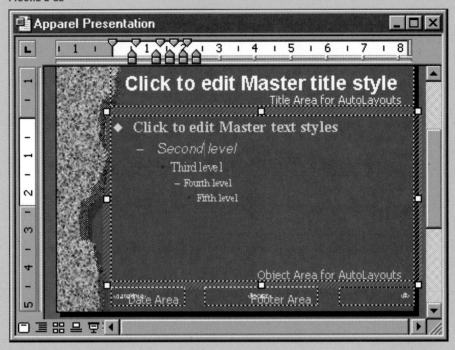

c. Right-click in a blank area of the presentation window, then click Ruler.

d. Click the Slide View button, then click the Save button on the Standard toolbar.

3. Add footers to slides.

a. Click View on the menu bar, then click Header and Footer.

b. Click the Date and time check box.

c. Click the Update automatically option button, click the Update automatically list arrow, then click the fourth option in the list.

d. Click the Slide number check box.

e. Click the Don't show on title slide check box.

f. Click the Notes and Handouts tab.

g. Click the Update automatically option button, click the Update automatically list arrow, then click the fifth option in the list.

h. In the Header text box, type "Apparel Division Report."

i. Click Apply to All.

j. Click the Notes Page View button. Notice the header and date information.

k. Click the Slide View button, then save your changes.

4. Adjust text objects.

a. Right-click anywhere in the main text object on Slide 2, then click Format AutoShape on the pop-up menu.

b. Click the Text Box tab.

c. Click the Text anchor point list arrow, click Middle, then click Preview.

d. In the Internal margin section, click the Left up arrow until 0.5 appears, then click Preview.

e. Click the Resize autoshape to fit text check box, then click Preview.

f. Click OK.

g. Move the pointer over the edge of the main text object, then click to select the entire object.

h. Click Format on the menu bar, then click Line Spacing.

i. In the Before paragraph section, click the up arrow until 0.3 appears, then click Preview.

j. Click OK.

k. Press ↑ four times to move the main text object up, then click the Save button on the Standard toolbar.

5. Use advanced drawing tools.

a. Drag the vertical scroll box to Slide 5.

b. Click the AutoShapes menu button on the Drawing toolbar, point to Connectors, then click the Elbow Connector button.

c. Position the cursor on the left side of the "Product Idea" diamond, then drag a connector line to the left side of the Review 1 diamond.

d. Click the AutoShapes menu button on the Drawing toolbar, point to Connectors, then click Straight Connector.

e. Position the cursor over the right side of the Review 1 diamond, then drag the connector line to the left side of the Review 2 diamond.

f. Click the AutoShapes menu button on the Drawing toolbar, point to Connectors, then click the Elbow Arrow Connector button.

g. Position the pointer over the right side of the Review 2 diamond, then drag the connector line to the point on the right side of the Product Idea diamond.

h. Press [Shift], then click the other two connector lines.

i. Click the Line Style button on the Drawing toolbar, click 3 pt, then click in a blank area of the slide.

j. Click the right connector line, click the Arrow Style button on the Drawing toolbar, then click More Arrows.

k. In the Arrows section, click the End size list arrow, click Arrow R Size 8, then click OK.

l. Click in a blank area of the slide, then save your changes.

6. Use advanced formatting tools.

a. Drag the vertical scroll box to Slide 1.

b. Press [Shift], right-click the text object in the lower right corner of the slide, then click Format AutoShape.

c. In the Fill section, click the Color list arrow, then click Fill Effects.

d. In the Colors section, click the One Color button, then click the Color1 option list arrow.

e. Click the second color cell from the right, then click the Light scroll arrow four times.

f. In the Variants section, click the bottom left variant, click OK, then click OK again.

g. Double-click the Format Painter button on the Standard toolbar, then drag the vertical scroll box to Slide 5.

h. Click each of the diamond objects, click the Format Painter button on the Standard toolbar, then click a blank area of the slide.

i. Press [Shift], click the Product Idea diamond object, click the 3-D button on the Drawing toolbar, then click the 3-D Style 14 button.

j. Click the 3-D button on the Drawing toolbar, then click 3-D Settings.

k. Click the Tilt Down button twice, then click the 3-D Settings toolbar Close button.

l. Double-click the Format Painter button on the Formatting toolbar, click the other two diamond objects, then click the Format Painter button again.

m. Select the three connector lines, then drag them slightly to the left so they connect the three objects.

n. Click in a blank area of the slide, then save your changes.

7. Use the Style Checker.

a. Click the Next Slide button.

b. Click Tools on the menu bar, then click Style Checker.

c. Click Options, then click the Visual Clarity tab.

d. In the Fonts section, double-click the number in the Title text size should be at least text box, then type "44".

e. In the Legibility section, click the Number of bullets should not exceed down arrow until 4 appears.

f. Click OK, deselect the Spelling check box, then click Start.

g. As the Style Checker finds inconsistencies, click Change to change them. Notice that your presentation changes.

h. Read the Style Checker Summary dialog box. Notice that the title text font is too small based on your adjustment to the Style Checker.

i. Click OK, press [Shift], then click the Slide View button.

j. Click anywhere in the Master title placeholder, then click the Increase Font Size button on the Formatting toolbar, then click the Slide View button.

k. Turn the Spelling option off and run the Style Checker again. Notice that the title text font size is no longer listed in the summary dialog box.

l. Click OK, then scroll through the presentation. Change the subtitle on the title slide so it is "A Nomad Ltd Division".

m. Save the presentation, print the presentation as Handouts (3 slides per page), then close the presentation.

▶ Independent Challenges

1. You are the owner of Premier Catering in New York City. You have built your business on banquets, private parties, wedding receptions, and special events over the last five years. To expand, you decide to cater to the local business community by offering executive meals and business luncheons. Use PowerPoint to develop a presentation that you can use to gain corporate catering accounts.

In this independent challenge, you will create an outline and modify the look of a presentation. Create your own material to complete the slides of the presentation. Assume the following about Premier Catering:

- Premier Catering has eight full-time employees and 10 part-time employees.
- Premier Catering handles catering jobs from 10 people to 1000 people.
- Premier Catering is a full-service catering business providing cost estimates, set-up, complete preparation, service personnel, and clean up.

To complete this independent challenge:

1. Open the file PPT E-3, then save it as Premier.
2. Think about the results you want to see, the information you need, and how you want to communicate the message.
3. Switch to Outline view and create a presentation outline. As you type, misspell words so PowerPoint can automatically correct them as you type.
4. Customize your presentation by formatting the Slide Master.
5. Use PowerPoint's advanced drawing and formatting tools to give your presentation a unique look.
6. Switch to the last slide and change the text anchor and line spacing to create the best look.
7. Review the Style Checker options and then check the style of the presentation.
8. Print and submit the slides of your final presentation.

2. You are the finance director at Splat Records in Los Angeles, California. Splat Records specializes in alternative music. As an emerging record company, your business is looking for investment capital to expand its talent base and increase sales. It is your responsibility to develop the outline and basic look for a standard presentation that the president can present to various investors.

In this independent challenge, you will complete an outline and choose a custom background for the presentation. You'll need to create a presentation consisting of at least six slides. Assume the following about Splat Records:

- Splat Records has been in business for six years.
- Splat Records currently has 12 recording contracts. Splat wants to double that during the next year and a half.
- Splat Records has two superstar recording groups at the present time: RIM and Blacknight.

To complete this independent challenge:

1. Open the file PPT E-4, then save it as Splat.
2. Think about the results you want to see, the information you need, and how you want to communicate the message.

3. Enter text into the title and main text placeholders of the slides. As you type, misspell words so PowerPoint can automatically correct them as you type.
4. Use advanced drawing and formatting tools to create a unique look.
5. Check the style of the presentation.
6. Print and submit the slides of your final presentation.

3. You work for Graphics +, a small multimedia software company in Silicon Valley that develops games and entertainment applications. Your primary job is to promote your company's computer software ideas to different venture capitalists and to secure money to develop products. Develop a 10- to 15-slide presentation that promotes a software product idea. Use PowerPoint clip art and shapes to enhance your slides. Use one of PowerPoint's templates or design one of your own. You can use one of the following three ideas that Graphics + has been developing, or you can develop one of your own.

1. "Cavern Adventures," an interactive game in which you lead a group of thrill seekers on one of 10 different cave adventures throughout the world
2. "Posse," an interactive game that puts you in one of six different historical situations, where you lead a "posse" of people chasing after a convicted murderer
3. "Spies," an adventure game in which you are a spy for the Axis Powers or the Allies during World War II; assume there are six different situations to choose from for each political side

Create your own company information, but assume the following:
- The product is designed for adults and children ages 13 and up.
- The cost of product development is estimated to be $250,000. Development time is four months.
- The retail price of the final product is designed to be $50, given the current product development cost estimate. For every $10,000 increase in product development cost, the base retail price goes up $2.
- The final presentation will be shown as a static presentation using color overheads.

To complete this independent challenge:

1. Think about the results you want to see, the information you need to create the slide presentation, and the message you want to communicate.
2. Plan the story line of the software product using five or more slides. Plan the beginning and ending slides. What do you want your audience to know about the product idea?
3. Use clip art, shapes, and a shaded background to enhance the presentation. Change the bullet and text formatting in the master text and title placeholders to fit the subject matter.
4. Save the presentation as Graphics
5. Submit your presentation plan and print the final slide presentation.

4. You are the vice president of sales for Redwood Timber Products Inc, a company based in Northern California that harvests redwood trees and sells a number of redwood products. As the vice president of sales, one of your responsibilities is to nurture and develop new business contacts with foreign countries. You are going to give a presentation at an international timber conference in Portland, Oregon, where many prospective foreign buyers will be in attendance.

Plan and create a 10- to 15-slide presentation that focuses on Redwood Timber Products Inc. Redwood Timber Products has been in business for over 75 years and employs a 320-person work force. Develop your own content, but assume the following:
- Redwood Timber Products harvests 75,000 acres per year and replants with 92,000 acres per year.
- Redwood Timber Products can harvest and deliver 400,000 tons of timber per month overseas.
- Redwood Timber Products uses Pacific Shipping Inc to deliver timber to overseas locations.
- Timber prices range from $10 to $16 per board foot depending on the size and grade (or quality) of the lumber. Lumber grades are designated with numbers as follows: "1" for top grade, "2" for middle grade, and "3" for bottom grade.
- Many of the attendees at the conference are from Middle Eastern countries.

The presentation will be shown with a projection screen and will last approximately 30 minutes.
To complete this independent challenge:

1. Think about the results you want to see, the information you need to create the slide presentation, what type of message you want to communicate, and the target audience.
2. Use the AutoContent Wizard to help you start an outline.
3. Log on to the Internet and use your browser to go to http://www.course.com. From there, click Student Online Companions, click the link for this textbook, then click the PowerPoint link for Unit E. Use the link there to research shipping costs, and include this information in your presentation.
4. Use clip art or pictures to enhance the presentation. Use culturally relevant symbols to appeal to your audience. Add or create a shaded background template for the presentation.
5. Format the content, then save the presentation as Redwood.
6. Submit your presentation plan and print the final slide presentation.

► Visual Workshop

Create two slides that look like the examples in Figures E-23 and E-24. Save the presentation as New Products. Save and print the Slide view of the presentation. Submit the final presentation output.

FIGURE E-23:

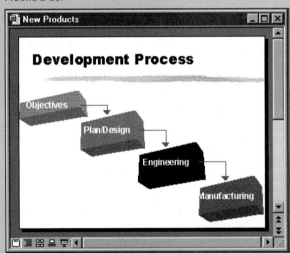

FIGURE E-24:

Enhancing
Charts

Objectives

- ► **Insert data from a file into a datasheet**
- ► **Format a datasheet**
- ► **Change a chart's type**
- ► **Customize a chart's 3-D view**
- ► **Customize a chart**
- ► **Work with chart elements**
- ► **Embed and format an organizational chart**
- ► **Modify an organizational chart**

A PowerPoint presentation is a visual communication tool. A slide that delivers information with a relevant graphic object has a more lasting impact than a slide with plain text. Graphs and charts often communicate information more effectively than words. Microsoft Graph and Microsoft Organization Chart are built-in PowerPoint programs that allow you to easily create and embed charts in your presentation.

In this unit, Carrie Armstrong updates the data and enhances the appearance of a Microsoft Graph chart, and then creates and formats an organizational chart showing the top company structure at Nomad Ltd.

Inserting Data from a File into a Datasheet

With Microsoft Graph, you can enter your own data into a datasheet using the keyboard or you can import existing data from a spreadsheet program like Microsoft Excel. The sales manager gave Carrie sales data in an Excel file. Carrie wants to insert this data as a chart on Slide 6. To do this, she will open Graph and import the updated data from Excel.

1. Start PowerPoint and open the presentation PPT F-1, save it as 97 Annual Report Revised Version 2, make sure the zoom is set for 36%, click the Restore Window button in the Presentation window, click Window on the menu bar, then click Fit to Page

   Move to Slide 6 to make changes to the chart on the slide.

2. Drag the vertical scroll box to Slide 6, then double-click the chart object

   Insert the data into the Graph datasheet from your Excel worksheet.

3. Click the first cell (upper left corner) in the datasheet

   This indicates where the imported data will appear in the datasheet.

4. Click the Import File button 📝 on the Graph Standard toolbar

   The Import File dialog box opens.

5. Locate the worksheet file PPT F-2, then click Open

   The Import Data Options dialog box opens. All the options are correctly marked, so just click OK.

6. Click OK

   Compare your screen to Figure F-1. The chart changes to reflect the new data you inserted into the datasheet. The data in Column D does not need to be included in the chart, so you can exclude it.

7. Double-click the Column D control box

   Control boxes are the gray boxes located along the edges of the datasheet, as shown in Figure F-2. The data in column D are grayed out, indicating that they're excluded from the datasheet and will not be displayed in the chart. To include data that you've previously excluded, double-click the control box again. Next, save your changes.

8. Click the Save button 🖫 on the Standard toolbar

> **QuickTip**
>
> You can change Graph options, such as how empty cells are plotted in the chart or the color of chart fills and lines, by choosing Options from the Tools menu.

FIGURE F-1: Datasheet showing imported data

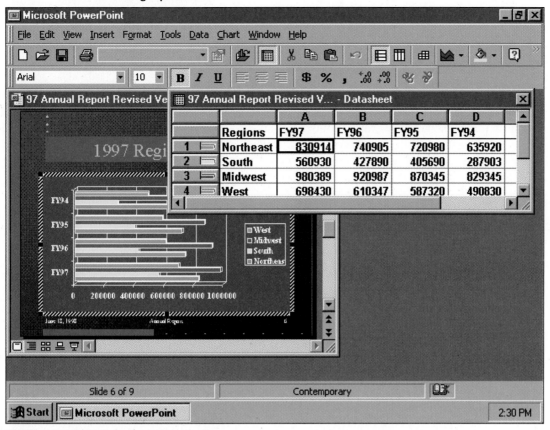

FIGURE F-2: Datasheet showing excluded column

		A	B	C	D	
	Regions	FY97	FY96	FY95	FY94	
1	Northeast	830914	740905	720980	635920	
2	South	560930	427890	405690	287903	
3	Midwest	980389	920987	870345	829345	
4	West	698430	610347	587320	490830	

Column D
control box

CLUES TO USE

Data series and data series markers

Each column or row of data in the datasheet is called a **data series**. Each data series has corresponding **data series markers** in the chart, which are graphical representations such as bars, columns, or pie wedges. Figure F-3 shows how each number in the West data series row appears in the chart.

FIGURE F-3: Graph chart and datasheet

West Data Series

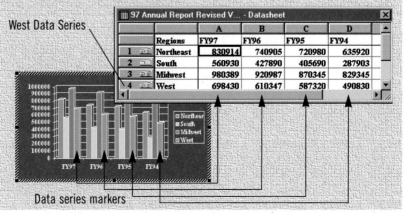

Data series markers

Formatting a Datasheet

Once you've imported the data from another file, it can be helpful to modify and format the datasheet to make your data easier to view and manipulate. With Graph, you can make simple formatting changes to the font, number format, and column size in your datasheet. To format the data in the datasheet, you must first select the data. 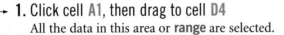 In this lesson, Carrie changes the size of the chart and the number format to display the sales numbers correctly, then she changes the chart to show the sales by region rather than by year.

Steps

Trouble?

If you can't see all the rows and columns, resize the datasheet window.

QuickTip

To quickly change the number format to Currency, click the Currency Style button $ on the Graph Formatting toolbar.

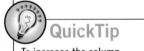

QuickTip

To increase the column width to fit the widest cell of data in a column, double-click ↔ over the control box border.

1. **Click cell A1, then drag to cell D4**
   All the data in this area or **range** are selected.

2. **Right-click the selection, then click Number on the pop-up menu**
   The Format number dialog box opens. The Category list on the left side of the dialog box displays the format categories. Change the datasheet numbers to the Currency format.

3. **In the Category list box, click Currency**
   Notice the sample number format at the top of the dialog box that shows you how the selected format code will display your data. Compare your Format number dialog box to Figure F-4.

4. **Click OK**
   The data in the datasheet and in the chart change to the new number format. Graph cannot display the numbers properly, however, because the new format increased the number of placeholders that each number has. Change all the column widths so the data can be displayed properly.

5. **With all the columns still selected, click Format on the menu bar, click Column Width, then click Best Fit**
   The column widths increase to accommodate the Currency format. Now, eliminate the numbers after the decimal point.

6. **Click the Decrease Decimal button 📉 on the Graph Formatting toolbar twice, then click anywhere in the datasheet**
   This chart would be more helpful if it displayed the Regions along the y-axis.

7. **Click Data on the menu bar, then click Series in Columns**
   The column icons now appearing in the column control boxes change to indicate that the data is shown in a series by column. Compare your datasheet to Figure F-5.

8. **Click the Close button in the datasheet**
   The datasheet closes, but Graph is still open. Save your changes.

9. **Click the Save button 💾 on the Standard toolbar**

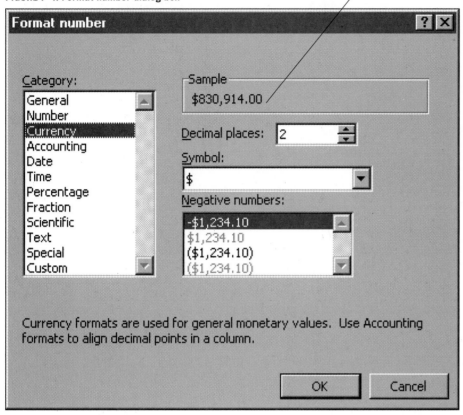

Sample box shows
how data will be
displayed

FIGURE F-4: Format number dialog box

Format number   ? X

Category: Sample
General $830,914.00
Number
Currency
Accounting   Decimal places: 2
Date
Time   Symbol:
Percentage $
Fraction
Scientific   Negative numbers:
Text   -$1,234.10
Special $1,234.10
Custom   ($1,234.10)
                             ($1,234.10)

Currency formats are used for general monetary values. Use Accounting
formats to align decimal points in a column.

                             OK   Cancel

Shows that data is
displayed in a series
by column

Column-box borders

FIGURE F-5: Datasheet showing formatted data

97 Annual Report Revised V... - Datasheet   X

	Regions	A FY97	B FY96	C FY95	D FY94
1	Northeast	$830,914	$740,905	$720,980	$63!
2	South	$560,930	$427,890	$405,690	$28
3	Midwest	$980,389	$920,987	$870,345	$82!
4	West	$698.430	$610.347	$587.320	$49!

CLUES TO USE

Formatting: datasheets and charts

You can format data in both datasheets and in charts created by Graph. Sometimes it's easier to view the numbers in the datasheet after they have been formatted; other times, you may want to manipulate the numbers after they have been placed into a chart to get a better picture. After you've formatted the data in the datasheet, the formatting changes will be reflected in the chart; however, formatting changes made to the data in the chart will not be reflected in the datasheet.

Changing a Chart's Type

Each chart has a specific type that defines how the chart graphically displays the data from the datasheet. There are over 20 chart type categories, including two-dimensional and three-dimensional graphs. Some of the most common chart types are area, bar, column, line, and pie charts. The type of chart you choose depends on the amount of information you have and how it's best displayed. For example, a chart with more than six or seven data series does not fit well in a pie chart. You can change a chart type quickly and easily by using the Chart Type command on the Chart menu. ◣▬▬▬ Carrie decides that a column chart on Slide 6 would communicate the information more clearly than a bar chart.

Steps 1 2 3 4

1. **With the chart still selected and Graph still open, click Chart on the menu bar, then click Chart Type**
   The Chart Type dialog box opens. Change the chart from a three-dimensional bar chart to a three-dimensional column chart.

2. **In the Chart type section, click Column, in the Chart sub-type section, click the sub-type shown in Figure F-6, then click OK**
   Now, customize the chart format by changing the column positions.

3. **Click the Chart Objects list arrow on the Standard toolbar, click Series "FY97", click Format on the menu bar, then click Selected Data Series**
   The Format Data Series dialog box opens as shown in Figure F-7. Change the color of the data series to green.

4. **In the Area section, click the green square in the second row, third column, then click the Options tab**
   The Options tab contains three sizing options that change the way the chart appears. **Gap depth** changes the size of the base area, or **floor**, of the chart; **Gap width** changes the distance between each group of data series; and **Chart depth** changes the size of the data series markers on the chart. Now, change the way the chart appears.

5. **Double-click the Gap depth text field, type 100, then click OK**
   Notice that the data series changes to a green color and the size of the chart floor enlarges. Go back now and change the other two chart sizing options.

6. **Right-click one of the columns in the FY97 data series, then click Format Data Series on the pop-up menu**
   The Format Data Series dialog box opens. Change the Gap width and Chart depth options.

7. **Double-click the Gap width text field, then type 200**

8. **Double-click the Chart depth text field, type 250, then click OK**

9. **Click the Save button 🖫 on the Graph Standard toolbar**
   Compare your chart to Figure F-8.

> **QuickTip**
>
> To easily change your chart's type, click the Chart Type button 🔳 on the Graph Standard toolbar.

Select this sub-type

FIGURE F-6: Chart Type dialog box

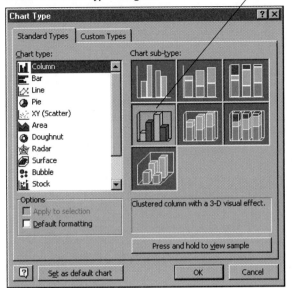

Select this color cell

FIGURE F-7: Format Data Series dialog box

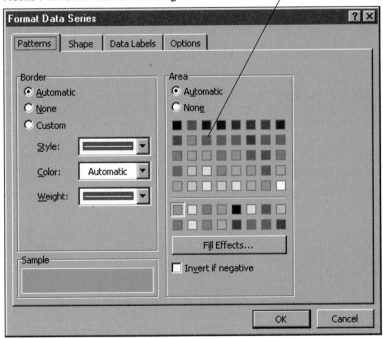

FIGURE F-8: Formatted chart

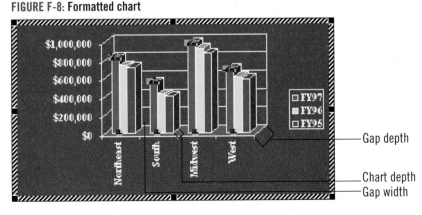

Gap depth

Chart depth
Gap width

Customizing a Chart's 3-D View

In Graph, every two-dimensional and three-dimensional chart format has a default position setting that determines the chart's placement on the slide. The 3-D formatting options allow you to creatively display your chart on the slide. Refer to Table F-1 for a description of the most common 3-D view options. One format option that you can change on most 3-D charts is the **elevation** or angle at which you view the chart. By changing the elevation, you can view a chart from above or below. Another option you can change is the **rotation** of the chart. This allows you to rotate that chart around so that you can get a clearer view of the data that interests you. ◀▬▬ Carrie experiments with the 3-D options by changing the elevation and rotation of her chart.

1. Click **Chart** on the menu bar, then click **3-D View**
   The 3-D View dialog box opens, as shown in Figure F-9. Change the elevation of the chart.

2. Click the **Elevation up arrow** twice, then click **Apply**
   The elevation setting changes to 25. Notice that the chart in the Preview box changes to show you how the chart looks with the new elevation setting. To see the changes on your slide, drag the dialog box up.

3. Drag the 3-D View dialog box up by its title bar until you see the chart in Slide 6
   Now, rotate the chart to the left to give it a more dramatic appearance.

4. Click the **Rotation left arrow** twice, then click **Apply**
   The rotation setting changes to 40. The new rotation setting moves the chart around to the left, which displays more of the side of the data series columns. To see how the perspective feature changes the chart format, you'll need to clear the Right angle axes check box.

5. Click the **Right angle axes check box** to clear it
   Notice that the Perspective option appears and the Preview box changes to show the default perspective setting. Change the perspective of the chart.

6. Click the **Perspective down arrow** until 50 appears, then click **Apply**
   The chart appears farther away. Turning the Right angle axes option off drastically changes the way this particular chart looks, so turn the option back on to reset the chart.

7. Click the **Right angle axes check box**, then click **Apply**
   The chart looks best with the current settings.

8. Click **OK**
   Compare your screen to Figure F-10. Save your changes.

9. Click the **Save button** 🔲 on the Standard toolbar

QuickTip

Click Default in the 3-D View dialog box to return your chart to its original settings.

FIGURE F-9: **3-D View dialog box**

Elevation up arrow

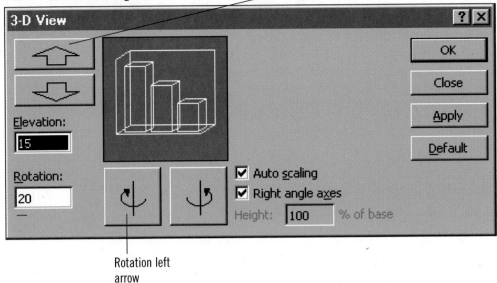

Rotation left
arrow

FIGURE F-10: **Formatted Chart**

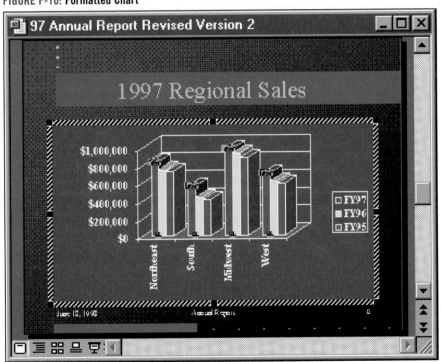

TABLE F-1: **Understanding the 3-D View options**

option	definition
Elevation	Controls the height or angle from which you view the chart; the elevation ranges from +90 degrees to -90 degrees
Rotation	Controls the horizontal rotation of the plot area; you can rotate your graph from 0 degrees to 360 degrees
Auto Scaling	Controls the scale of a chart automatically; helps keep the size of the chart proportional when changing a two-dimensional chart to a three-dimensional chart
Right Angle Axes	Controls the orientation of the axes; when this option is checked, the axes of the chart appear at right angles to each other
Perspective	Controls the distance perspective; the higher the perspective, the farther away the chart appears; only available when the Right Angle Axes option is turned off

Customizing a Chart

PowerPoint 97

Graph provides many advanced formatting options so that you can customize your chart to emphasize the information you think is important. For example, you can add gridlines to a chart, change the color or pattern of data markers, and format the axes. ⬥ Carrie wants to improve the appearance of her chart, so she makes several formatting changes.

Steps

1. **Click Chart on the menu bar, then click Chart Options**
   The Chart Options dialog box opens. First, add major and minor gridlines to the x-axis. Gridlines help separate and clarify the data series markers.

2. **Click the Gridlines tab in the Category (X) axis section, click the Major gridlines check box, then click the Minor gridlines check box**
   Gridlines appear on the floor and back of the chart in the Preview box. Compare your screen to Figure F-11. Adding minor gridlines increases the number of gridlines in the chart. Now, add the data table to the chart.

3. **Click the Data Table tab, click the Show data table check box, then click OK**
   Adding the data table dramatically decreased the size of the chart, so undo your last action.

4. **Click Chart on the menu bar, click Chart Options, click the Show data table check box to deselect it, then click OK**
   Next, add data labels to one of the data series to make the series easier to identify.

Trouble?

If the incorrect formatting dialog box opens, you double-clicked the wrong chart element. Close the dialog box, then double-click the correct chart element.

5. **Double-click one of the FY97 data markers in the chart, click the Data Labels tab in the Format Data Series dialog box, click the Show value option button, then click OK**
   Each data marker's value from the datasheet is displayed, as shown in Figure F-12. Now, finish the formatting of the chart by modifying the z-axis. In a three-dimensional chart, the vertical axis is the z-axis.

6. **Right-click one of the values on the z-axis, click Format Axis on the pop-up menu, then click the Scale tab**
   The Scale tab in the Format axis dialog box opens. Change the major unit number to better display the values on the z-axis.

7. **Double-click 200000 in the Major unit text field, type 100000, then click OK**
   Notice that the values on the z-axis change to the new unit scale. Now, check to see how your chart looks on the slide.

Time To

✔ Save

8. **Click a blank area of the slide**
   Compare your screen to Figure F-13.

FIGURE F-11: Chart options dialog box

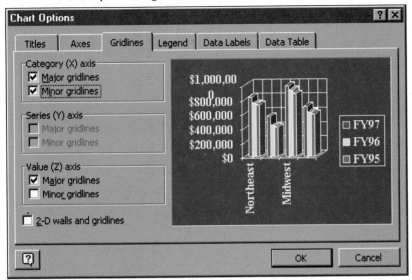

FIGURE F-12: Chart showing data marker labels

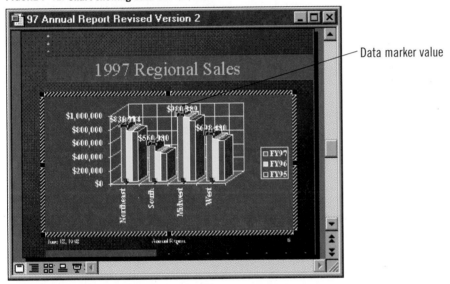

Data marker value

FIGURE F-13: Modified chart

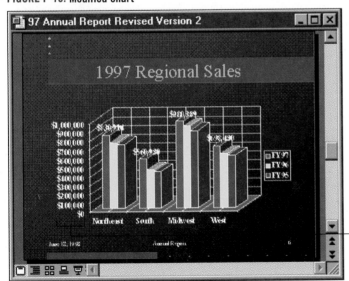

Modified z-axis

Working with Chart Elements

Chart elements are objects you can add and format to help display or highlight certain information in your chart. Chart elements include legends, arrows, shapes or lines, text objects, and chart titles. ▰▰▰ Carrie decides to add a text object and an arrow to draw attention to particularly strong sales from the Midwest sales region.

Steps

1. **Double-click the Graph chart object**
   Graph opens and displays the chart from the previous lesson. Display the Graph Drawing toolbar, then add a text object to the chart.

2. **Right-click the Graph Formatting toolbar, click Drawing on the pop-up menu, then click the Text Box button 🄰 on the Drawing toolbar**
   The pointer changes to +. Due to the limited blank space in the chart, create the text box over the top of the chart.

Trouble?

If the text object is not where you want it, refer to the Clues to Use, then reposition the object.

3. **Position + over the top right side of the chart, drag to create a text box, then type Over Goal**
   Compare your screen to Figure F-14. After typing the text into the text box, it's apparent that the text is difficult to read. Change the color and size of the text.

4. **Drag I over the text to select it, click Format on the menu bar, then click Text Box**
   The Format Text Box dialog box opens.

Trouble?

Resize the text box if necessary to accommodate the larger font size.

5. **Click the Color list arrow, click the red box in the last row, scroll down the Size list, click 22, click OK, then click in a blank area of the chart**
   Now, draw an arrow to connect the new text object to a data marker in the chart.

6. **Click the Arrow button ↖ on the Drawing toolbar, position + to the left of the word "Over," then drag an arrow to the top of the Midwest data markers**
   Modify the arrow slightly to make it stand out better.

7. **Click the Arrow Style button ⇄ on the Drawing toolbar, click More Arrows, then in the Line section, click the Color list arrow**
   Change the arrow line color to yellow and change the arrow format.

8. **Click one of the yellow boxes in the color palatte, click the Weight up arrow until 2 pt appears, then click OK**

9. **Click a blank area of the slide, then click the Save button 💾 on the Standard toolbar**
   Compare your screen to Figure F-15.

FIGURE F-14: Chart showing new text object

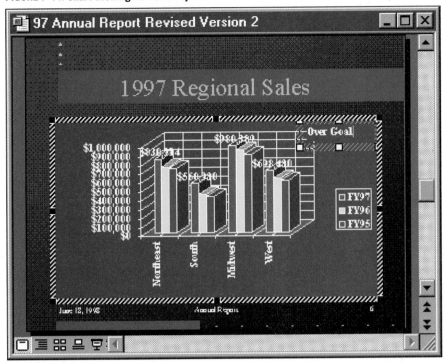

FIGURE F-15: Chart showing added elements

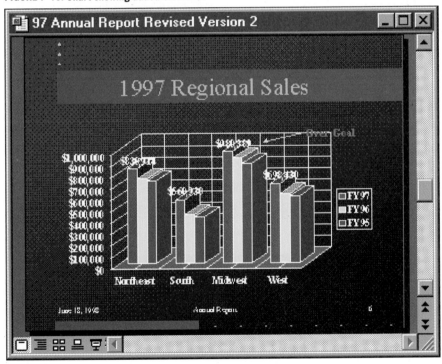

CLUES TO USE

Moving and sizing chart elements

To move a chart element, such as an arrow or legend, you must first select the object to display its resize handles, then drag the object to a new location. Make sure that the cursor is over the border when you drag, not over the resize handle. To change the size of a chart element, click the object to display its resize handles, then drag a resize handle.

Embedding and Formatting an Organizational Chart

You can create an organizational chart by using the Object command on the Insert menu or by changing the layout of your slide to the Organization Chart slide AutoLayout. Once you open Microsoft Organization Chart, a series of connected boxes called **chart boxes** appears. Each chart box has placeholder text that you replace with the names and titles of people in your organization. Carrie is satisfied with her graph and now turns her attention to creating an organizational chart showing Nomad's top management structure. Follow Carrie as she creates a basic organizational chart.

1. **Drag the vertical scroll box to Slide 8, click New Slide on the Common Tasks toolbar, click the Organization Chart AutoLayout, then click OK**

   A new slide appears displaying the Organization Chart placeholder. Use the Organization Chart placeholder to insert a new organizational chart.

2. **Type Nomad Ltd, then double-click the org chart placeholder**

   The text you type is entered into the title placeholder and the default organizational chart appears in a separate window, as shown in Figure F-16. The default organizational chart displays a chart title and four chart boxes. The open chart box at the top of the window is a **Manager chart box** and the three chart boxes below it are **Subordinate chart boxes**. Notice that the Manager chart box is selected and ready to accept text.

QuickTip

You can also press [Enter] to move to the next placeholder in a chart box.

3. **Type Bill Davidson, press [Tab], type President, then click a blank area of the Organization chart window**

   Now fill in the three subordinate chart boxes.

4. **Enter the information in the Subordinate chart boxes shown in Figure F-17**

   Click each chart box to enter the first line of text, then press [Tab] to move from line to line. Now, format the chart boxes using Organization Chart's formatting tools.

5. **Click Edit on the Organization Chart menu bar, point to Select, then click All**

   All the chart boxes are selected and ready to be formatted.

6. **Click Boxes on the Organization Chart menu bar, click Color, click the fifth color cell from the left in the top row, then click OK**

   The chart boxes change to a deep blue color. Now change the chart box connector line style.

7. **Click Lines on the Organization Chart menu bar, point to Thickness, click the third line in the menu, then click in a blank area of the chart window**

   Notice that the connector line between the chart boxes is thicker. Now embed the organizational chart in your slide.

8. **Click File on the menu bar, then click Exit and Return to 97 Annual Report Revised Version 2**

   A Microsoft Organization Chart alert box opens to confirm your desire to update your slide with the organizational chart.

Time To

✔ Save

9. **Click Yes to update the presentation, then click a blank area of the Presentation window**

   Compare your screen to Figure F-18.

FIGURE F-16: Default organizational chart

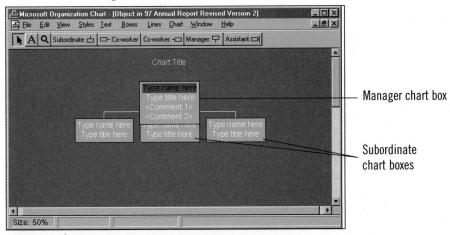

Manager chart box

Subordinate chart boxes

FIGURE F-17: Organizational chart showing filled-in chart boxes

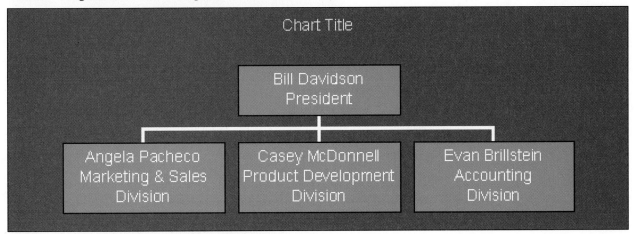

FIGURE F-18: Organizational chart embedded on the slide

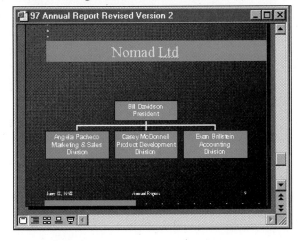

CLUES TO USE

Changing chart styles

In Organization Chart you can change the way chart boxes are grouped together by clicking a group style on the Styles menu. Figure F-20 illustrates how each Styles button displays subordinate chart boxes relative to the Manager chart box.

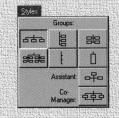

FIGURE F-19: Styles Menu

Modifying an Organizational Chart

If the organizational chart you want to create requires more than the four default chart boxes, you can add up to nine chart boxes in a row and thirteen chart boxes in a column to accommodate more information. Note, however, that each chart box you add automatically decreases the size of all the chart boxes so that the organizational chart fits on the slide. After you add all the chart boxes you need for your chart, you can rearrange them as desired. Carrie needs to add two chart boxes to her organizational chart.

1. Double-click the organizational chart
The Organization Chart window opens, displaying the organizational chart you created in the last lesson. Maximize the window to make it easier to work with all the chart boxes.

2. Click the Microsoft Organization Chart window Maximize button
The Organization Chart window fills the screen. Now, add a co-worker chart box.

3. Click the Right Co-worker button `Co-worker: ─□` on the Organization Chart toolbar
The pointer changes to ─□

4. Click the Evan Brillstein chart box, type Michael Belmont, press [Tab], type Travel, press [Tab], type Division, then click in a blank area of the Organization Chart window
Compare your screen to Figure F-20. Now, add a subordinate chart box to the chart.

5. Click the Subordinate button `Subordinate: □` on the Organization Chart toolbar, then click the Michael Belmont chart box
A small blank chart box appears.

6. Type Barry Cheda, press [Tab], type Executive Director, then click in a blank area of the Organization Chart window
Change the placement of the Michael Belmont chart box to another position on the chart.

7. Drag the Michael Belmont chart box on top of the Casey McDonnell chart box until the pointer changes to ◁, release the mouse button, then click in a blank area of the Organization Chart window
You may have to experiment with the placement of the chart box until the pointer changes to ◁ . Compare your organizational chart to Figure F-21. Notice that the subordinate chart box moves with the Co-worker chart box to the new location in the chart. When you move a chart box, all of its subordinate chart boxes move with it, which makes it easy to rearrange the organizational chart. See Table F-2 for an explanation of chart box placement arrows.

8. Click File on the menu bar, then click Exit and Return to 97 Annual Report Revised Version 2, click Yes to update the presentation, click a blank area of the Presentation window, click Slide Layout on the Common Tasks toolbar, then click Reapply

9. Click the Slide Sorter View button ▦, then click the Maximize button in the Presentation window
Compare your screen to Figure F-22.

QuickTip

See the Organization Chart on-line Help for information on keyboard commands you can use to create and edit chart boxes.

Trouble?

When you move a chart box, make sure the correct placement arrow appears before you release the mouse button.

Time To

✔ Save
✔ Run the slide show
✔ Print handouts (3 slides per page)
✔ Close the presentation

FIGURE F-20: Organizational chart showing new co-worker chart box

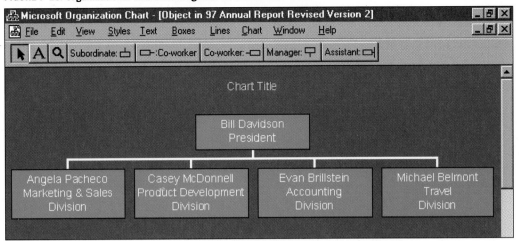

FIGURE F-21: Organizational chart showing rearranged chart boxes

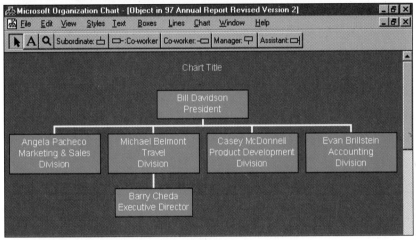

FIGURE F-22: Final presentation in Slide Sorter view

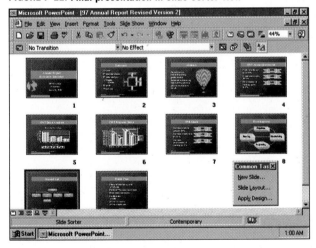

TABLE F-2: Chart box placement arrows

arrow	placement
⇨	Places a chart box to the right of another chart box
⇦	Places a chart box to the left of another chart box
⊤	Places a chart box below another chart box

Practice

▶ Concepts Review

Label each of the elements of the PowerPoint window shown in Figure F-23.

FIGURE F-23

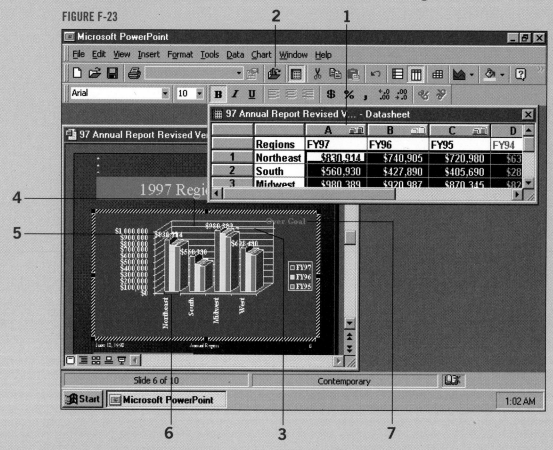

Match each of the terms with the statement that describes its function.

8. A row or column of data in a datasheet
9. How a chart graphically displays data
10. Graphical representation of a data series
11. Size of a chart floor
12. The angle at which you view a chart
13. Distance between each data series group

a. Data series markers
b. Chart type
c. Data series
d. Elevation
e. Gap width
f. Gap depth

Select the best answer from the list of choices.

14. In Graph, clicking a column control box
    a. Selects all column data markers in a chart
    b. Selects an entire column of data in the datasheet
    c. Switches the chart format to 3-D column
    d. Controls the format of the datasheet

15. **Which of the following statements about Graph charts is incorrect?**
    a. There are two-dimensional and three-dimensional chart type categories.
    b. You can change the size and format of data markers.
    c. You can format every element of a chart.
    d. The type of chart you choose does not depend on the data you have.

16. **What does the elevation option in the 3-D View dialog box control?**
    a. The angle of the chart
    b. The rotation of the chart
    c. The perspective of the chart
    d. The dimension of the chart

17. **Which of the following is true about an organizational chart?**
    a. You can create a chart by using the Organization Chart command on the Insert menu.
    b. The default organizational chart displays two subordinate chart boxes.
    c. Adding chart boxes to your chart increases the size of all the chart boxes.
    d. Chart boxes have placeholder text that you type over.

18. **Based on what you know of organizational charts, which of the following data would best fit in an organizational chart?**
    a. A company's division structure
    b. A company's database mailing list
    c. A company's annual financial numbers
    d. Spreadsheet data

▶ Skills Review

1. **Insert data from a file into a datasheet.**
    a. Start PowerPoint and open the presentation PPT F-3, then save it as OutBack Report.
    b. Drag the vertical scroll box to Slide 3, then double-click the Graph chart.
    c. Click the first cell.
    d. Click the Import File button on the Graph Standard toolbar.
    e. Locate the file PPT F-4, then click Open.
    f. Make sure "Sheet 1" is selected, then click OK.
    g. Double-click the Column A control box. Column A is excluded from the datasheet and does not appear in the chart.
    h. Double-click the Column A control box again.

2. **Format a datasheet.**
    a. Click cell A1, drag to cell D4 to select the range, right-click the selection, then click Number on the pop-up menu.
    b. In the Category list box, click Accounting.
    c. Click the Decimal places down arrow twice to remove the places after the decimal point.
    d. Click OK.
    e. Select all the columns in the datasheet, click Format on the menu bar, click Column Width, click Best Fit, then click anywhere in the datasheet.
    f. Click the datasheet Close box, then click the Save button.

3. Change a chart's type.

a. Right-click a blank area of the chart, then click Chart Type on the pop-up menu.

b. Click the Custom Types tab, then click each of the chart types in the Chart type list box. Notice how each chart type displays your data.

c. Click the Standard Types tab, click the Cylinder chart type, then click OK.

d. Click the Chart Objects list arrow, then click Series "Outlets".

e. Click Format on the menu bar, then click Selected Data Series.

f. Click the Options tab.

g. Double-click the Gap depth text field, then type "50".

h. Double-click the Gap width text field, then type "175".

i. Double-click the Chart depth text field, type "350" then click OK.

4. Customize a chart.

a. Right-click a blank area of the chart, then click Chart Options on the pop-up menu.

b. Click the Gridlines tab.

c. In the Category (X) axis section, click the Major gridlines check box, then click the Minor gridlines check box.

d. In the Value (Z) axis section, click the Major gridlines check box, then click OK.

e. Right-click the Z-axis (Value Axis), then click Format Axis.

f. Click the Scale tab, double-click the Major Unit text field, then type "300".

g. Click the Font tab, then in the Size list box, click 20.

h. Click OK.

i. Right-click the X-axis (Category Axis), then click Format Axis.

j. Click the Font tab, then in the Size list box, click 16.

k. Click OK.

l. Right-click an Outlets data series marker (dark blue), then click Format Data Series.

m. In the Area section, click the tan color cell (sixth row, sixth column), then click OK.

n. Save your changes.

5. Work with chart elements.

a. Right-click the legend, then click Format Legend on the pop-up menu.

b. Click the Font tab, then in the Size list box, click 16.

c. Click the Patterns tab, then in the Area section, click Fill Effects.

d. Click the Texture tab, click the Green marble square, then click OK.

e. Click the Placement tab, click the Top radio button, then click OK.

f. Click the Chart Objects list arrow on the Graph Standard toolbar, then click Plot Area.

g. Drag the left bottom corners of the plot area.

h. Right-click the Formatting toolbar, then click Drawing on the pop-up menu.

i. Click the Text Box button on the Drawing toolbar, position the cursor near the top of the chart over the West data series markers, then drag a text box.

j. Type Sales Goal Reached, then select the text.

k. Right-click the selection, then click Format Text Box on the pop-up menu.

l. Click the Color list arrow, click the red color cell in the last row, then click OK.

m. Press [Shift], right-click the selection box of the text object, then click Format Text Box on the pop-up menu.

n. Click the Font tab, click the Background list arrow, click Automatic, then click OK.

o. Click anywhere in the chart to deselect the text object, then, if necessary, resize the text object and drag it to a better position in the chart.

6. Customize a chart's 3-D view.
   a. Right-click a blank area of the chart, then click 3-D View.
   b. Drag the 3-D View title bar to the top of the screen until you see the chart.
   c. Click the Elevation up arrow until 25 appears.
   d. Click the Rotation left arrow until 40 appears, then click Apply.
   e. Click OK.
   f. Click in a blank area of the slide, then click the Save button on the Standard toolbar.

7. Embed and format an organizational chart.
   a. Click the Next Slide button.
   b. Click Slide Layout on the Common Tasks toolbar, click the Organization Chart AutoLayout, then click Apply.
   c. Double-click the Organization Chart placeholder, then click the Organization Chart window Maximize button.
   d. Type "Tanya Bryceson," press [Tab], then type "Division Manager."
   e. In the Subordinate chart boxes, type the names and titles shown in Table F-3.

TABLE F-3

W. Paul Jones III	Sherline Montgomery	David Von Rotz
Accounting Manager	Design Manager	Product Manager

   f. Click Edit on the menu bar, point to Select, then click Lowest Level.
   g. Click Boxes, point to Border Style, then click the third line style down in the first column.
   h. Click the Manager chart box, click Boxes on the menu bar, point to Border Style, then click the fourth line style down in the first column.
   i. Click File on the menu bar, then click Exit and Return to Outback Report.
   j. Click Yes to update the presentation, click a blank area of the Presentation window, then save your changes.

8. Modify an organizational chart.
   a. Double-click the organizational chart.
   b. Click the Organization Chart window Maximize button.
   c. Click the Assistant button on the Organization Chart Standard toolbar, then click the Tanya Bryceson chart box.
   d. Type "Lisa Musante," press [Tab], then type "Special Assistant."
   e. Add a Subordinate chart box to each manager chart box.
   f. In the Subordinate chart boxes, type the names and titles shown in Table F-4.

TABLE F-4

Robert Garcelon	Lori Heredia	Wendy Peterson
Account Specialist	Style Designer	Finance Supervisor

   g. Click in a blank area of the Organization Chart window.
   h. Drag the David Von Rotz chart box over the W. Paul Jones III chart box, then place the David Von Rotz chart box to the left of the W. Paul Jones III chart box.
   i. Drag the Wendy Peterson chart box over the Robert Garcelon chart box, then place the Wendy Peterson chart box to the right of the Robert Garcelon chart box.
   j. Click File on the menu bar, then click Exit and Return to Outback Report.
   k. Click Yes to update the presentation.
   l. Click Slide Layout on the Common Tasks toolbar, then click Reapply.
   m. Click the Slide Sorter View button, then run through your slide show in Slide Show view.
   n. Save your changes, print Slides 3 and 4, then close the presentation.

▶ Independent Challenges

1. You work for Larsen Concepts, a business consulting company that helps small and medium-sized businesses organize or restructure themselves to be more efficient and profitable. You are one of six senior consultants who work directly with clients. To prepare for an upcoming meeting with executives at ComSystems, a mobile phone communications company, you create a brief presentation outlining Larsen's typical investigative and reporting techniques, past results versus the competition, and the company's business philosophy.

The following is a sample of the type of work you perform as part of your duties at Larsen: You usually investigate a client's business practices for two weeks and analyze all relevant records. Once the initial investigation stage is complete, you submit a client recommendation report to your boss that describes the known problem areas, the consequences of the problems, the reasons for the problems, the recommended solutions, the anticipated results for each solution, the anticipated cost to the client for each solution, and Larsen's final professional recommendation. After the client recommendation report is approved by your boss, you prepare a full report for the client. If the client approves a particular plan, you develop a maintenance schedule (usually one year or less) to make sure the plan is implemented correctly.

To complete this independent challenge:

1. Open the file PPT F-5, then save it as Larsen Presentation.
2. Think about the results you want to see, the information you need, and how you want to communicate the message. Sketch how you want your presentation to look.
3. Create two organizational charts on Slides 3 and 4. Use the information above to create two flow charts (Phase 1 and Phase 2) showing the various stages of investigation and reporting.
4. Create a Graph chart on Slide 5 that shows how Larsen compares with two competitors. For example, you might illustrate the satisfaction level of Larsen clients compared to its competitors' clients.
5. Add supplemental objects to enhance the presentation.
6. Format the text on the slides. Modify the master views to achieve the look you want.
7. Add a template and shaded background to finish the presentation.
8. Spell check the presentation.
9. Print the slides of the presentation, then submit your presentation plan and printouts.

2. This year you have been selected by your peers to receive a national teaching award for the educational program for handicapped children that you created in your home state of Connecticut. In accepting this award, you have the opportunity to give a presentation describing your program's results since its introduction. You will give the presentation at an educator's convention in Washington, D.C.

Plan and create a color slide presentation describing your results. Create your own data, but assume the following:
- Over the last four years, 3,548 children in 251 classrooms throughout Connecticut participated in your program.
- Children enrolled in your program have shown at least a 7% improvement in skills for every year the program has been in effect.
- Children ages 4 through 16 have participated in the program.
- Money to fund the program comes from the National Education Association (NEA) and the State of Connecticut Public Schools Department. The money goes to each participating school district in the state.
- Funding per child is $2,867.45 per school year. Funding for children in the regular public school system is $3,950 per year.

To complete this independent challenge:

1. Think about the results you want to see, the information you need to create the slide presentation, and how your message should be communicated.
2. Create a color slide presentation using Microsoft Graph and Microsoft Organization Chart to build some of your slides. Think about how you can effectively show information in a chart.
3. Use clip art, shapes, and a shaded background to enhance the presentation. Change the bullet and text formatting in the master text and title placeholders to fit the subject matter.
4. Save the presentation as Teaching Award.
5. Submit your presentation plan and print the final slide presentation.

3. LabTech Industries is a large company that develops and produces technical medical equipment and machines for operating and emergency rooms around the United States. You are the business manager for the company and one of your assignments is to prepare a presentation for the stockholders on the profitability and efficiency of each division in the company.

Plan and create a slide presentation that shows all the divisions and divisional managers of the company. Also, graphically show how each division performed in relation to its previous year's performance. Create your own content but assume the following:

- The company has seven divisions: Administration, Accounting, Sales and Marketing, Research and Development, Product Testing, Product Development, and Manufacturing.
- Four divisions increased productivity by at least 12%.
- The presentation will be given in a boardroom using a projector.

To complete this independent challenge:

1. Think about the results you want to see, the information you need to create the slide presentation, what type of message you want to communicate, and the target audience.
2. Use Outline view to create the content of your presentation.
3. Use Microsoft Graph and Microsoft Organization Chart to create charts to help display the information you want to communicate.
4. Use clip art, pictures, or a shaded background to enhance the presentation.
5. Format the content, then save the presentation as LabTech Industries.
6. Submit your presentation plan and print the final slide presentation.

4. You are in your first year of graduate school where you are earning a Masters in Business Administration (MBA). The final project in your first semester sales and marketing class is to create a sales or marketing presentation and then present it to the entire class during finals week. You decide to use PowerPoint to help you create a professional-looking presentation.

In this independent challenge, you'll need to develop a presentation that convinces your audience that they need to have the product you are selling. Create your own information using the basic presentation provided on your Student Disk. Assume the following about this final project assignment: (1) Your presentation topic is on a new type of pen computing software called NotesWriter produced by Romedia. NotesWriter is a word-processing program for a Windows-compatible computer with an integrated pen or an attached tablet (personal communicator) with a pen. You can create, edit, and send handwritten notes, faxes, e-mail notes, and other messages using this software. (2) The primary feature of NotesWriter is its ability to allow the user to write and edit naturally with a pen and then send the note as a fax or an e-mail message. (3) The assignment requires a 6- to 10-slide presentation that adequately explains the topic.

To complete this independent challenge:

1. Open the file PPT F-6, then save it as NotesWriter.
2. Think about the results you want to see, the information you need, and how you want to communicate the message. Plan the presentation using an outline.
3. Log onto the Internet and use your browser to go to http://www.course.com. From there, click Student Online Companions, click the link for this textbook, then click the PowerPoint link for Unit F. Use the links you find there to research data on pen commuting products to use in your presentation.
4. Use the information on the second and third slides to create charts.
5. Add between 3 and 5 slides to the presentation that adequately explain the product features, the target market, and the market need.
6. Enhance the presentation with objects, a shaded background, or other items that improve the look of the presentation.
7. Add a template and then change the master views, if necessary, to fit your information.
8. Spell-check the presentation.
9. Print the slides of the presentation, then submit your presentation plan and printouts.

▶ Visual Workshop

Create two slides that look like the examples in Figures F-24 and F-25. Save the presentation as Semiphore. Save and print Slide view of the presentation. Submit the final presentation output.

FIGURE F-24

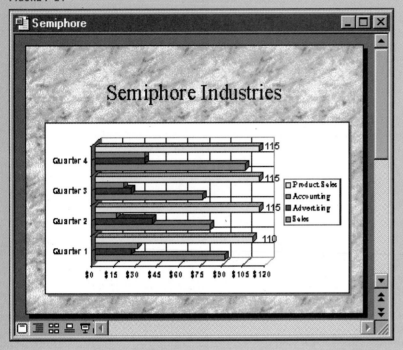

FIGURE F-25

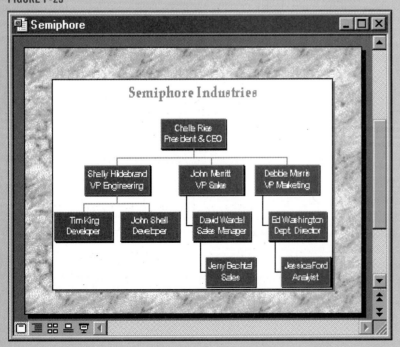

Working

with Embedded and Linked Objects and Hyperlinks

Objectives

- ► **Embed a picture**
- ► **Embed a table**
- ► **Embed a worksheet**
- ► **Link an Excel worksheet**
- ► **Update a linked Excel worksheet**
- ► **Insert a movie**
- ► **Insert a sound**
- ► **Insert a hyperlink**

PowerPoint offers many ways to add graphic elements to a presentation. In this unit you will learn how to embed or link objects created in other programs. **Embedded** and **linked** objects are created in another program, known as a **source program**, and then stored in or linked to the PowerPoint presentation. In this unit, Karen Craig, the executive director for New Directions, Nomad Ltd's travel subsidiary, creates a brief presentation using embedded and linked objects that outlines a new product proposal for a magazine on a CD-ROM called *CD Travel*™ *Magazine*. When Karen is finished with her presentation, she will give it to Carrie Armstrong, who plans to link it to the Annual Report Executive Summary presentation.

Embedding a Picture

There are several methods for inserting pictures into PowerPoint slides. You can enbed over 20 different types of pictures using the Insert Picture command. As you work with pictures, especially photographs, be aware that frequently a presentation's color scheme will not match the colors in the picture. In order to make the picture look good in the presentation, you may need to customize the presentation's color scheme, recolor the picture, or change the presentation's template. ✐ Karen wants to embed a picture in a slide. She will make sure that the photo-graph looks good with the slide color scheme.

Steps

1. Start PowerPoint, open the presentation PPT G-1, save it as CD Travel, click the Restore Window button in the Presentation window, click Window on the menu bar, then click Fit to Page
   Move to Slide 2 to embed a picture.

2. Click the Next Slide button 🔽, click Insert on the menu bar, point to Picture, click From File, select the file PPT G-2, then click OK
   A picture of a tropical island harbor appears in the middle of the slide and the Picture toolbar opens. Resize the picture and position it on the slide.

3. Drag the picture to the right side of the slide, drag the picture's resize handles to match the size of Figure G-1, then click on a blank area of the Presentation window
   Compare your screen to Figure G-1. The current color scheme is a little dark for the picture, so experiment with a different color scheme for this slide.

   Trouble?
   If your picture size doesn't look like the picture in Figure G-1, drag the resize handle again until the picture matches the figure.

4. Right-click a blank area of the Presentation window, then click Slide Color Scheme on the pop-up menu
   The Color Scheme dialog box opens. Notice that there are six standard color schemes to choose from. Experiment with the standard color schemes to see if any look good with the picture.

5. Drag the Color Scheme dialog box title bar to the upper right corner of the PowerPoint window so that you can see part of the picture

6. In the Color schemes section, click each standard color scheme option, then click Preview
   As you click a color scheme option and then click Preview, the color scheme is applied to the slide. The middle color scheme in the bottom row fits best with the color and contrast of the picture.

7. In the Color Schemes section, click the middle color scheme option in the bottom row, then click Apply
   Make sure you do not click Apply to All. The color scheme for slide 2 changes, as shown in Figure G-2. Save your changes.

8. Click the Save button 💾 on the Standard toolbar

FIGURE G-1: Slide showing resized picture

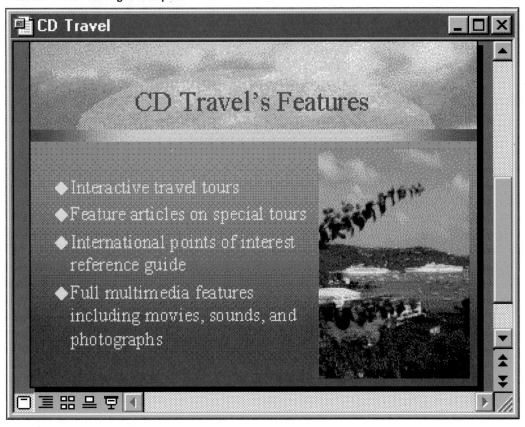

FIGURE G-2: Slide showing new color scheme

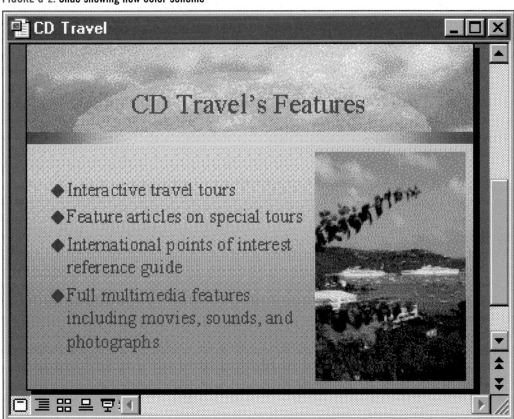

Embedding a Table

Sometimes a table is the best way to provide information in an organized and concise manner. You create tables in PowerPoint by embedding a Microsoft Word table in your PowerPoint slide. You can use formatting features of both Word and PowerPoint to call attention to important information and to make the table visually appealing. 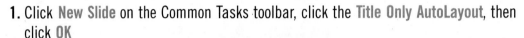 Karen decides to add a new slide with a table showing competitive market analysis information for *CD Travel Magazine*.

1. **Click New Slide on the Common Tasks toolbar, click the Title Only AutoLayout, then click OK**
   A new Slide 3 appears. Now create the table for the presentation.

QuickTip

You can also embed a Word table by choosing the Table AutoLayout.

2. **Click the Insert Microsoft Word Table button ▦ on the Standard toolbar, then drag to create a 6 × 4 Table, as shown in Figure G-3**
   Microsoft Word opens and displays a blank table with six rows and four columns in the middle of the slide. Notice that the Microsoft Word menu bar and toolbars replace PowerPoint's menu bar and toolbars. Increase the size of the table to accommodate the information you will enter.

3. **Resize the table object so it occupies most of the slide as shown in Figure G-4, then enter the data shown in Figure G-4 into your blank table**

Trouble?

If your insertion point scrolls out of view as you are entering the data, resize the columns before you enter the rest of the data.

4. **Click in a blank area of the Presentation window, double-click the table object to open Word again and redisplay the table, then use ←→ to drag each column marker on the horizontal ruler so that the words wrap as shown in Figure G-4**
   Use the Tab key to move from cell to cell in your table. If necessary, use the vertical scroll bar to view the last line of the table. Now format the table using Microsoft Word formatting features.

5. **Click Table on the menu bar, then click Table AutoFormat, in the Formats section click Simple 2, then click OK**
   The new table format adds lines to the table and changes the row and column headings to bold. The horizontal and vertical table lines may not appear in Slide view. They should appear in Slide Show view. Now change the text alignment of Columns 2 through 4.

6. **Drag to select Columns 2 through 4, click the Center button ▤ on the Formatting toolbar, then adjust column widths as necessary to accomodate the new formatting**
   The data in Columns 2 through 4 move to the center of the cells. Compare your screen to Figure G-4. Next, add a fill color to the table so it is easier to see.

Trouble?

If the table has extra blank space on the bottom or the sides, or if it is very small, double-click the table and drag the borders of the table object to eliminate extra space between the table and the object borders. Double-click the table, then click it once and resize it as necessary.

7. **Click in a blank area of the Presentation window, click the table once to select it, click the Fill color list arrow on the Drawing toolbar, then click the light purple box labeled Follow Fills Scheme Color**
   The table fills with the purple color. Now move and resize the table.

8. **Drag the table to the lower section of the slide, drag the table's resize handles so the table fills as much of the lower section as possible, leaving about ¼" of space above and below it, then drag the table to center it horizontally on the slide**
   Complete this slide by adding a title.

9. **Click the title placeholder, type Market Research Analysis, click in a blank area of the Presentation window, then click the Save button ▤ on the Standard toolbar**
   Compare your screen to Figure G-5.

FIGURE G-3: Insert Microsoft Word Table button selected

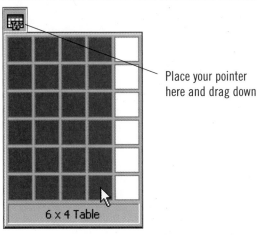

Place your pointer here and drag down

6 x 4 Table

FIGURE G-4: Formatted Microsoft Word table

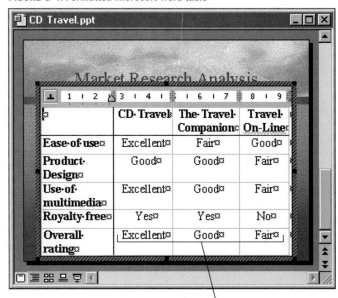

Columns are centered

FIGURE G-5: Slide showing embedded table

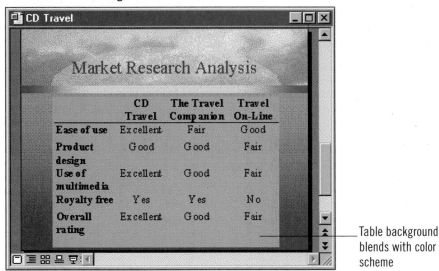

Table background blends with color scheme

Exporting a presentation to Microsoft Word

FIGURE G-6: Send To dialog box

Sometimes you need the features of a word-processing program like Word to create detailed speaker's notes or handouts. Using the PowerPoint Send To command, you can copy or link a presentation into a Microsoft Word document. Click File on the menu bar, point to Send to, and then click Microsoft Word. In the Send To dialog box, shown in Figure G-6, select one of the layout options. A new Word document opens with your embedded presentation, using the layout you selected. If you plan to modify the presentation, click the Paste link option button.

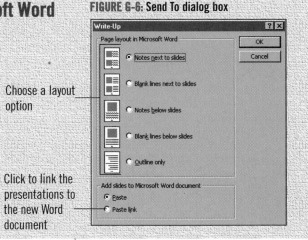

Choose a layout option

Click to link the presentations to the new Word document

WORKING WITH EMBEDDED AND LINKED OBJECTS AND HYPERLINKS PP G-5

Embedding a Worksheet

Sometimes a spreadsheet is the best way to present information that PowerPoint is not designed to create. For example, you may need to show an income and expense summary for each quarter of the year. For large amounts of data, it's easier to create a worksheet using a spreadsheet program. Then you can embed the workbook file in your PowerPoint presentation, and edit it using Excel tools. Excel is the workbook file's source program, the program in which the file was created. PowerPoint is the **target program**. Karen created an Excel workbook with the budget allocation data for *CD Travel Magazine*. She wants to include this worksheet in her presentation, so she embeds the workbook in a slide.

1. Click New Slide on the Common Tasks toolbar, click the Object AutoLayout, then click OK
   A new Slide 4 appears. Before you embed the workbook file, create a title for the new slide.

2. Type Budget Allocation, then click in a blank area of the Presentation window
   Now that the title is in place, embed the Excel workbook file.

3. Double-click the object placeholder, and in the Insert Object dialog box, click the Create from file option button, click Browse, locate the file PPT G-3, click OK, then click OK in the Insert Object dialog box
   The worksheet containing the budget allocation data appears on the slide. Notice that the Total row is not filled in yet. Because the worksheet is embedded, you can edit the worksheet using Excel tools. Use the Microsoft Excel Sum **function** (a presupplied formula) to automatically calculate the category totals.

4. Double-click the spreadsheet to open Microsoft Excel, click cell B5, click the AutoSum button [Σ] on the Excel Formatting toolbar, then press [Tab]
   The total, 115,000, appears in cell B5, which is the total of the Phase 1 category. Now copy the formula to enter the totals for the other three categories.

5. Click cell B5, then drag the selection handle in the lower right corner of cell B5 (you might need to scroll the worksheet down to see it) to cell E5
   The total for each column appears, because you have copied the sum formula you entered in B5. Now format the headings in bold.

6. Drag to select cells A2 through A5, press and hold [Ctrl], select cells B1 through E1, click the Bold button [B] on the Formatting toolbar, then click any cell to deselect the cells
   The column and row headings are now bold, as shown in Figure G-7. The original Budget Allocation worksheet, however, remains in its original form, without the totals and the new formatting. You have edited only the copy of the worksheet you embedded in the presentation. Now redisplay PowerPoint and fill the embedded spreadsheet with a color that matches the presentation color scheme.

7. Click in a blank area of the Presentation window to redisplay PowerPoint, click the worksheet object once, then click the Fill color button [🖌] on the Drawing toolbar
   The embedded worksheet fills with the same color you used to fill the embedded table in the last lesson. Resize the worksheet object.

8. Drag the lower corners of the embedded worksheet so it fills the width of the slide, then click a blank area of the Presentation window to deselect the object
   Compare your screen to Figure G-8.

FIGURE G-7: Formatted Excel worksheet

Headings are now bold

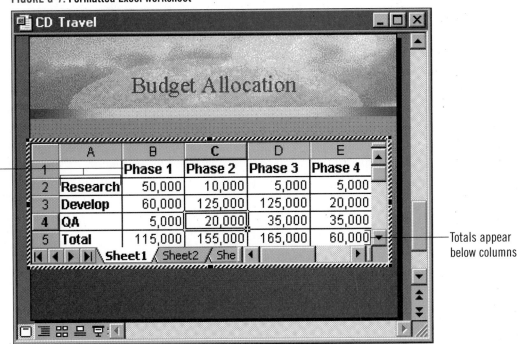

Totals appear below columns

FIGURE G-8: Embedded Microsoft Excel worksheet on slide

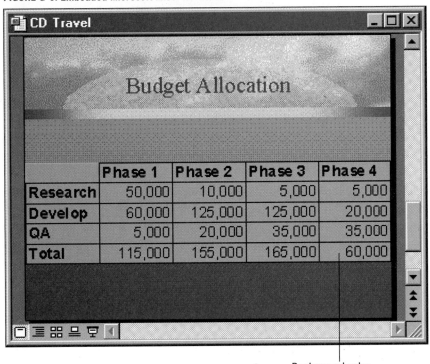

Background color added

CLUES TO USE

Embedding part of a worksheet

You can copy and paste only part of a worksheet into a PowerPoint slide. Open the Excel workbook and copy the cells you want to include in your presentation. Open the PowerPoint presentation, and paste the cells on a slide. To edit the information, double-click the pasted copy to open Excel, and edit it with Excel tools as you did in this lesson.

WORKING WITH EMBEDDED AND LINKED OBJECTS AND HYPERLINKS

Linking an Excel Worksheet

Objects like Excel worksheets can also be connected to your presentation by establishing a **link** between the source file that created the object and the PowerPoint presentation that displays the object. When you link an object to a PowerPoint slide, a representation (picture) of the object, not the actual object itself, appears on the slide. Unlike an embedded object, a linked object is stored in its source file, not on the slide. When you link an object to a PowerPoint slide, any changes made to the source file are automatically reflected in the linked representation in your PowerPoint presentation. Use linking when you want to include an object, such as an accounting spreadsheet, that may change over time and when you want to be sure your presentation contains the latest information. See Table G-1 for suggestions on when to use embedding and linking. Some of the objects that you can link to PowerPoint include movies, Microsoft Excel worksheets, and PowerPoint slides from other presentations. Karen needs to link to her presentation an Excel worksheet created by the Accounting Department manager earlier in the year.

1. Click New Slide on the Common Tasks toolbar, make sure the Object AutoLayout is selected, click OK, then type Division Annual Budget in the title placeholder
   Next, link a worksheet to the new slide to show the New Directions annual budget for 1998.

2. Double-click the object placeholder
   The Insert Object dialog box opens.

3. Click the Create from file option button, click Browse, locate the file Division Budget, click OK, then click the Link check box to select it
   Compare your screen to Figure G-9.

4. Click OK
   The image of the linked worksheet appears on the slide. Add a background fill to the worksheet object.

5. With the worksheet still selected, click the Fill Color list arrow on the Drawing toolbar, then click the pink box on the far right
   A background fill color appears behind the worksheet, as shown in Figure G-10. Now save and close the presentation.

6. Click the Save button 🖫 on the Standard toolbar, then click the Presentation window Close button
   PowerPoint remains open but the Presentation window closes.

TABLE G-1: Embedding vs. linking

embed	link
When you are the only user of an object and you want the object to be a permanent part of your presentation	When you want your object to always have the latest information from its source file
When you don't want to create a separate file for your object	When the object's source file is shared on a network or when other users have access to the file and can change it
When you want to access the object in its source program in the future, even when the original file is not available	When you want to keep your presentation file size small
When you want to update the object manually while working in PowerPoint	

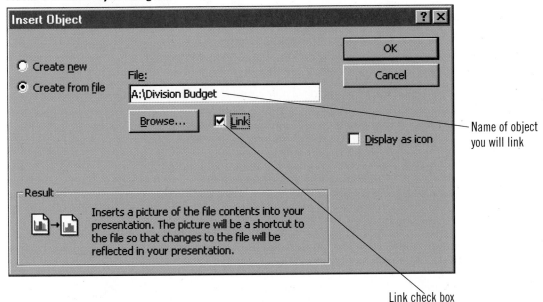

Name of object you will link

Link check box

FIGURE G-10: Linked worksheet with background fill color

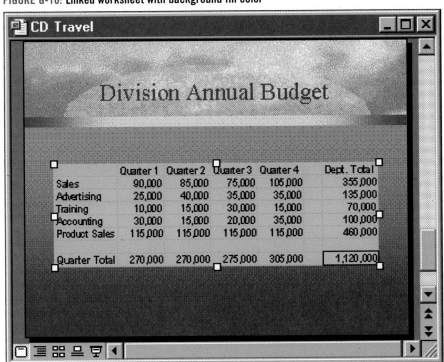

Linking objects using Paste Special

You can also link an object or selected information from another program into PowerPoint by copying and pasting the information. This technique is useful when you want to link part of a worksheet rather than the entire file. For example, you may want to link a worksheet from a Microsoft Excel workbook that contains both a worksheet and a chart. To link just the worksheet, open the Microsoft Excel workbook file that contains the worksheet, select the worksheet, then copy it to the Clipboard. Open the PowerPoint presentation, click Edit on the menu bar, click Paste Special, click the Paste link option button, then click OK.

Updating a Linked Excel Worksheet

To edit or change the information in a linked object, you must open the object's source program. For example, you must open Microsoft Word to edit a linked Word table or you must open Microsoft Excel to edit a linked Excel worksheet. You can open the Source program by double-clicking the linked object in the PowerPoint slide as you did with embedded objects or by clicking the Start menu, which you will do here. When you work in the source program, you can close your PowerPoint presentation or leave it open. Karen needs to update some of the data in the Microsoft Excel worksheet, so she opens Excel, changes some data, and then updates the linked object in PowerPoint.

Steps

QuickTip

To open or edit a linked object in your presentation, the object's source program and source file must be available on your computer or network.

1. Click the Start button on the taskbar, point to Programs, and click Microsoft Excel
The Microsoft Excel program opens.

2. On the Microsoft Excel Standard toolbar, click the Open button 📂, locate the file Division Budget, then click Open
The Division Budget worksheet opens. Insert the updated figures for the Sales budget.

3. Click cell E2, type 95000, click cell C2, type 80000, then press [Enter]
The Department Total for Sales is automatically recalculated and now reads $340,000 instead of $355,000. Now close Microsoft Excel and return to the linked worksheet in PowerPoint.

4. Click the Close button in the Microsoft Excel program window, then click Yes to save the changes
Microsoft Excel closes and the PowerPoint window appears.

5. Click 📂 on the Standard toolbar, locate the file CD Travel, then click Open
A Microsoft PowerPoint message box opens, telling you that the CD Travel presentation has links and asking if you want to update them. See Figure G-11. This message appears whether or not you have changed the source file.

6. Click OK, restore your Presentation window to the size used in this book, then drag the vertical scroll box to Slide 5
Compare your screen to Figure G-12. The linked Excel worksheet shows the new Department Total for Sales, $340,000. The changes you made in Excel were automatically made in this linked copy when you reopened the worksheet. Save your changes.

7. Click the Save button 💾 on the Standard toolbar

FIGURE G-11: PowerPoint update links message box

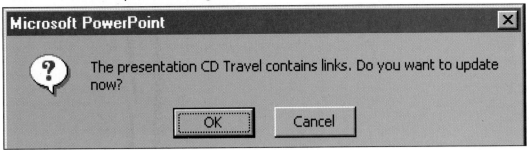

FIGURE G-12: Slide showing updated linked worksheet

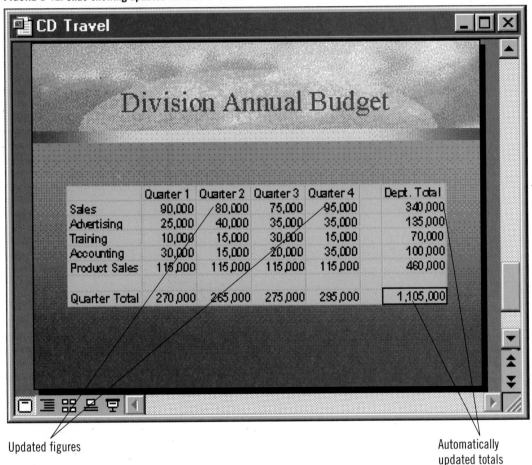

Updated figures

Automatically
updated totals

CLUES TO USE

Updating links when both files are open

You do not have to close the target file to update the links. If you change the source file, when you switch back to the presentation file, the link will be updated. If you want to update the links manually, click Edit on the menu bar, then click Links to open the Links dialog box. See Figure G-13. If the Manual check box is selected, the links in the target file will not be updated unless you select the link in this dialog box and click Update Now.

FIGURE G-13: Links dialog box

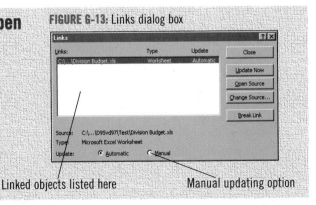

Linked objects listed here

Manual updating option

PowerPoint 97

Inserting a Movie

In your presentations, you may want to use special effects to illustrate a point or capture the attention of your audience. Microsoft Media Player, a video editing program that comes with PowerPoint, allows you to run and edit movies. When you embed a movie, it becomes a PowerPoint object, so you can change or edit it to fit the style of your presentation. There are two basic types of movies: digital video and animation. **Digital video** refers to a live-action or full-motion movie captured by a video camera. An **animation** is a movie that sets graphics (clip art or drawn objects) in motion. Karen continues developing her presentation by embedding an animated movie and then changing its playback options.

QuickTip
You can also use the Text and Media Clip Auto Layout to insert a movie on a slide.

1. Click **New Slide** on the Common Tasks toolbar, click the **Text & Object AutoLayout**, click **OK**, then type **International Distribution** in the title placeholder
Before embedding the animation, enter the main points for the slide in the main text placeholder.

2. Click the main text placeholder, type **United States**, press **[Enter]**, type **Western Europe**, press **[Enter]**, type **Australia**, press **[Enter]**, type **Asia**, press **[Enter]**, type **South America**, then resize and reposition the text object on the slide so it appears as shown in Figure G-14
Now embed the animation.

3. Double-click the **object placeholder**, click the **Create from file option button**, click **Browse**, select the file **PPT G-4**, click **OK**, then click **OK**
The movie appears on the right side of the slide, as shown in Figure G-14. Play the movie to make sure it works properly.

4. Double-click the **movie object**
The Globe movie plays once through. You can modify an embedded movie the same way you modify any embedded file. Change some playback options now.

5. Right-click the **movie object**, then click **Edit Video Clip Object** on the pop-up menu
The Microsoft Media Player program window opens, as shown in Figure G-15. You can easily edit your movie with the Microsoft Media Player control bar that appears below the menu bar.

6. Click **Edit** on the menu bar, then click **Options**
The Options dialog box opens. First, hide the movie control bar so it won't show while the movie plays.

7. In the OLE Object section, click the **Control Bar On Playback check box** to deselect it
You can set the movie to play continuously until you stop it, and to rewind to the beginning after you stop it.

8. Click the **Auto Repeat check box** to select it, click **OK**, then click in a blank area of the Presentation window
The Microsoft Media Player program window closes. Notice that the movie control bar is no longer visible. Resize the movie object so it occupies more of the slide.

Trouble?
If your movie object seems small, reapply the Text & Object AutoLayout using the Slide Layout button on the Common Tasks toolbar.

9. Drag the corner resize handles and reposition the movie object so it fills the right half of the slide
Now, run the movie again to view the changes.

10. Double-click the **movie object**, view the movie for a while, click in a blank area of the Presentation window to stop the movie, then click the **Save button** on the Standard toolbar

FIGURE G-14: Slide showing embedded movie object

Step 2

Double-click movie object to begin animation

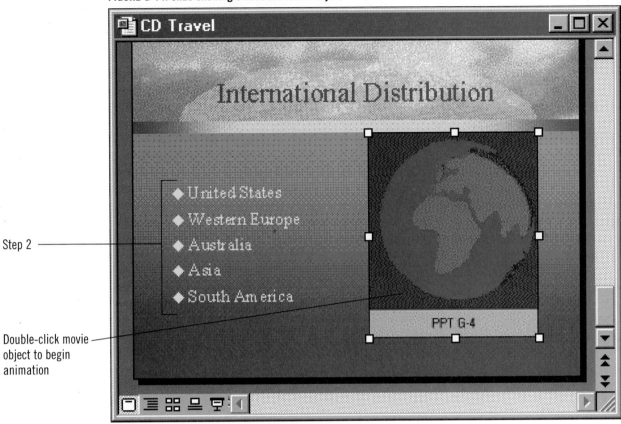

FIGURE G-15: Microsoft Media Player program window

Microsoft Media Player control bar

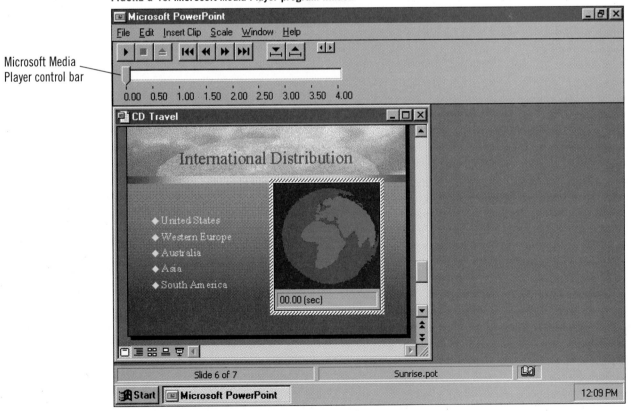

PowerPoint 97

Inserting a Sound

PowerPoint allows you to embed sounds in your presentation just as you embed movies. When adding sounds to your presentation, it is a good idea to think about how a sound can help you present your message. Use sound to enhance the message of a slide. For example, if you are creating a presentation about a raft tour of the Colorado River, you might embed a river sound on a slide showing a photograph of people white-water rafting. You can embed several different types of sounds in your presentation, but you'll need a sound card and speakers installed on your computer to play the sounds. In this lesson, Karen embeds a sound on Slide 2 of her presentation to enhance the picture on the slide.

1. Drag the vertical scroll box to Slide 2

2. Click Insert on the menu bar, point to Movies and Sounds, then click Sound from File
   The Insert Sound dialog box opens.

Trouble?

The sound icon you see may be different from the one illustrated in Figure G-16, depending on your sound card software.

3. Select the file PPT G-5, then click OK
   A small sound icon appears on the slide, as shown in Figure G-16. Enlarge the icon so it is easier to see.

4. Click Format on the menu bar, click Picture, then click the Size tab
   The Size tab opens in the Format Picture dialog box.

5. In the Scale section, double-click the Height setting and type 150, then click OK
   The sound icon enlarges to 150% of its original size. Now move the sound icon down to the bottom of the slide.

6. Drag the sound icon to the lower-right corner of the Presentation window
   Compare your screen to Figure G-17. Now play the sound.

Trouble?

If you do not hear a sound, your computer may not have a sound card installed. See your instructor or technical support person for help.

7. Double-click the sound icon
   The sound of a camera clicking plays. Save your changes.

8. Click the Save button 🖫 on the Standard toolbar

Inserting sounds and movies from the Clip Gallery

You can also insert sounds and movies from the Microsoft Clip Gallery. Make sure the Office 97 CD-ROM is in the CD drive or that all the clip art images from the Office 97 CD-ROM have been imported to the Clip Gallery. Click Insert on the menu bar, point to Movies and Sounds, click Movie from Gallery or click Sound from Gallery, select the clip you want to include in the presentation, then click Insert. If you insert movies and sounds using this method, the Office 97 CD-ROM must be in the CD drive. If PowerPoint cannot find the file, then you need to locate it manually.

FIGURE G-16: Slide showing small sound icon

Sound icon

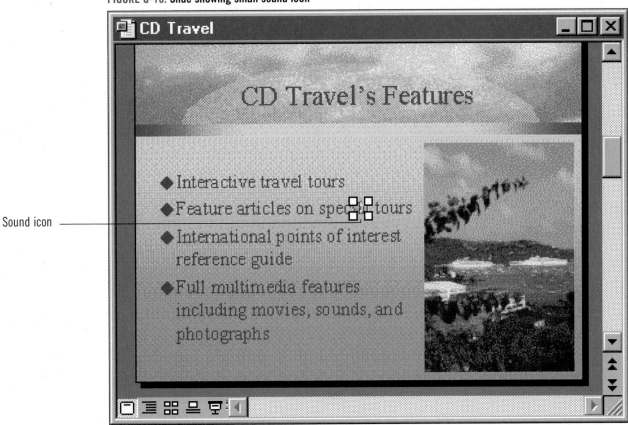

FIGURE G-17: Slide showing scaled and repositioned sound icon

Sound icon

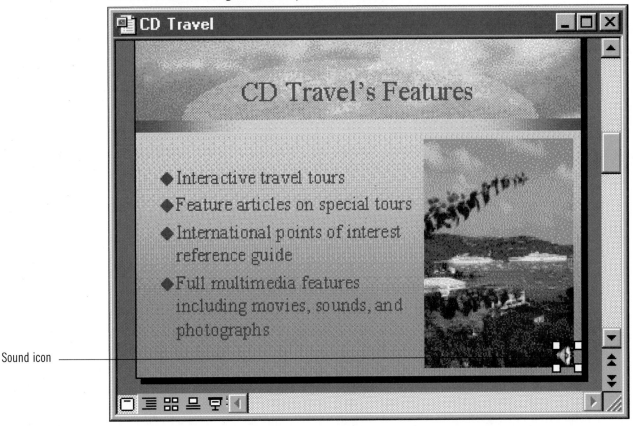

Inserting a Hyperlink

Often you will want to display a document that either won't fit on the slide, or that is too detailed for your presentation. In these cases, you can insert a **hyperlink**, which is a specially formatted word, phrase, or graphic that you click during your slide show to "jump to," or display, another document. The **target document**, the file your hyperlink displays on the screen when you click it, can be a Word, Excel, or Access file, another slide in your current presentation, another PowerPoint presentation, or an address on the World Wide Web. Inserting a hyperlink is similar to linking because you can change the object in the source program after you click the hyperlink. Karen decides to use a hyperlink to display a recent product review, which is in a Word document.

1. Go to Slide 6, click New Slide on the Common Tasks toolbar, click the Bulleted List AutoLayout, click OK, then type Product Reviews in the title placeholder
   Enter the names of three magazines that have recently reviewed *CD Travel Magazine*.

2. Click the main text placeholder, type Travel World, press [Enter], type Armchair Traveler, press [Enter], and type Vacation Monthly
   Now format the text box.

3. Click the border of the text box to select the entire text object, click the Font Size list arrow, click 48, drag the lower-right corner of the text box up and to the left to resize it to fit the text, and then center the text box on the slide
   To be able to click on a magazine name to display the review during the slide show, make the second magazine title a hyperlink to the review from that magazine.

4. Highlight Armchair Traveler, click the Insert Hyperlink button 🖳 on the Standard toolbar, click Browse at the top of the dialog box, locate the file PPT G-6, click OK, click OK in the Insert Hyperlink dialog box, then click in a blank area of the Presentation window
   Now that you have made the magazine title a hyperlink, the title automatically changes to hyperlink formatting, which is underlined blue text. Change the background color of the slide, so the blue text will be more readable.

5. Right-click in a blank area of the Presentation window, click Slide Color Scheme on the pop-up menu, click the Standard tab, click the scheme with the dark pink background in the bottom row on the left, then click Apply
   Make sure you do not click Apply to All. The hyperlink is now visible on the slide. See Figure G-18. Now test the hyperlink.

6. Click the Slide Show button 🖵, then click the Armchair Traveler hyperlink
   The Word document containing the review appears on the screen in Full Page View. See Figure G-19. The Web toolbar appears at the top of the screen. Now return to the presentation.

7. Click the Back button ⇐ on the Web toolbar
   The Product Reviews slide reappears in slide show view. The hyperlink is now light purple, indicating that the hyperlink has been used.

8. Click once to end the slide show, press [Ctrl][Home], click the Slide Sorter View button 🔳, then click the Maximize button in the Presentation window
   Compare your screen to Figure G-20. Evaluate the presentation, then save and print it.

9. Run through the entire slide show making sure you click the Sound icon on Slide 2, the Movie object on Slide 6, and the hyperlink on Slide 7, spell-check the presentation, save your changes, print the slides of the presentation, close the presentation, right-click the Word program button on the taskbar, then click Close on the pop-up menu

QuickTip

The hyperlink will only take you to the target document when you are in slide show view.

FIGURE G-18: **The hyperlink to the product review**

Underlined blue text is a hyperlink

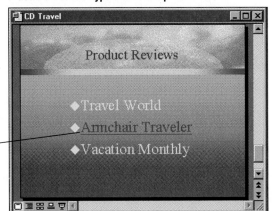

FIGURE G-19: **The product review displays during the slide show**

Web toolbar

Back button

FIGURE G-20: **Final presentation in Slide Sorter view**

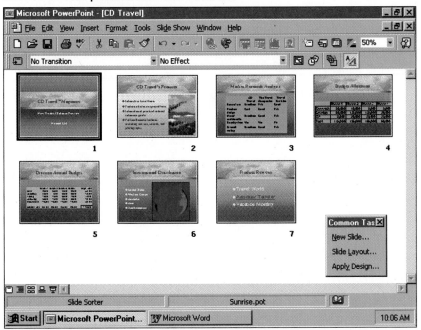

Practice

► Concepts Review

Label each of the elements of the PowerPoint window shown in Figure G-21.

FIGURE G-21

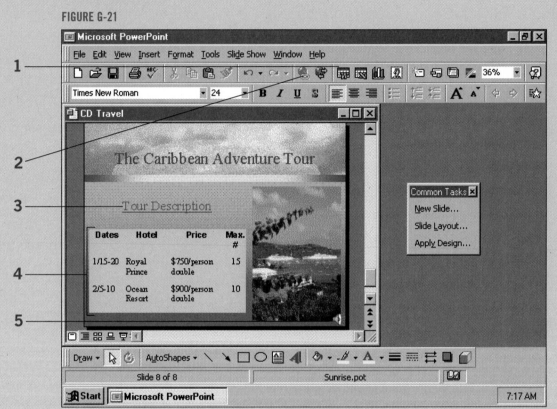

Match each of the terms with the statement that describes its function.

6. An object created in another program and then stored in PowerPoint
7. The program in which an embedded object is created
8. A scanned photograph or piece of line art
9. A word or object you click to display another file
10. The connection between a source file and a PowerPoint presentation

a. Picture
b. Embedded object
c. Link
d. Source program
e. Hyperlink

Select the best answer from the list of choices.

11. Which of the following objects are you able to embed into PowerPoint?
    a. Digital movies
    b. Photographs
    c. Microsoft Excel worksheets
    d. All of the above
12. Which statement about embedded objects is false?
    a. You can format embedded objects in their source program.
    b. Embedded objects are not dependent on a source file.
    c. Embedded objects are not a part of the presentation.
    d. Embedded objects increase your presentation file size more than linked objects do.

13. Which statement about linked objects is true?

   a. To edit a linked object, you must open its source file.

   b. A linked object is an independent object embedded directly to a slide.

   c. You can access a linked object even when the source file is not available.

   d. A linked object substantially increases the size of your presentation file.

▶ Skills Review

If you complete all of the exercises in this unit, you may run out of space on your Student Disk. To make sure you have enough disk space, please copy files PPT G-7, PPT G-8, PPT G-9, and ND Profit onto a new disk and use the new disk to complete the rest of the exercises in this unit. If you do not have access to the Office 97 CD-ROM or if the complete set of clip art images has not been imported to the Clip Art Gallery, then you should also copy the files PPT G-2, PPT G-4, and PPT G-5.

1. Embed a picture.

   a. Start PowerPoint, open the presentation PPT G-7, then save it as New Directions 97.

   b. Click the Next Slide button twice.

   c. Click Insert on the menu bar, point to Picture, then click Clip Art.

   d. Click the Pictures tab, click the Sports & Leisure category, click the photo of the rock climber, then click Insert. (If this image is not available, use the Insert Picture From File command and insert the file PPT G-2 again.)

   e. Click the Crop button on the Picture toolbar, position the cropping tool pointer over the right middle sizing handle, drag the handle to the left to crop out the right half of the picture, then click the Crop button to deselect it.

   f. Drag the picture to the right side of the slide, resize the picture so it is slightly taller than the bulleted list, then use the [Arrow] keys on the keyboard to make minor adjustments to the picture's position.

   g. Click the More Contrast button on the Picture toolbar three times to make the image in the photo stand out more.

   h. Save your changes.

2. Embed a table.

   a. Click the Previous Slide button, click New Slide on the Common Tasks toolbar, click the Title Only AutoLayout, then click OK.

   b. Type "New Directions at a Glance."

   c. Click the Insert Microsoft Word Table button on the Standard toolbar and drag to select a 5 x 3 table.

   d. Enter the information shown in Figure G-22. Don't worry about the column widths now.

FIGURE G-22

Adventure	Sailing	International Tours
Kayaking	Hawaii	Trans-Siberian Railway
Alaskan Lakes	South China Sea	China
U.S. by Air	Black Sea	African Safari
Hot Air Balloon	World Tour	Black Forest

   e. Click in the Presentation window, then double-click the table to redisplay it.

   f. Drag to select all three columns, then click the Center button on the Formatting toolbar.

g. Click Table on the menu bar, click Table AutoFormat, click Simple 3, then click OK.

h. Drag the column dividers so that the columns are sized as in Figure G-22, then resize the table object border so it fits the table as closely as possible.

i. Click in a blank area of the Presentation window, resize the table so it fills the lower portion of the slide, then drag the table so it is centered below the slide title.

j. With the table still selected, click the Fill Color list arrow, and select the turquoise box on the far right.

k. Click the Save button on the Standard toolbar.

3. Embed a worksheet.

a. Drag the vertical scroll box to Slide 4.

b. Click New Slide on the Common Tasks toolbar, click the Object AutoLayout, then click OK.

c. Type "Projected Division Income."

d. Double-click the object placeholder, click the Create from file option button, then click Browse.

e. Locate the file PPT G-8, then click OK twice.

f. Double-click the worksheet, click cell B4, click the AutoSum button on the Excel Standard toolbar, then press [Tab].

g. Drag to select cells B4 through E4, click Edit on the menu bar, point to Fill, then click Right.

h. Leave cells B4 to E4 selected, hold down [Ctrl], drag to select cells B1 through E1, release [Ctrl], and click the Bold button on the Formatting toolbar.

i. Drag to select cells B1 through E1, then click the Center button in the Formatting toolbar.

j. Click on the slide outside the worksheet, then click the worksheet and drag its lower-right resize handle until the worksheet is almost as wide as the slide.

k. Reposition the worksheet using the keyboard arrow keys, so it is centered horizontally and vertically.

l. With the worksheet selected, click the Fill Color button on the Drawing toolbar.

m. Save your changes.

4. Link an Excel worksheet.

a. Click New Slide on the Common Tasks toolbar, click the Object AutoLayout, then click OK.

b. Type "Projected Division Profit."

c. Double-click the object placeholder, click the Create from file option button, then click Browse.

d. Locate the file ND Profit, click OK, click the Link check box, then click OK.

e. Drag the object's lower resize handles so that it fills the slide width.

f. Use the keyboard arrow keys to reposition the object so it is centered horizontally.

g. With the worksheet still selected, click the Fill Color button on the Drawing toolbar.

h. Save and close the New Directions 97 presentation.

5. Update a linked Excel worksheet.

a. Click the Start button on the taskbar, point to Programs, then click Microsoft Excel.

b. On the Excel Standard toolbar, click the Open button, locate the file ND Profit, then click Open.

c. Click cell B2, type "2550900," then press [Enter].

d. Click cell D3, type "95000," click cell B4, type "220300," click cell D7, type "1780800," then press [Enter].

e. Click the Excel Program window Close button, then click Yes to save the changes.

f. Click the Open button on the PowerPoint Standard toolbar, locate the file New Directions 97, then click Open.

g. Click OK to update the linked object.

h. Drag the vertical scroll box to Slide 6. View your changes.

i. Click the linked worksheet, click Edit on the menu bar, click Links, examine the link information, then click Close.

j. Save the presentation.

6. Embed a movie.

a. Drag the vertical scroll box to Slide 2.

b. Click Insert on the menu bar, point to Movies & Sounds, then click Movie from Gallery.

c. Scroll down to find the Globe movie, select it, then click Insert. (If this movie is not available, insert the movie file PPT G-4.)

   d. Double-click the movie object.
   e. Right-click the movie object, then click Edit Movie Object.
   f. Click the Loop until stopped check box, then click OK.
   g. Click in a blank area of the Presentation window, then resize the movie object so it fills the right side of the screen.
   h. Double-click the movie object, click outside the movie object, then save the presentation.

7. **Embed a sound.**
   a. Click the Next Slide button twice.
   b. Click Insert on the menu bar, point to Movies and Sounds, then click Sound from Gallery.
   c. Click the Charge sound, then click Insert. (If this sound is not available, insert the sound file PPT G-5.).
   d. Click Format on the menu bar, click Picture, click the Size tab.
   e. In the Scale section, double-click the Height setting, type "150", then click OK.
   f. Drag the sound icon to the bottom right of the slide.
   g. Double-click the sound icon to test it.
   h. Click the Save button on the Standard toolbar.

8. **Insert a hyperlink.**
   a. Drag the vertical scroll bar to the last slide in the presentation, click New Slide on the Common Tasks toolbar, click the Bulleted List AutoLayout, and click OK.
   b. Type "Testimonials" in the Title placeholder.
   c. Click the main text placeholder and type "George Sanders, Medford, Oregon," and press [Enter].
   d. Type "Jorge Fonseca, Orem, Utah."
   e. Click the edge of the main text placeholder, click the Font Size list arrow, and click 48.
   f. Drag the lower-right corner of the text box up and to the left to resize it to fit the text, and then center the text box on the slide using the keyboard arrow keys.
   g. Highlight the text in the George Sanders bullet, click the Insert Hyperlink button on the Standard toolbar, and, under Link to file or URL, click Browse.
   h. Select the file PPT G-9, click OK, then click OK again.
   i. Click on the slide outside the text box.
   j. Click the Slide Show button, then click the hyperlink.
   k. After you view the Testimonial, click the Back button on the Web toolbar.
   l. Click the slide background to leave Slide Show view, then save the presentation.
   m. Run the spell checker, view the entire presentation in Slide Show view, print the slides, close the presentation, right-click the Word program button on the taskbar, then click Close on the pop-up menu.

► # Independent Challenges

1. Quincy Engineering is a mechanical and industrial design company that specializes in designing manufacturing plants in the United States and Canada. Most of the work that Quincy Engineering does is refitting manufacturing plants that are old and outdated. As the company financial analyst, you have been asked by Quincy Engineering's board of directors to investigate and report on a possible contract to design and build a large manufacturing plant in Brazil. Because Quincy Engineering has never worked overseas, the board of directors wants to make sure that they can make a minimum profit on the deal. It is your job to provide a recommendation to the board.

In this challenge, you'll need to enhance the presentation to make it look professional. Create your own information using the basic presentation provided and assume the following about Quincy Engineering:

- The Brazilian company can offer a contract for no more than $23 million for this entire project.
- The new manufacturing plant in Brazil will be 75,000 square feet in size. The projected cost for Quincy Engineering to design and build the plant in Brazil is $350.00 per square foot based on a four-phase schedule; planning and design, site acquisition and preparation, construction phase 1, and construction phase 2.
- Factors that helped determine Quincy Engineering's cost to build the plant include: Quincy Engineering payroll

for 15 people in the United States and payroll for 10 people in Brazil for 18 months; materials cost; hiring of one construction company in the United States and two in Brazil to construct the plant; travel and lodging costs.

- The board of directors requires at least a 4% profit margin to go ahead with a proposal.

To complete this independent challenge:

1. Open the file PPT G-10, then save it as Quincy 1.
2. Think about what results you want to see, what information you need to create the slide presentation, and how your message should be communicated. In order for your presentation to be complete, it must include the following objects: (1) embedded Word table; (2) embedded Excel worksheet; (3) linked table, worksheet, chart, or other object; (4) embedded picture; and (5) hyperlink.
3. Use Microsoft Word and Microsoft Excel to embed, link, or hyperlink objects into your presentation. Use the preceding assumptions to develop related information that would be appropriate for a table or worksheet.
4. All slides should be titled and have main text where appropriate.
5. The last slide in the presentation should be your recommendation to pursue the contract or not, based on the financial data you present.
6. Submit your presentation plan and print the final slide presentation.

2. You are the director of operations at The Franklin Group, a large investment banking company in Texas. Franklin is considering merging with Redding Industries Inc, a smaller investment company in Arizona, to form the tenth largest financial institution in the United States. As the director of operations, you need to present some financial projections regarding the merger to a special committee formed by Franklin to study the proposed merger.

Create your own information using the basic presentation provided on your Student Disk. Assume the following facts about the merger between Franklin and Redding:

- Franklin earned a $19 million profit last year. Projected profit this year is $26 million. Projected profit next year with the merger with Redding is $36 million. Franklin's operating expenses run about $30 million a year. Redding's operating expenses run about $19 million a year.
- Redding earned $8 million in profit last year. Projected profit this year is $10 million. Projected profit next year with the merger is $18 million.
- Franklin has an 18% share of the market without Redding. Redding has a 6% share of the market without Franklin. Combined, the companies would have a 24% share of the market.
- With the merger, Franklin would need to cut $7.6 million from its annual operating costs and Redding would need to cut $2 million from its annual operating costs.

To complete this independent challenge:

1. Open the file PPT G-11, then save it as Merger.
2. Think about what results you want to see, what information you need to create the slide presentation, and how your message should be communicated. In order for your presentation to be complete, it must include the following objects: (1) embedded Word table; (2) embedded Excel worksheet; (3) linked table, worksheet, chart, or other object; (4) embedded picture; and (5) a hyperlink.
3. Use Microsoft Excel to embed or link a worksheet to your presentation. Use the preceding assumptions to develop related information that would be appropriate for a worksheet. For at least one worksheet, use the profit and operating expense figures to create your own revenue figures. (Revenue minus operating expenses equals profit.)
4. Use Microsoft Word to create a table showing market share analysis between Franklin, Redding, and two other companies that you create. Illustrate the market share figures with and without the merger.
5. All slides should be titled and have main text where appropriate. Create slides as necessary to make the presentation complete.
6. Create another slide or presentation that you can branch to your presentation.
7. Submit your presentation plan and print the final slide presentation.

3. You are the communications director at Johnson & Associates, a large advertising agency in southern Florida. One of your company's clients is New Directions, the travel subsidiary of Nomad Ltd. One of your jobs is to create a sales presentation for the New Directions account that promotes New Directions' new products and tours for 1998. The presentation will be shown to large groups at the annual travel trade show held every year in Miami, Florida.

Plan and create a presentation that promotes New Directions' products and tours. Use the information you know about New Directions from this unit as a basis for your presentation. You may want to open the presentations you created in this unit for more information. Create your own data, but assume the following:

- New Directions is offering four new international tours for 1998: (1) Trans-Siberian Railway; (2) China; (3) African Safari; and (4) the Black Forest.
- New Directions wants to vigorously promote its Adventure tour series. The new Adventure tours for 1998 include: the Colorado River Kayak tour; the Yosemite Rock Climbing tour; the Southern States Hot-Air Balloon tour; the US by Air tour; and the Alaskan Lakes tour.
- New products include: the *CD Travel Magazine*; the *Travel Encyclopedia*; and the *Traveler's Handbook*.

To complete this independent challenge:

1. Think about what results you want to see, what information you need to create the slide presentation, and how your message should be communicated. In order for your presentation to be complete, it must include the following objects: (1) embedded Word table; (2) embedded Excel worksheet; (3) linked table, worksheet, chart, or other object; (4) embedded picture; (5) embedded movie and sound; and (6) a hyperlink.
2. Use the information provided and the information in the presentations you created in this unit to help you develop the content for your presentation. Use the movies and sounds provided for you with the student files for this text, or if you have access to the Microsoft Office CD-ROM, choose another appropriate movie (and sound) to embed into your presentation. (Feel free to embed another movie or sound if you have access to other media sources.)
3. Use Microsoft Word and Microsoft Excel to embed, link, or hyperlink objects into your presentation. Use the preceding assumptions to develop related information that would be appropriate for a table or worksheet.
4. All the slides should be titled and have main text where appropriate.
5. Create another slide or presentation that you can branch to from your presentation. To help you create a branch, you can customize the New Directions 97 presentation you created in the Skills Review portion of this unit.
6. Add a template, background shading, or other enhancing objects to make your presentation look professional.
7. Save the presentation as Johnson Presentation.
8. Submit your presentation plan and print the final slide presentation.

4. You have just been promoted to the position of sales manager at DWImports, a U.S. company that exports goods and professional services to companies in Japan, South Korea, China, and the Philippines. One of your new responsibilities is to give a presentation at the biannual finance meeting showing how the Sales Department performed during the previous six-month period.

Plan and create a short slide presentation (six to eight slides) that illustrates the Sales Department's performance during the last six months. Identify the existing accounts (by country) and then identify the new contracts acquired during the last six months. Create your own content, but assume the following:

- The majority of goods and services being exported are: food products (such as rice, corn, and wheat); agriculture consulting; construction engineering; and industrial designing and engineering.
- The company gained five new accounts in China, South Korea, and the Philippines.
- The Sales Department showed a $5 million profit for the first half of the year.
- Department expenses for the first half of the year were $3.5 million.
- The presentation will be given in a boardroom using a projection machine.

To complete this independent challenge:

1. Think about what results you want to see, what information you need to create the slide presentation, and how your message should be communicated. In order for your presentation to be complete, it must include the following objects: (1) embedded Word table; (2) embedded Excel worksheet; (3) linked table, worksheet, chart, or other object; (4) embedded picture; (5) embedded movie and sound; and (6) hyperlink.
2. Use the movies and sounds provided for you on your Student Disk, or if you have access to the Microsoft Office CD-ROM, choose another appropriate movie (and sound) to embed into your presentation. (Feel free to embed another movie or sound if you have access to other media sources.)

3. Use Microsoft Word and Microsoft Excel to embed, link, or hyperlink objects into your presentation. Use the preceding assumptions to develop related information that would be appropriate for a table or worksheet.

4. Log on to the Internet and use your browser to go to http://www.course.com. From there, click Student Online Companions, click the link for this textbook, then click the PowerPoint link for Unit G. Use the link there to find relevant information about trade between the U.S. and the Asia-Pacific area, and any issues that might have influenced the sales climate during the last six months.

5. All the slides should be titled and have main text points where appropriate.

6. Add a template, background shading, or other enhancing objects to make your presentation look professional.

7. Save the presentation as Imports.

8. Submit your presentation plan and print the final slide presentation.

▶ Visual Workshop

Create two slides that look like the examples in Figures G-23 and G-24. Save the presentation as Year End Report. Save and print Slide view of the presentation. Submit the final presentation output.

FIGURE G-23

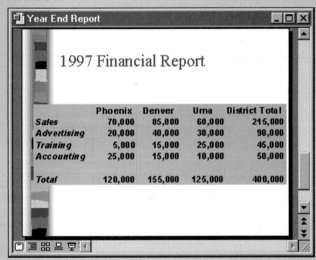

FIGURE G-24

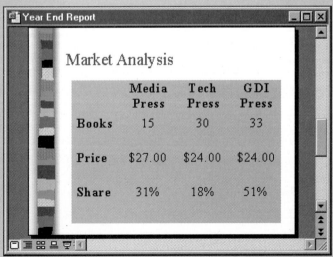

Using
Slide Show Features

Objectives

- ► **Animate charts and sounds**
- ► **Set up a slide show**
- ► **Create a custom show**
- ► **Hide a slide during a slide show**
- ► **Use the Meeting Minder**
- ► **Rehearse slide timings**
- ► **Use the Pack and Go Wizard**
- ► **Use the Microsoft PowerPoint Viewer**

After all the work on your presentation is complete, you need to produce the final output that you will use when you give your presentation. You probably have realized by now that PowerPoint offers several options for your presentation output. You can create 35mm slides, overhead transparencies, audience handouts, or you can show your presentation on a computer using Slide Show view. Slide Show view turns your computer screen into a projector that displays your slides one by one in an **on-screen presentation.** Carrie Armstrong finishes the Annual Report Executive Summary by adding special effects. She then produces an on-screen presentation to show Bill Davidson, the president of Nomad Ltd.

Animating Charts and Sounds

As you know, you can animate text and objects in PowerPoint by determining how and when bullets or pictures appear during a slide show. You can add more interest to your slide shows by animating charts, sounds, and videos. For example, instead of displaying the entire chart at one time, you can animate the individual bars in a bar chart and specify when you want them to appear. Then you can add a sound effect to accompany the appearance of each one. You can animate sounds and videos to play at predetermined times during and after each slide. 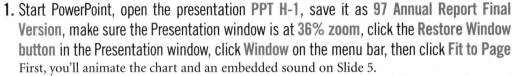 Carrie added a sound icon to Slide 5, the slide containing the bar chart of the 1997 Sales Analysis. Now she'd like to animate the bar chart and add the embedded applause sound effect on that slide.

Steps

1. Start PowerPoint, open the presentation **PPT H-1**, save it as **97 Annual Report Final Version**, make sure the Presentation window is at **36% zoom**, click the **Restore Window button** in the Presentation window, click **Window** on the menu bar, then click **Fit to Page**
   First, you'll animate the chart and an embedded sound on Slide 5.

2. Drag the vertical scroll bar to go to **Slide 5**, click the chart to select it, click **Slide Show** on the menu bar, click **Custom Animation**, then click the **Chart Effects tab**
   The Custom Animation dialog box opens, similar to Figure H-1. You'll animate each data series in the chart to "dissolve in" gradually, accompanied by the sound of a cash register.

3. In the Introduce chart elements list box, select **by Series**; in the top Entry animation and sound list box, select **Dissolve**; and in the bottom Entry animation and sound list box, select **Cash Register**
   Compare your screen to Figure H-1.

4. Click **Preview** and watch the Preview window to see how the chart will appear with the settings you've chosen
   Now set the timing so that each chart element appears three seconds after the previous one.

5. Click the **Timing tab**, in the Start animation section, click the **Automatically option button**, change the setting to **3 seconds** after previous event, then click **OK**
   Now add the embedded applause sound to the slide animation.

6. Right-click the **sound icon**, click **Custom Animation** on the pop-up menu, then click the **Play Settings tab**
   Set the applause sound animation effect so that it plays after the chart animation has finished, hide the sound icon, and pause the slide show while the embedded sound plays.

7. Click to select the check boxes for **Play using animation order** and **Hide while not playing**, and make sure that the **Pause slide show option button** is selected
   See Figure H-2. Now set the applause sound to play 2 seconds after the chart appears.

8. Click the **Timing tab**, click the **Automatically option button** in the Start animation section, change the setting to **2 seconds**, click **OK**, then deselect the icon
   See Figure H-3. Now view the slide show to see the full effect of your changes. Several of the slides have transition and animation effects already applied to them.

9. Press **[Ctrl][Home]**, click the **Slide Show button** 🖵 , click the left mouse button to advance through the slide show, making sure you wait to view the animation effects on each slide

Trouble?

If your computer does not have a sound card, you will not be able to hear the sound effects. You can still continue with the lesson.

QuickTip

Use animations to emphasize only the most important points in your presentation. Too many animations and sounds will distract audience attention from your message.

Time To

✔ Save

FIGURE H-1: Chart Effects tab in the Custom Animation dialog box

Objects listed here will be animated

Chart Effects tab

Preview window

Step 4

Select how elements will appear and with what sound

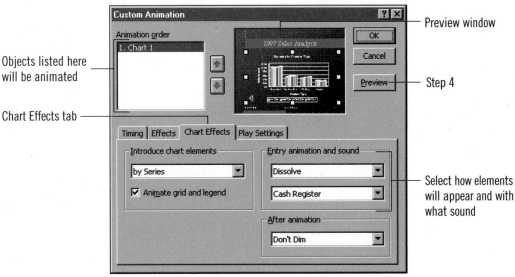

FIGURE H-2: Play Settings tab in the Custom Animation dialog box

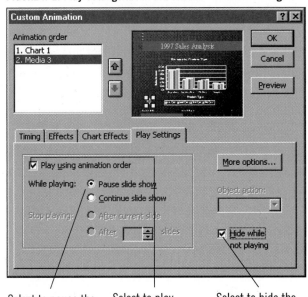

Select to pause the slide show while sound plays

Select to play sound according to the Animation order list

Select to hide the sound icon in Slide Show view

FIGURE H-3: Final chart

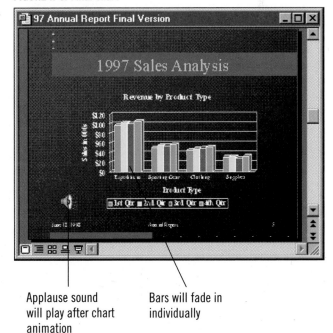

Applause sound will play after chart animation

Bars will fade in individually

CLUES TO USE

Adding voice narrations

If your computer has a sound card and a microphone, you can record a voice narration that plays with your slide show. To record a voice, click Slide Show on the menu bar, then click Record Narration. If you want the recording to be linked to the presentation, click the Link narrations in check box. If you do not select this option, the recording will be embedded in the presentation. Then start recording.

PowerPoint 97

Setting Up a Slide Show

With PowerPoint, you can create a slide show that runs automatically. Viewers can then watch the slide show individually on a public computer at a convention or a trade show on a free-standing computer called a **kiosk**. You can create a self-running slide show that loops, or runs through the entire show, without users touching the computer. You can also let viewers advance the slides at their own pace by pressing the spacebar, clicking the mouse, or clicking an on-screen control button called an Action button. Carrie prepares the Annual Report presentation so shareholders can view it at a table during the open house after Bill Davidson's presentation.

1. Click Slide Show on the menu bar, click Set Up Show, and under Show Type, click the Browsed at a kiosk (full screen) option button to select it
   The Set Up Show dialog box opens, similar to Figure H-4. When the kiosk option is selected, the slide show will run continuously until you press [Esc] to end the show. Include all the slides in the presentation, and have PowerPoint advance the slides at time intervals you set.

QuickTip

When you set up a slide show in a public area, you should think about where you'll set up the show, who will monitor the area, and how to prevent viewers from changing the presentation.

2. In the Slides section, make sure the All option button is selected, and in the Advance slides section, click the Using timings, if present option button
   Compare your screen to Figure H-4. Next, specify that you want a 5 second pause between slides.

3. Click OK, click the Slide Sorter View button 📇, press [Ctrl][A] to select all the slides, click Slide Show on the menu bar, click Slide Transition, in the Advance section, click the Automatically after check box to select it, type 5, then click Apply to All
   The slide show will now display the slides automatically using the timing you entered, and it will not advance if someone clicks the mouse or presses [Spacebar].

Trouble?

Although transition icons appear in Slide Sorter view, the settings in the Set Up Show dialog box override the transition effects. If you want, you can reapply the transition effects to the slides.

4. Click the Slide Show button 🖵, view the self-running presentation through to the end, let it start again, and then press [Esc]
   Now set up a show that lets users click a button to move to the next slide.

5. Click Slide Show on the menu bar, click Set Up Show, in the Advance slides section, click the Manually option button, then click OK
   Now place a button on each slide that is actually a hyperlink to the next slide.

6. Double-click Slide 1, click Slide Show on the menu bar, point to Action Buttons, click the Action Button: Forward or Next button ▷, and drag the pointer to draw a button in the lower right corner of Slide 1
   The Action Settings dialog box opens. See Figure H-5.

7. Make sure the Hyperlink to option button is selected and that Next Slide is selected in the list box, then click OK
   Compare your screen to Figure H-6. Now copy the hyperlink button to all the slides.

8. With the button selected, press [Ctrl][C] to copy it, click the Next Slide button ⬍, press [Ctrl][V] to paste the button on Slide 2, then repeat for each slide that follows
   Now view the slide show using the hyperlink buttons to move from slide to slides.

QuickTip

You must be in Slide Show view to use the hyperlink buttons.

9. Press [Ctrl][Home], click the Slide Show button 🖵, click the hyperlink buttons to move from slide to slide, then press [Esc] after you have viewed the last slide
   Make sure you wait for the animated objects to appear on the slides. There are some tasks you can't do during a slide show with the kiosk setting active, so turn this feature off for now.

10. Click Slide Show on the menu bar, click Set Up Show, click the Presented by a speaker (full screen option button), click OK, then save your changes

FIGURE H-4: Set Up Show dialog box

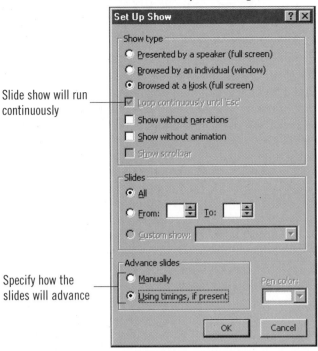

Slide show will run continuously

Specify how the slides will advance

FIGURE H-5: Action Settings dialog box

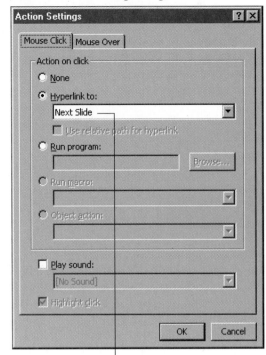

Indicates where the hyperlink jumps to

FIGURE H-6: Slide 1 with the hyperlink button to the next slide

User clicks hyperlink button to advance to next slide in Slide Show view

CLUES TO USE

Presenting a slide show on two screens

PowerPoint lets you connect two computers so you can control a slide show on one computer while showing it on another. The speaker can view the presentation on a laptop computer, while the audience views a computer with a large-screen monitor. To do this, you connect the two computers with a special cable, and install PowerPoint 97 on both computers. During the presentation, you can use the Slide Navigator and other tools available on the slide show pop-up menu that help you manage your slide show on the speaker's computer screen, without displaying them on the audience monitor.

Creating a Custom Show

Often when you create a slide show, you need to create a custom version of it for a different audience or purpose. For example, you might create a 20-minute presentation about a new product to show to potential customers who will be interested in the product features and benefits. Then you could create a 5-minute version of that same show for an open house for potential investors, containing only selected slides from the longer show. ◤━━ Bill Davidson wants a reduced version of the slide show that he can present to the sales force, so Carrie creates a custom slide show containing only the slides relating to sales goals and performance.

Steps

1. **Click Slide Show on the menu bar, click Custom Shows, then click New in the Custom Shows dialog box**
   The Define Custom Show dialog box opens, with the slides in your current presentation in the Slides in presentation list box on the left. Select the slides that give information about sales.

2. **Click Slide 3. Mission, press and hold [Shift], click Slide 7. 1998 Goals to select Slides 3 through 7, then click Add**
   The five selected slides move to the Slides in custom show list box, indicating that they will be included in the new presentation. See Figure H-7.

3. **Select the existing text in the Slide show name text box, then type Sales Presentation**
   Now change the slide order in the custom show.

4. **In the Slides in custom show list, click the Mission slide, click the Slide Order down arrow ↓ 4 times to move the Mission slide to the bottom of the list, then click OK**
   The Custom Shows dialog box lists your new presentation. Preview the custom show, which starts with the 1997 Accomplishments slide and ends with the Mission slide.

5. **Click Show, view the slide show, clicking the hyperlink button to move from slide to slide; when you reach the Mission slide, press [Esc] to end the custom show**
   Because the slide show is not set up to loop continuously, clicking the hyperlink button on the Mission slide doesn't do anything.

6. **Click Close in the Custom Shows dialog box**
   You return to the presentation in Slide view. Now view the custom show, starting at the title slide, as the president would at the actual presentation to the sales force. To show a custom slide show, you must first open the show you used to create it. You then go to the custom show, which is not saved as a separate slide show on your disk, even though you assigned it a new name.

Trouble?

If you right-click the title slide and no shortcut menu appears, you probably forgot to return the Set Up Show option to Presented by a speaker (full screen). Press [Esc], click Slide Show on the menu bar, click Set Up Show, and select that option now.

7. **Press [Ctrl][Home] to go to Slide 1, click the Slide Show button ☐, right-click the slide, point to Go, point to Custom Show, then click Sales Presentation as shown in Figure H-8**

8. **Use the hyperlink buttons to move from slide to slide and press [Esc] after viewing the Mission slide**
   Now print the slides in the custom show and save your changes.

9. **Click the Save button ☐ on the Standard toolbar, click File on the menu bar, click Print, click the Custom Show option button, make sure Sales Presentation is listed in the list box, click the Print what list arrow, select Slides (without animations), then click OK**

FIGURE H-7: Define Custom Show dialog box

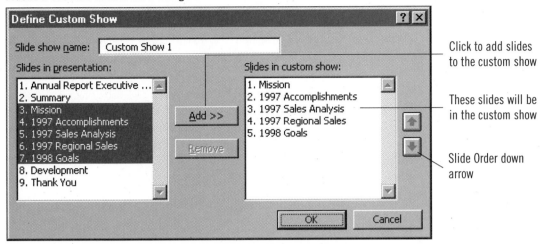

Click to add slides to the custom show

These slides will be in the custom show

Slide Order down arrow

FIGURE H-8: Switching to the custom slide show

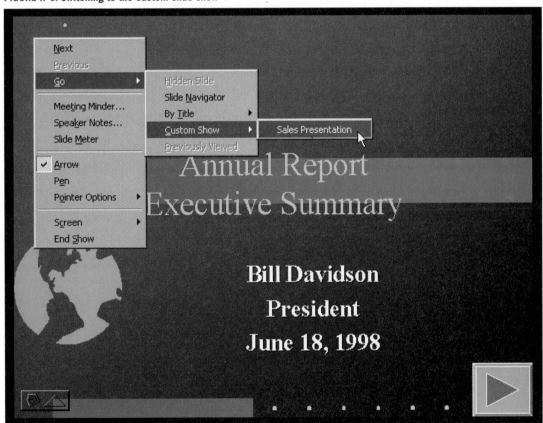

CLUES TO USE

Using action buttons to hyperlink to a custom slide show

You can also use action buttons to switch from the "parent" show to the custom show. Click Slide Show on the menu bar, point to Action Buttons, and choose any action button. Drag the pointer to draw a button on the slide, in the Action Settings dialog box, select

Custom Show in the Hyperlink list box. Select the name of the custom show to which you want to hyperlink and click OK. When you run the show, click the hyperlink button you created to run the custom show.

Hiding a Slide During a Slide Show

Another method of customizing a slide show for an audience is to hide slides you don't need or want to see. Hidden slides are not deleted from the presentation; they just don't appear during a slide show. You know a slide is hidden when there is a line through the slide number in Slide Sorter view. Carrie decides to learn how to hide slides so she can quickly teach the president in case he wants to hide any of the slides when he gives the presentation.

Steps

QuickTip

To hide a slide in Slide view, click Hide Slide on the Slide Show menu.

1. **Click the Slide Sorter View button ⊞, and click Slide 8**
   The presentation appears in Slide Sorter view, and Slide 8 is selected.

2. **Click the Hide Slide button 🔲 on the Slide Sorter toolbar**
   The slide number under Slide 8 now has the hide symbol on it, as shown in Figure H-9. To test the Hide Slide feature, view Slides 7, 8, and 9 in Slide Show view.

3. **Click Slide Show on the menu bar, then click Set Up Show**
   The Set Up Show dialog box opens, similar to Figure H-10.

4. **In the Slides section, type 7 in the From box, make sure 9 appears in the To box, compare your screen to Figure H-10, then click OK**
   Before you can display the slide show without Slide 8, you must first delete the hyperlink buttons you inserted earlier, since they will override the slide sequence that you set here.

5. **Double-click Slide 1, click the hyperlink button, press [Delete], click the Next Slide button ⏷, and repeat the procedure to delete the hyperlink button from each slide in the presentation**
   Now run slides 7 through 9 in Slide Show view.

6. **Click the Slide Show button 🖵, view the animation effects on Slide 7, then press [Spacebar] once to move to Slide 9**
   PowerPoint displays Slide 7, skips over Slide 8, and shows Slide 9. Replay the same slide show, but this time display Slide 8.

QuickTip

To display a hidden slide during a slide show, you can also right-click the slide before the hidden one, point to Go on the pop-up menu, then click Hidden slide.

7. **Press [PgUp] twice to redisplay Slide 7, press [H] to display Slide 8, then press [Spacebar] to display Slide 9**
   Pressing [H] tells PowerPoint to display Slide 8. Now turn the Hide Slide feature off.

8. **Press [Esc], click the Slide Sorter View button ⊞, click Slide 8, then click 🔲**
   The Hide symbol no longer appears over the slide number. Now reset the slide show setup so that the entire show will display in Slide Show view.

9. **Click Slide Show on the menu bar, click Set Up Show, in the Slides section click the All option button, click OK, then click the Save button 🖫 on the Standard toolbar**
   The next time you run the slide show, all the slides will appear.

FIGURE H-9: Slide showing Hide symbol

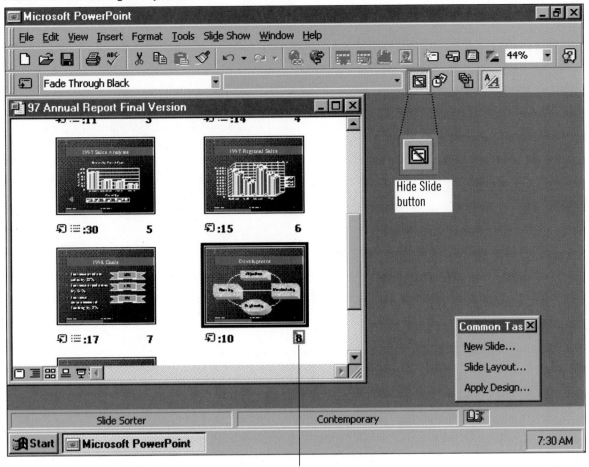

Hide symbol

FIGURE H-10: Set Up Show dialog box

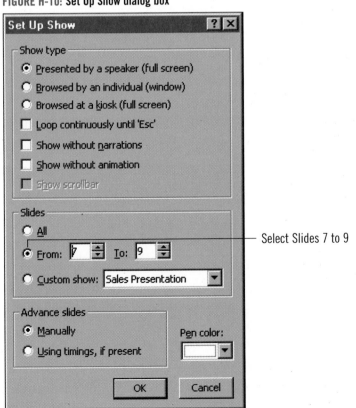

Select Slides 7 to 9

USING SLIDE SHOW FEATURES PP H-9 ◄

Using the Meeting Minder

Occasionally, it's helpful to assign tasks or take notes as you present a slide show to make sure people follow up on meeting items. PowerPoint makes that task easy with the Meeting Minder. The Meeting Minder is a dialog box you use in Slide Show view to enter information related to the slides in your presentation. The action items you enter are automatically added to a new slide at the end of your presentation. You can export the action items to a Microsoft Word document to edit them or to make them part of another document. Carrie practices adding action items with the Meeting Minder so she can teach the president how to use it.

Steps 123 4

1. Click the **Slide View button** 🖼, then press **[Ctrl][Home]** to go to Slide 1
Slide 1 appears. Enter an action item.

2. Click the **Slide Show button** 🖵, right-click the slide, click **Meeting Minder** on the pop-up menu, then click the **Action Items tab**
The Meeting Minder dialog box opens and displays the Action Items tab, similar to Figure H-11. Enter an action item that will help with meeting follow-up.

3. Type **1. Review meeting minutes with president**, press **[Tab]**, type **Carrie** in the Assigned To text box, double-click the **Due Date text box**, type **6/22/98**, compare your screen to Figure H-11, then click **Add**
The action item you entered appears in the list box on the Action Items tab. If you were to enter any more action items, they would be added to this list.

4. Click **OK**
Now view the last slide to make sure the item was added to a new slide at the end of the presentation.

5. Right-click the slide, point to **Go** on the pop-up menu, point to **By Title**, then click **10 Action Items** on the list of slides
The new Action Items slide appears, with the action item you entered in the Meeting Minder. See Figure H-12. Now export your meeting notes to a Microsoft Word document.

6. Right-click the slide, select **Meeting Minder** on the pop-up menu, click the **Action Items tab**, then click **Export**
The Meeting Minder Export dialog box opens.

7. Make sure that the **Send meeting minutes and action items to Microsoft Word check box** is selected, then click **Export Now**
Microsoft Word starts and opens a new Word document containing your Meeting Minder action items. See Figure H-13. You can edit and print this document just as you would any Word document. Now print and save the document, then return to your PowerPoint presentation.

8. Click the **Print button** on the Word Standard toolbar, click the **Close button** in the Word program window, click **Yes** to save the document, then save it as **Action Items** to the drive and folder where you are storing the files for this unit
Your PowerPoint presentation reappears in Slide Show view.

9. Click the left mouse button once to end the slide show
If PowerPoint on your computer is set to show a black slide at the end of the presentation, then you will need to click twice to end the slide show.

Trouble?
If you receive an error message telling you that PowerPoint will be shut down, click Close to exit, restart the program, open 97 Annual Report Final Version, and start this lesson again. If it happens a second time, try restarting your computer.

FIGURE H-11: Meeting Minder dialog box

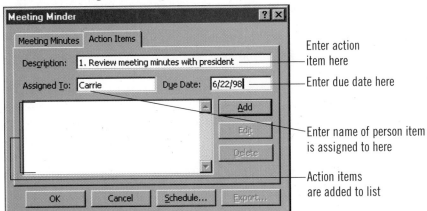

Enter action item here

Enter due date here

Enter name of person item is assigned to here

Action items are added to list

FIGURE H-12: New Action Items slide at end of presentation

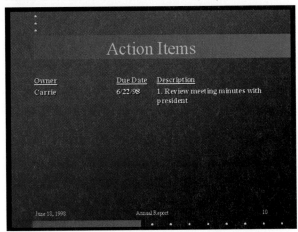

FIGURE H-13: Action Items after exporting to Microsoft Word

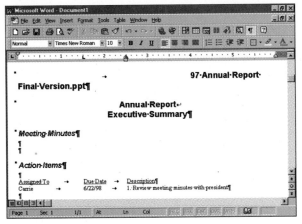

Keeping track of Meeting Minutes and Speaker Notes

You can also use the Meeting Minder to keep a record of meeting minutes you type during the slide show. Right-click any slide in Slide Show view, click Meeting Minder, click the Meeting Minutes tab, then type notes in the text box. You can export meeting minutes to Microsoft Word the same way you export action items. You can also create speaker notes by clicking the Speaker Notes command on the Slide Show view pop-up menu. Type any items you want to remember, and they will automatically be transferred to the Speaker Notes section of that slide.

Rehearsing Slide Timings

Whether you are creating a self-running slide show or you're planning to talk about the slides as they appear, you should rehearse the slide timings, the amount of time each slide stays on the screen. Your presentation will be smoother if you rehearse your slide show and set an appropriate slide timing for each slide. If you assign slide timings to your slides without actually running through the presentation, you will probably discover that the timings do not allow enough time for each slide or point in your presentation. To set accurate slide timings, use PowerPoint's Rehearse Timings feature. As you run through your slide show, the Rehearsal dialog box shows you how long the slide stays on the screen. As soon as you decide enough time has passed, click the mouse to move to the next slide. Carrie learns how to rehearse slide timings so she can show the president, who might want to set appropriate slide timings while he rehearses.

1. Click the **Slide Sorter View button** ⊞, then click **Slide 1**
   Before you continue through the steps of the lesson, you may want to read the steps and comments that follow first, so you are aware of what happens during a slide show rehearsal.

2. Click the **Rehearse Timings button** 🖼 on the Slide Sorter toolbar
   Slide Show view opens, displaying Slide 1. The Rehearsal dialog box appears in the lower-right corner of the screen, as shown in Figure H-14.

3. When you feel an appropriate amount of time has passed for the presenter to speak and for the audience to view the slide, click the **Forward arrow** in the Rehearse dialog box or click your mouse anywhere on the screen
   Slide 2 appears.

4. Click the **Forward arrow** at an appropriate interval after all the information on Slide 2 appears, then click the **Forward arrow** again to view Slide 3

5. Continue through the rest of the slides in the presentation
   Be sure to leave enough time to present the contents of each slide thoroughly. At the end of the slide rehearsal, a Microsoft PowerPoint message box opens asking if you want to save the slide timings. If you save the timings, the next time you run the slide show, the slides will appear automatically at the intervals you specified during the rehearsal.

6. Click **Yes** to save the timings
   A second message box opens. This message box asks if you want to review your timings in Slide Sorter view.

7. Click **Yes** to review the timings, then click the Presentation window **Maximize button**
   Slide Sorter view appears showing the new slide timings, as shown in Figure H-15. Your timings will be different. Run the slide show to see how the new slide timings work. When you run the slide show, it will run by itself, using the timings you rehearsed. The rehearsed timings override any previous timings you set.

8. Click the **Slide Show button** 🖳, view the presentation with your timings, then save your changes
   Now print the slide show as Handouts (6 slides per page)

9. Click **File** on the menu bar, click **Print**, click the **All option button**, click the **Print what list arrow**, click **Handouts (6 slides per page)**, then click **OK**

QuickTip

If you are called away during the rehearsal and too much time has elapsed, click Repeat to restart the timer for that slide.

QuickTip

To override slide timings, click your mouse to advance to the next slide or open the slide show pop-up menu.

FIGURE H-14: Rehearsal dialog box

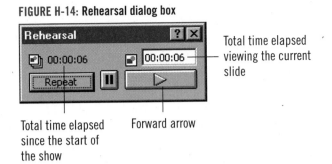

Total time elapsed viewing the current slide

Total time elapsed since the start of the show

Forward arrow

FIGURE H-15: Final presentation in Slide Sorter view showing new slide timings

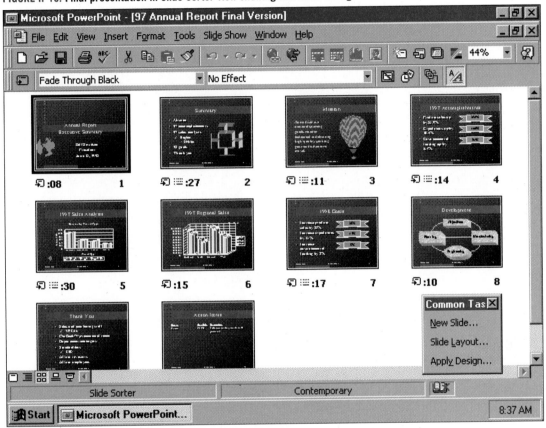

CLUES TO USE

Using the Slide Meter

The Slide Meter measures the time you take to present the information on the slide in relation to the rehearsed slide timing you set. You can use the Slide Meter while practicing your presentation to help determine if your rehearsed slide timings are accurate. To open the Slide Meter, switch to Slide Show view, right-click, then click Slide Meter on the pop-up menu. The Slide Meter dialog box opens, as shown in Figure H-16, and immediately begins recording the slide time. If you need to make adjustments to a slide time, you can open the Slide Transition dialog box and make the changes there.

FIGURE H-16: Slide Meter dialog box

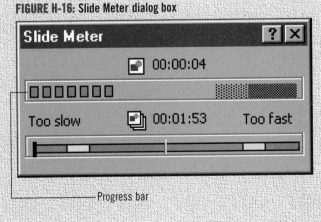

Progress bar

Using the Pack and Go Wizard

Occasionally you need to present your slide show using another computer. To transport everything to the new computer, you use the Pack and Go Wizard. The Pack and Go Wizard compresses and packages all the necessary files (such as your presentation, embedded objects, linked objects, and fonts) that you'll need to take a presentation on the road. You can also package the PowerPoint Viewer. PowerPoint Viewer is a program that allows you to view a slide show even if PowerPoint is not installed on the computer. Carrie packages the Annual Report presentation using the Pack and Go Wizard.

1. **Create a new folder on your hard drive called PackNGo**
   When you run the Pack and Go Wizard, you will save your packaged presentation in this new folder. You will delete this folder from your hard drive at the end of the next lesson. PowerPoint Viewer is available in several versions. Older versions of the Viewer will not run PowerPoint 97 presentations. Save your presentation as a PowerPoint 95 & 97 Presentation so that the steps in this lesson will work no matter which version of the Viewer you have.

2. **Click File on the menu bar, click Save As, in the Save As dialog box, change the Save in list box to the PackNGo folder on your hard drive, click the Save as type list arrow, click PowerPoint 95 & 97 Presentation, edit the File name so it is 97 Annual Report Viewer Version, then click Save**
   Now open the Pack and Go Wizard.

3. **Click File on the menu bar, click Pack and Go, read the screen, then click Next**
   The Pick files to pack screen in the Pack and Go Wizard dialog box opens, as shown in Figure H-17. You indicate here which presentation you would like to package.

4. **Make sure the Active presentation check box is selected, then click Next**
   The Choose destination screen opens. Select the PackNGo folder on your hard drive as the destination for the packaged presentation.

5. **Click the Choose destination option button, click Browse, locate and click the PackNGo folder, then click Select**
   See Figure H-18. In the Links screen, you'll include the TrueType fonts in your packaged presentation and any linked files. Although your presentation doesn't include any linked files, leave this option checked whenever you're not sure if there are linked files.

6. **Click Next, make sure the Include linked files checkbox is selected, click the Embed TrueType fonts check box to select it, then click Next**
   The Viewer screen in the Wizard opens. You want to package the PowerPoint Viewer with your presentation so you can run it from any compatible computer. The PowerPoint Viewer program is available on the Office 97 CD-ROM.

7. **Insert the Office 97 CD-ROM into the disk drive, click the Viewer for Windows 95 or NT option button, click Next, read the Finish screen, then click Finish**
   The Pack and Go Wizard packages the Annual Report presentation. After the presentation is packaged, a message box opens telling you that the Pack and Go Wizard has finished.

8. **Click OK**
   Now close PowerPoint.

9. **Close the presentation, then exit PowerPoint**

QuickTip

If your original presentation is on your hard disk, you can place the packaged version directly on a floppy disk. If the presentation is too big for one disk, PowerPoint 97 lets you save across multiple floppy disks.

Trouble?

If you are working on a network, ask your instructor where you can locate the PowerPoint Viewer file. You can also download the latest version of Viewer from the Product News link on the Microsoft Web Site (http://www.microsoft.com).

FIGURE H-17: Pick files to pack screen in the Pack and Go Wizard

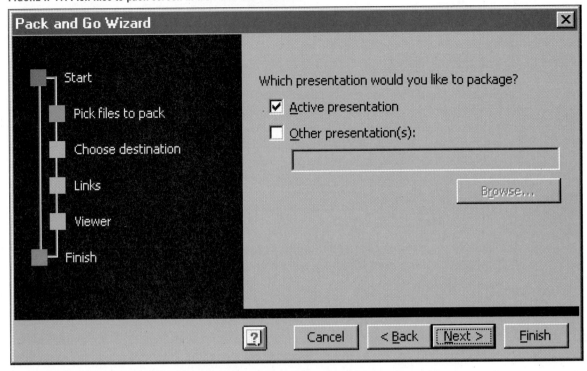

FIGURE H-18: Choose destination screen in the Pack and Go Wizard

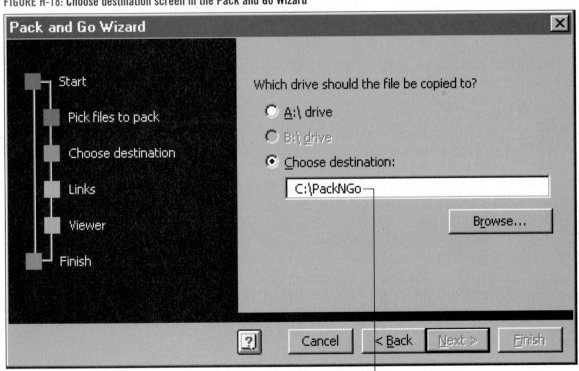

Your destination path
may be different

Using the Microsoft PowerPoint Viewer

The Microsoft PowerPoint Viewer is a program that displays a slide show on compatible computers that do not have PowerPoint installed. All you need to show a presentation using the Viewer is a computer running Windows 95 or Windows NT, a copy of PowerPoint Viewer, and the PowerPoint presentation itself. The content of a presentation can't be altered using the Viewer. PowerPoint Viewer is a free program distributed by Microsoft that can be copied onto any compatible computer. Carrie practices locating and using the PowerPoint Viewer to show her presentation.

Steps

1. **Open the PackNGo folder you created in the previous lesson**
   The Pack and Go Wizard supplies a special setup program that automatically decompresses the packaged file.

2. **Double-click the Pngsetup icon in the PackNGo folder window**
   The Pack and Go Setup dialog box appears. Indicate the destination folder for your extracted file.

3. **In the Destination folder text box, click after the backslash, type the path to your PackNGo folder ending with the folder name PackNGo (the same way it appears in the Source Folder line), click OK, click Yes to unpack the presentation to the PackNGo directory, then click OK in the warning box that opens**
   The presentation you previously saved as a PowerPoint 95 and 97 presentation has been overwritten with the newly unpacked files. Next a message box opens telling you that the installation was successful and asking if you want to view the slide show.

Trouble?

You may see messages that the Viewer cannot play the sound you embedded. Click OK and continue.

4. **Click Yes**
   When you use Viewer, preview your slide show before the actual presentation to make sure everything works the way you expect. The Viewer displays the Annual Report presentation without opening PowerPoint. The presentation runs with the slide timings set during the rehearsal. When the presentation is complete, the presentation and the Viewer close. Now change the settings so that you can advance the slides manually.

5. **In the PackNGo folder window, double-click the Ppview32 icon**
   The Microsoft PowerPoint Viewer dialog box opens, similar to Figure H-19.

6. **Select the file 97 Annual Report Viewer Version**
   A preview of the Annual Report presentation appears in the Preview window. Now tell the Viewer that you want to have access to the pop-up menu and end with a black slide. Since this will not be a kiosk presentation, you won't need to protect it with a password.

Trouble?

If you see a truncated file name, for example 97annu~1, in the PowerPoint viewer dialog box, select it and continue with the steps.

7. **Select the check boxes Popup Menu on Right Mouse Click, Show Popup Menu Button, and End With Black Slide**
   Ending with a black slide is a visual cue to the audience that the presentation is ending. Now change the way the slides advance.

8. **Click the Show SlideShow Dialog check box, then click Show**
   The Advanced Slide Show Settings dialog box opens, similar to figure H-20.

9. **Click the Manual Advance option button, click Show, then click the left mouse button to progress through the slide show**
   PowerPoint Viewer displays your show. The timing of the animated objects' appearance on the slides was overridden by selecting the Manual Advance option in the Advanced Slide Show Settings dialog box. After you view the last slide, you are returned to the Microsoft PowerPoint Viewer dialog box.

10. **Click Exit, then delete the PackNGo folder and its contents from the hard drive**

FIGURE H-19: Microsoft PowerPoint Viewer dialog box

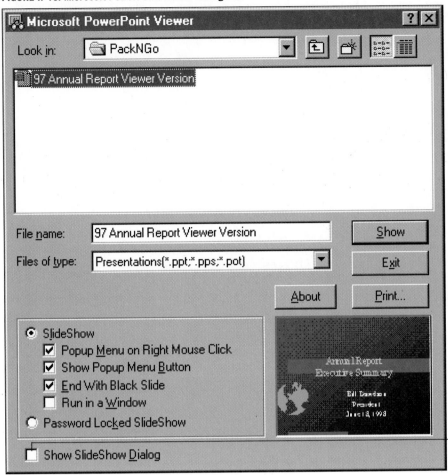

Click to show only
selected slides or
to change slide
advance method

FIGURE H-20: Advanced Slide Show Settings dialog box

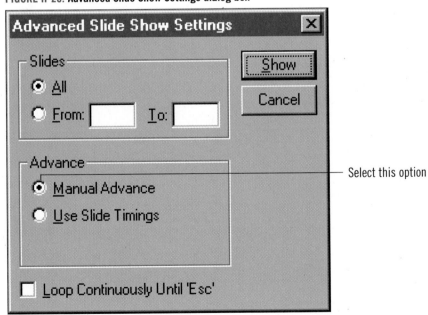

Select this option

Practice

▶ Concepts Review

Label each of the elements of the PowerPoint window shown in Figure H-21.

FIGURE H-21

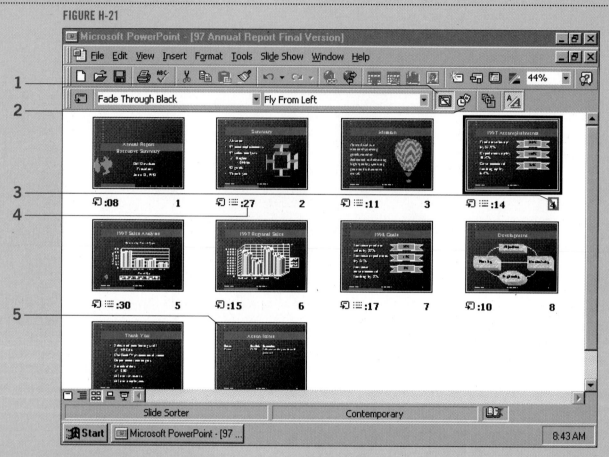

Match each of the terms with the statement that describes its function.

6. A presentation created from selected slides in another presentation
7. Program that runs a slide show on other computers
8. A free-standing public computer that runs a slide show
9. A dialog box that lets you keep track of meeting minutes and action items during a slide show
10. Packages a presentation to take it on the road

a. Microsoft PowerPoint Viewer
b. kiosk
c. custom show
d. Pack and Go Wizard
e. Meeting Minder

Select the best answer from the list of choices.

11. In Slide Sorter view, what does a box with a line through it indicate when it is over a slide number?
  a. The slide is first in the presentation.
  b. The slide is deleted.
  c. The slide appears last in a slide show.
  d. The slide won't appear in a slide show.

12. **Which of the following is not a Meeting Minder feature?**
    a. You can enter text directly to the notes pages of your presentation.
    b. You can export text to Microsoft Word.
    c. You can enter text that is placed on a new slide in your presentation.
    d. You can print the text you enter in the Meeting Minder.

13. **Which of the following statements is true about rehearsing your slide timings?**
    a. Rehearsing the slides in your presentation gives each slide the same slide timing.
    b. During a rehearsal, you have no way of knowing how long the slide stays on the screen.
    c. If you give your slides random slide timings, you may not have enough time to adequately view each slide.
    d. If you rehearse your presentation, someone on another computer can set the slide timings.

14. **When you want to have a slide show run continuously and automatically at a kiosk, you should**
    a. Use the Set Up Show dialog box to choose the appropriate settings
    b. Click Custom Animation on the Slide Show menu, and choose the Automatically option button
    c. Insert hyperlink buttons on all the slides
    d. Add a voice narration and save the presentation using the Pack and Go Wizard

► Skills Review

1. **Animate charts and sounds**
   a. Open the presentation PPT H-2, and save it as Division Final.
   b. Go to Slide 6 and click the sound icon to select it.
   c. Click Slide Show on the menu bar, click Custom Animation, and click the Timing tab.
   d. Click the Animate option button, then click the Automatically option button, then set the timing to 1 second.
   e. Click the Play Settings tab, select the check boxes Play using animation order and Hide while not playing.
   f. Select the Pause slide show option button, then click OK.
   g. Right-click the chart to select it, click Custom Animation on the pop-up menu, then click the Timing tab.
   h. Click the Animate option button, click the Automatically option button, then set the timing to 2 seconds.
   i. Click the Chart Effects tab, in the Introduce chart elements list box, select by Category, in the top Entry animation and sound list box, select Wipe Down, then in the bottom list box, select Drum Roll.
   j. Click Preview, watch the Preview box, watch the Preview box, then click OK.
   k. Save your changes, click the Slide Show button, view the animation effects, then press [Esc].

2. **Set up a slide show**
   a. Click Slide Show on the menu bar, click Set Up Show, then click the Browsed at a kiosk (full screen).
   b. In the Advance Slides section, click the Using timings if present option button, then click OK.
   c. Switch to Slide Sorter view, select all the slides, click Slide Show on the menu bar, click Slide Transition, click the Automatically after check box, set the timing to 3 seconds, then click Apply to All.
   d. Run the slide show all the way through, then press [Esc] to end the presentation.
   e. Click Slide Show on the menu bar, click Set Up Show, then click the Manually option button.
   f. Click the Presented by a speaker (full screen) option button, then click OK.
   g. Move to Slide 1 in Slide view, click Slide Show on the menu bar, point to Action Buttons, click the Action Button: Forward or Next button, then drag to draw the button on Slide 1 in the lower right corner.
   h. In the Action Settings dialog box, click OK.
   i. Copy the action button to the Clipboard, then paste it onto all of the slides except the last one.
   j. Move to Slide 6, click Slide Show on the menu bar, point to Action Buttons, click the Action Button: Back or Previous button, then drag to draw the button in the lower left corner of Slide 6. Resize the button so it is the same size as the button you created in step g.
   k. In the Action Settings dialog box, click OK.

l. Copy the button to the Clipboard, then copy it to all of the slides except the first one.

m. Press [Ctrl][Home], then run through the slide show using the hyperlink buttons you inserted. Move forward and backward through the presentation, watching the animation effects as they appear.

n. When you have finished viewing the slide show, press [Esc] to end the show, then save your changes.

3. Create a custom show

a. Click Slide Show on the menu bar, click Custom Shows, then click New

b. Click Slide 3, press and hold [Shift], click Slide 5, then click Add.

c. Select the Adventure Tours slide in the Slides in custom show list, then click the Slide Order up arrow.

d. Select the existing text in the Slide show name text box, type New Customer Presentation, then click OK.

e. Click Show, click the hyperlink buttons to move among the three slides, then click [Esc] to end the slide show.

f. Click Close in the Custom Shows dialog box.

g. Move to Slide 1, click the Slide Show button, right-click Slide 1, point to Go, point to Custom Show, then click New Customer Presentation.

h. View the custom slide show, press [Esc] to end the show, then save your changes.

4. Hide a slide during a slide show

a. Delete the hyperlink buttons from all the slides.

b. Click the Slide Sorter View button.

c. Click Slide 2, then click the Hide Slide button on the Slide Sorter toolbar.

d. Click Slide Show on the menu bar, click Set Up Show, in the Slides section, type 1 in the From box, type 3 in the To box, then click OK.

e. Click the Slide Show button, then click through the selected slides. Slide 2 does not appear in the slide show.

f. Click the Slide Show button, press [H], then view the animation on Slide 2.

g. Move through the rest of the slide show, select Slide 2, then click the Hide Slide button on the Slide Sorter toolbar.

h. Click Slide Show on the menu bar, click Set Up Show, click the All option button, then click OK.

5. Use the Meeting Minder

a. Click Slide 1, then click the Slide Show button.

b. Click the left mouse button to move to Slide 2, and wait for the animation effects to appear.

c. Right-click, click Meeting Minder, then click the Meeting Minutes tab.

d. In the text box, type the following items. (Press [Enter] after typing each sentence.)
   "Research the type of tour and the target audience."
   "Explore the tour features: projected costs, special equipment, weather considerations, profit margin."
   "Promote and advertise the tour."

e. Click the Action Items tab.

f. Type "1. Review tour philosophy with sales staff", press [Tab], type [Your First Name] in the Assigned To text box, press [Tab], change the Due Date to one week from today's date, click Add, then click OK. (Note: The Assigned To text box will accept a maximum of 10 characters.)

g. Click the left mouse button once, then open the Meeting Minder again.

h. Click the Action Items tab, then type "2. Review Int. tours figures for 1997", enter your name and the date as described in step f, click Add, then click OK.

i. Click through the rest of the presentation until Slide 7 appears.

j. Open the Meeting Minder, click the Action Items tab, click Export, then click Export Now.

k. Save the Microsoft Word document as ND Action, print the document, then exit Word.

l. Click your mouse once to end the slide show.

6. Rehearse slide timings

a. Click Slide 1, then click the Rehearse Timings button on the Slide Sorter toolbar.

b. Click through the presentation setting new slide timings, then save your new timings and review them.

c. Save your changes.

d. Click File on the menu bar, click Print, click the Custom Show option button, click the Print what list arrow, select Slides without animations, then click OK.

e. Open the Print dialog box again, and print all the slides as Handouts (3 slides per page).

7. Use the Pack and Go Wizard

a. Create a new folder on your hard drive and name it PackNGo2.

b. Click File on the PowerPoint menu bar, click Save As, change the Save in list box to the PackNGo2 folder, click the Save as type list arrow, click PowerPoint 95 & 97 Presentation, edit the file name so it is Division Final Viewer Version, then click Save.

c. Click File on the menu bar, click Pack and Go, then click Next.

d. In the Pick files to pack screen, make sure the Active presentation check box is selected, then click Next.

e. In the Choose destination screen, click the Choose destination option button, click Browse, locate and click the PackNGo2 folder on the hard drive, click Select, then click Next.

f. In the Links screen, click the Embed TrueType Fonts check box, then click Next.

g. Make sure the Office 97 CD-ROM is in the disk drive, then in the Viewer screen, click the Viewer for Windows 95 or NT option button, click Next, then click Finish.

8. View a packaged presentation

a. Open PackNGo2 folder, double-click the Pngsetup file, then in the Destination Folder text box, type the path to your PackNGo2 folder ending with the name "PackNGo2".

b. Click OK, then click OK again.

c. Click Yes to show your packaged presentation, then view the slide show. (You may not be able to play the sounds or the movie.)

d. Double-click the Pptview32 icon in the PackNGo2 folder.

e. Select the file Division Final Viewer Version (the file name may be truncated).

f. Select the following check boxes: Popup Menu on Right Mouse Click, End With Black Slide, and Show SlideShow Dialog, then click Show.

g. Click the Manual Advance option button, then click Show.

h. Click the left mouse button or press [Spacebar] to move through the slide show.

i. Click Exit, then delete the PackNGo2 folder from your hard drive.

▶ Independent Challenges

1. If you complete all of the exercises in this unit and the Skills Review, you may run out of space on your Student Disk. If so, copy the files referenced in the Independent Challenges to a new disk. You work for Pacific Tours, an international tour company that provides specialty tours to destinations in the Pacific Ocean region. You have to develop presentations that the sales force can use to highlight different tours at conferences and meetings.

In this challenge, you will use some of PowerPoint's advanced slide show features such as slide builds and interactive settings to finish the presentation you started. Create at least two additional slides for the basic presentation provided on your Student Disk using your own information. Assume the following about Pacific Tours:

- Pacific Tours has a special (20% off regular price) on tours to Bora Bora and Tahiti during the spring of 1998.
- Over the years, Pacific Tours has built a successful business selling tour packages to the major islands of the Pacific: Philippines, Japan, Australia, and New Zealand.

To complete this independent challenge:

1. Open the file PPT H-3, then save it as South Pacific.
2. Use the assumptions provided to help you develop additional content for your presentation. Use pictures, movies, and sounds provided on the Office 97 CD-ROM or from other media sources to complete your presentation.
3. Animate the chart and have an appropriate sound effect play as each chart element appears.
4. Create a custom version of the show that can be shown at a trade show kiosk.
5. Rehearse slide timings.
6. Use the Meeting Minder to create Action Items that could result from your presentation.
7. Package your presentation, then use the viewer to present your packaged presentation to the class.
8. Submit your presentation plan and print the final slide presentation and all related documents.

2. You work for WorldWide Travel Services, a travel service company. WorldWide Travel is a subsidiary owned by Globus Inc. Every year in October, WorldWide Travel needs to report to Globus Inc on the past year's activity.

Create your own information using the basic presentation provided on your Student Disk. Assume the following:

- WorldWide purchased major routes from Canada to Asia and the Far East from Canadian AirTours.
- WorldWide's operating expenses run $6 million a quarter.
- Ten new tour packages to Eastern Europe were created this year. Two of the new tours are The Great Wall Tour and The Trans-Siberian Rail Tour.
- WorldWide added 30 employees during the year.

To complete this independent challenge:

1. Open the file PPT H-4, then save it as WorldWide.
2. Use the assumptions provided to help you develop additional content for your presentation. Use pictures, movies, and sounds provided on the Office 97 CD-ROM or from other media sources to complete your presentation.
3. Animate the chart, and have an appropriate sound effect play as each chart element appears.
4. Rehearse slide timings.
5. Create a version of your show to run continuously at a conference kiosk, using the timings that you rehearsed.
6. Create a custom version of the show for a specific audience of your choice, with only selected slides, and rearrange the order of the slides appropriately.
7. Use the Meeting Minder to create meeting minutes, then export the minutes to Microsoft Word. Save the Word document as WorldWide Minutes.
8. Package your presentation, then use the Viewer to present your packaged presentation to the class.
9. Submit your presentation plan and print the final slide presentation and all related documents.

3. You are the assistant director of operations at American Shipping Line Inc, an international marine shipping company based in San Francisco, California. American Shipping handles 65% of all the trade between Asia, the Middle East, and the West Coast of the United States. You need to give a quarterly presentation to the company's operations committee that outlines the type and amount of trade American Shipping handled during the previous quarter.

Plan and create a 10- to 15-slide presentation that details the type of goods American Shipping carried, how much was carried, what companies (foreign and domestic) purchased goods, what companies (foreign and domestic) sold goods, and how much revenue American Shipping earned. You also need to identify the time it took to deliver the goods to their destinations and the delivery cost. Create your own content, but assume the following:

- American Shipping hauled cars and trucks from Tokyo to San Francisco during the last quarter. A car carrier ship can hold 143 cars or 126 trucks.
- American Shipping hauled large tractor equipment and parts made by Caterpillar Tractor and Massey-Ferguson. One shipload went to South Korea and one load went to Saudi Arabia.
- Typical household goods carried by American Shipping include electronic equipment, appliances, toys, and furniture.
- The cost of hauling goods by ship is $3,380 a ton. American Shipping owns five cargo ships that can operate at one time. All five ships were in operation during the last quarter.
- American Shipping hauled a total of 980,000 tons during the last quarter.

To complete this independent challenge:

1. Use clip art or shapes to enhance your presentation.
2. Use the assumptions provided to help you develop the content for your presentation. Use movies and sounds provided on the Office 97 CD-ROM or from other media sources to complete your presentation.
3. Use Word and Excel to embed or link objects into your presentation. Use the preceding assumptions to develop related information that would be appropriate for a table or worksheet.
4. Set transitions and animations, and rehearse slide timings.
5. Use the Meeting Minder to create action items and then export the items to Microsoft Word.
6. Save the presentation as Shipping.
7. Package your presentation, then use the Viewer to present your packaged presentation to the class.
8. Submit your presentation plan and print the final slide presentation and all related documents.

4. You work for Discover Industries, an aerospace and defense contractor in Maryland. You need to prepare a presentation to present to the U.S. Congress outlining your company's competency and ability to build a permanent space station.

Plan and create a slide show presentation that gives a general outline of Discover's space station production plan. Create your own information, but assume the following:

- The space station production costs for the first year are estimated at $25 billion. Each year after the first, until the project is completed, is estimated to cost $16 billion. The space station would take eight years to build. Discover could begin production in 1999.
- Discover Industries has three production facilities: in Livermore, California; Tulsa, Oklahoma; and Bremerton, Washington. The California production facility produces rocket propulsion and satellite systems. The Oklahoma production facility produces the space station module (frame, structure, and furnishings). The Washington production facility produces the communication, directional guidance, and living environment systems.
- Aerospace Systems Inc is the subcontractor that Discover Industries uses to assemble and deliver the space station to orbit. Estimated cost to assemble and deliver the space station to orbit is $215 billion. It will take approximately 14 space shuttle payloads over a two-and-a-half-year period to get the entire space station into orbit.

To complete this independent challenge:

1. Use the assumptions provided to help you develop the content for your presentation. Use movies and sounds provided on the Office 97 CD-ROM or from other media sources to complete your presentation.
2. Log on to the Internet and use your browser to go to http://www.course.com. From there, click Student Online Companions, click the link for this textbook, then click the PowerPoint link for Unit H. Use the link there to find information, photographs, videos, and sound to enhance your presentation. (The videos may be very large files.)
3. Use Word and Excel to embed, link, or hyperlink objects into your presentation. Use the preceding assumptions to develop related information that would be appropriate for a table or worksheet.
4. Create and add a chart with information about Discover, and animate the chart elements. Make the appearance of each chart element be accompanied by an appropriate sound effect.
5. Add a template, background shading, or other enhancing objects to make your presentation look professional.
6. Rehearse slide timings.
7. Create Action Items and then export the items to Microsoft Word. Print the Action Items.
8. Save the presentation as Space.
9. Package your presentation, then use the Viewer to present your packaged presentation to the class.
10. Create a custom version of the slide show that will run continually at a kiosk at a company meeting.
11. Create a custom version of the slide show for an audience of your choice.
12. Submit your presentation plan and print the final slide presentation and all related documents.

► Visual Workshop

Create the slides shown in Figures H-22 and H-23. The clip art is on the Office 97 CD-ROM. Set transitions, animations, and slide timings. Insert a hyperlink and create a target slide for the hyperlink to jump to. Create a title slide. Adjust the background of all the slides to match the figures. Submit the final presentation output.

FIGURE H-22

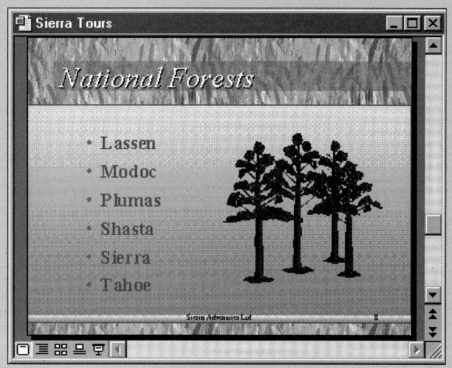

FIGURE H-23

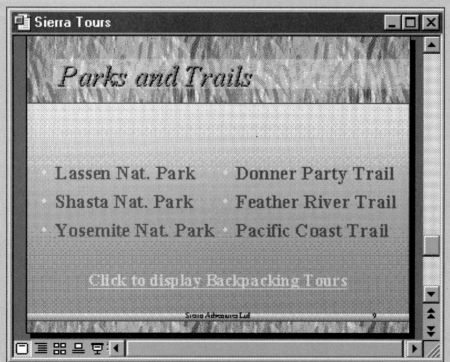

Working

with Special PowerPoint Features

Objectives

- ► Import text from Word
- ► Export a presentation to 35mm slides
- ► Set custom options
- ► Save a presentation for use on the Internet
- ► Use Presentation Conferencing as the presenter
- ► Use Presentation Conferencing as the audience

Information in your PowerPoint presentations often relates to subjects that you've written about or that you'll want to use in other ways. For example, you may want to create a presentation using information from a report you've already written on the subject. Once you have learned the essential features of PowerPoint, you can use the special features of PowerPoint to extend a presentation's usefulness and increase your productivity. Carrie Armstrong is preparing a presentation on proposed whitewater rafting tours for New Directions, a travel subsidiary of Nomad Ltd. She uses the special features of PowerPoint to create the presentation and make it available to others.

Importing Text from Word

You may want to create a presentation on a subject you wrote about earlier using Microsoft Word. For example, suppose you wrote a business plan using Word. You could create a PowerPoint presentation by importing the business plan outline from your Word document. This would save you retyping time. PowerPoint automatically creates slides containing the items from your outline, using styles from the Word document to determine where to put information on each slide. Carrie is helping the New Directions travel subsidiary create a presentation on proposed whitewater rafting tours. She opens an existing presentation and then adds more slides using a Word outline. Then she applies the New Directions company template.

1. Start PowerPoint, open the presentation PPT I-1, save it as Rafting, make sure the presentation window is at 36% zoom, click the Restore window button in the presentation window, click Window on the menu bar, then click Fit to Page
   The presentation has two slides. First, change a tab setting on Slide 1 to improve the look of the slide.

2. Click in the text box containing the text New Directions, click View on the menu bar, then click Ruler if it is not already selected
   The horizontal ruler appears at the top of the page, showing the margin and tab settings for the text box. A small box to the left of the ruler contains tab marker choices.

3. Click the tab box until you see the center-aligned tab marker ⊥, then click at the 3⅜" point on the Ruler
   A center-aligned tab marker appears at the 3⅜" point on the ruler, which is approximately the midpoint of the text box. When you tab text over to this marker, the text will automatically be centered across the point on the ruler where the marker appears.

4. Click to the left of the text New Directions, then press [Tab]; repeat this procedure with the text A Subsidiary of Nomad Ltd
   The company title and subtitle are now centered in the text box and on the slide. Next, go to the slide that will precede the slides from the outline.

5. Click the Next Slide button ⬇ to display Slide 2, click Insert on the menu bar, then click Slides from Outline
   The Insert Outline dialog box opens.

6. Click the Files of type list arrow, scroll down if necessary, select All Outlines, click the file PPT I-2 as shown in Figure I-1, click Insert, then scroll through the 11 slides to see how PowerPoint added the outline information to the presentation
   The outline items are inserted into the presentation on Slides 3 through 11. The first-level outline items are slide titles. The second-level heads became bullets, and the third-level heads become sub bullets. Next, you'll apply the New Directions template.

7. On the Common Tasks toolbar, click Apply Design, then double-click PPT I-3 from your Student Disk
   The presentation now uses the New Directions template. View all the slides to check their content and layout.

8. Click the Slide Sorter View button 🔠, then set the Zoom to 36%
   See Figure I-2. Now, print the first two slides in color.

9. Click File on the menu bar, click Print, under Print range, click the Slides option button, type 1-2 in the Slides text box, click the Black and White check box in the Print What section to remove the check mark and deselect it, then click OK

10. Save the presentation, then view the slide show

FIGURE I-1: The Insert Outline dialog box

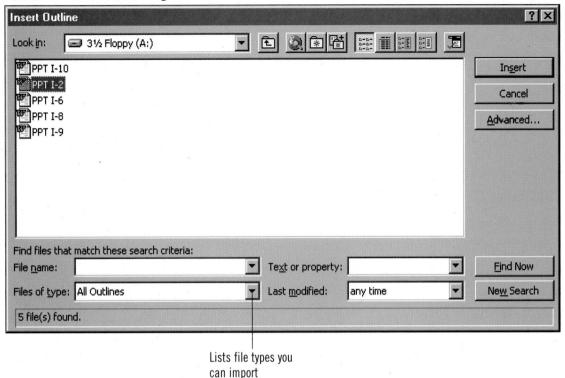

Lists file types you
can import

FIGURE I-2: Presentation with imported Word items and template applied

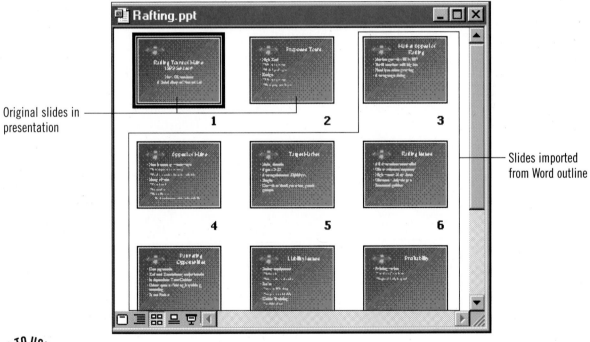

Original slides in
presentation

Slides imported
from Word outline

CLUES TO USE

Exporting a PowerPoint outline to Word

When you want to make a longer written document using the information in your presentation, you can easily export a PowerPoint outline to Word. Click the Outline view button, then click File on the menu bar, then click Save as. In the Save as type list box, select Outline/RTF, name the file, then click Save. PowerPoint saves the outline as an .RTF (Rich Text Format) file, which you can open using Word and then edit as you would any Word document.

Exporting a Presentation to 35mm Slides

You may want to show your presentation to a large audience. If so, using a 35mm slide projector will ensure that your presentation is readable from a distance. You can easily create 35mm slides from a PowerPoint presentation by sending your presentation to a **service bureau**, which is a graphics services business that produces and mounts slides. You can send your presentation on disk, by modem, or through the Internet. From PowerPoint, you can send your slides directly to a service bureau called Genigraphics, using the Genigraphics Wizard; however, you will not actually send your presentation in this lesson. ✎ Carrie decides to practice sending the New Directions presentation to Genigraphics in case the New Directions manager wants to show the presentation at the stockholders' meeting.

1. Make sure the **Rafting** presentation is open and in Slide Sorter view
   First, delete one slide that Carrie doesn't want in the presentation.

2. Click **Slide 11**, click **Edit** on the menu bar, then click **Delete slide**
   The presentation now contains 10 slides with only the information Carrie needs for the presentation. Next, you'll size the presentation correctly for 35 mm slides, which is 11.25" by 7.5".

3. Click **File** on the menu bar, click **Page Setup**, click the **Slides sized for list arrow**, click **35mm Slides**, then click **OK**
   The slides change to the new dimensions. Now, start the Genigraphics Wizard.

4. Click **File** on the menu bar, point to **Send to**, then click **Genigraphics**
   The Genigraphics Wizard starts and displays an introductory screen. (If the Genigraphics command is not available, the Genigraphics Wizard is not installed on your computer. See your instructor or technical support person.)

5. Read the screen, then click **Next** to display the Output products or services screen

6. Click the **Display Pricing Information button**, read the information and click **OK**, then click the **35mm slides** option and click **Next**
   The next screen asks which presentation you want to send and how you want to send it to Genigraphics. See Figure 1-3.

7. Make sure **Rafting** is selected, click **Send via Internet connection**, then click **Next**
   Now, the Wizard asks how you want your slides mounted and how many sets you want.

8. Click **Plastic mounts**, make sure **1** is selected, then click **Next**
   Then you can choose whether you want to include hidden slides, if you want a slide for each build image or not, and what turnaround time you want. Because the presentation has no hidden slides or build steps, these items are dimmed. On the left side of the screen, there is also a toll-free telephone number you can call to obtain current price information.

9. In the **Turnaround list box**, select **Plan ahead: in by 5 PM; back in 3 - 7 bus. days**, then click **Next**
   The next two Wizard screens ask you for ordering information. If you were actually ordering slides, you would enter your name, address, and shipping information in the screen shown in Figure I-4. The next screen asks you for credit card and billing information. PowerPoint would automatically send your order to Genigraphics and bill the account you specified. *Do not enter a credit card number and do not click Finish.*

10. Click the **Cancel button**, then click File on the menu bar, click **Page Setup**, click the **Slides sized for list arrow**, click **On-Screen**, then click **OK**
    The new slides return to their original dimensions.

QuickTip

To create overhead transparencies instead of slides for your presentation, choose the Overheads option in this step to format the presentation appropriately. When completing the Genigraphics Wizard, click the Overheads option instead of the 35mm option.

QuickTip

If you enter billing information, be aware that as soon as you click Finish, your order will be sent to Genigraphics using the information and presentation you specified. Do not click Finish if you do not want to be personally responsible for paying for the order.

FIGURE I-3: The Genigraphics Wizard

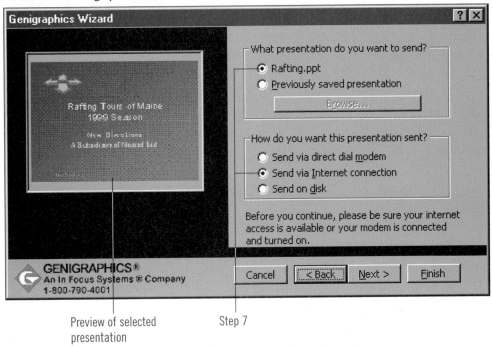

Preview of selected presentation

Step 7

FIGURE I-4: The screen you would use to enter billing information

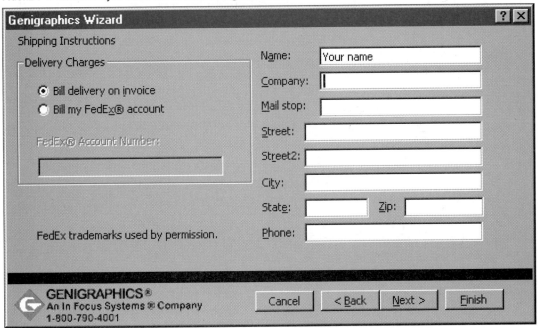

CLUES TO USE

Saving slides in .WMF format

You can use PowerPoint slides as graphics in other documents and manipulate them like any image by using the control buttons on the Picture toolbar. For example, you might want to use the title slide of your presentation on the title page of a Word document about the same subject. Then your document will have graphic interest (and color, if you have a color printer) without your knowing a graphics program. To create .WMF (Windows Metafile) files from your presentation, click File on the menu bar, click Save as, and under Save as type, select Windows Metafile (*.WMF). You can save the current slide or all slides in your presentation. If you save all slides, PowerPoint creates a separate .WMF file for each one.

Setting Custom Options

Once you have learned PowerPoint basics, you may want to customize certain program settings so you can use the program as efficiently as possible. The seven tabs in the Options dialog box let you control, for example, automatic editing features, as well as which dialog boxes appear on the screen when you start a new presentation or insert a new slide.   Carrie wants to customize several options to match the way she has learned to work with PowerPoint.

Steps

1. Make sure the Rafting presentation is open in Slide Sorter view

2. Click Tools on the menu bar, then click Options
   The Options dialog box opens, displaying seven tabs. See Table I-1 for a summary of the commands on each tab. First, change the appearance of the Slide Show window.

3. Click the View tab
   You can learn what any option does by using the What's This feature of online Help.

4. In the Slide Show section, right-click the Show Pop-up menu button, then click What's This?
   A pop-up help window describing the option opens. See Figure I-5.

5. Click anywhere on the tab to close the Help window, then click the Show pop-up menu check box to remove the check and deselect it
   The next time you run a slide show, the pop-up menu in the lower-left corner will not appear. However, you will still be able to right-click to see the pop-up menu because that option is still checked. Now, change some editing settings.

6. Click the Spelling tab, then under Suggest, click the Always check box to deselect it
   The next time you spell-check a presentation, PowerPoint will not suggest possible replacement words, which will speed up the spell-check process. Now, customize some printing options.

7. Click the Print tab, then look under Options for current document only
   See Figure I-6.

8. Click to select Use the most recently used printer settings
   The next time you print this presentation using the Print button on the toolbar, PowerPoint will use the most recent settings in the Print dialog box. For example, if you select this, and you last printed only handouts, clicking the Print button will again print only handouts.

9. Click OK or, if you are working in a lab, click Cancel
   The dialog box closes.

QuickTip

Note that this setting only applies to the current presentation.

FIGURE I-5: View tab in Options dialog box with pop-up help

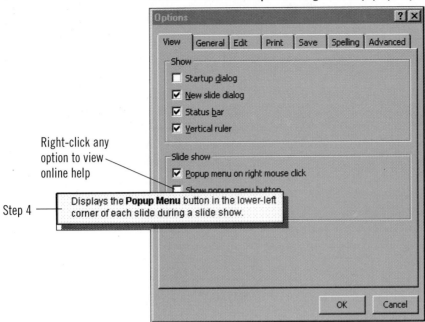

Right-click any
option to view
online help

Step 4

FIGURE I-6: Print tab in Options dialog box

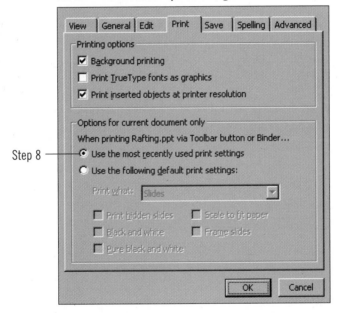

Step 8

TABLE I-1: Tabs in the Options Dialog Box (Tools Menu)

tab	lets you control
View	What you see in the Presentation and Slide Show windows
General	Settings that affect how the overall program runs
Edit	Editing by having PowerPoint perform some features automatically
Print	Printing options for all documents or the current document
Save	What appears when you save and how PowerPoint saves files
Spelling	What appears and what PowerPoint flags during a spell-check
Advanced	What happens when you export pictures and save files

Save a Presentation for Use on the Internet

You can place any PowerPoint presentation on the World Wide Web. Viewers can then look at your presentation over the Internet, just as they would if they were seeing it in PowerPoint. To prepare your presentation for the Web from within PowerPoint, you only need to save it in HTML (Hypertext Markup Language) file format. Internet Assistant's HTML Wizard lets you customize the appearance of your presentation, such as the page style, colors, and button styles. The HTML Wizard saves your slide as a set of linked Web pages, like the pages of a book, and groups them in a folder with the same name as the presentation. Users can click any hyperlinks in your presentation, as they would with any Web page, to jump to related information. To make the New Directions proposal easily available to investors, Carrie wants to put the rafting presentation on the company Web page, so she uses the HTML Wizard to convert it.

1. Make sure the **Rafting** presentation is open, then double-click **Slide 2**
   Next, insert two hyperlinks to Slide 10 on Slide 2 of the presentation.

2. Select the text **High End**, click the **Insert Hyperlink button** 🔗, click the **Browse button** next to the Named location in file text box, click **10. Proposed Trips for 1999 Season**, click **OK**, then click **OK**; repeat this procedure to create another hyperlink from the text **Budget** to Slide 10

3. While still in Slide 2, click the **Slide Show View button** 🖥, then test the hyperlinks
   Notice that since you were in Slide 2 when you clicked the Slide Show View button, the slide show starts at Slide 2. Also, notice that the Slide Show pop-up menu button does not appear, because you turned off this option in the previous lesson.

QuickTip

To save time when creating your presentation, you can use one of the PowerPoint online templates designed for online viewing, which include linked action buttons on each slide.

4. Click **File** on the menu bar, click **Save as HTML**, read the first Wizard screen, click **Next**, make sure **New Layout option button** is selected, then click **Next**
   The Wizard lets you choose the page style for your Web page. You can use a standard style, or you can use frames, which display different parts of the page in separate boxes. Because not all Internet browsers let you view frames, you'll choose the Standard style.

5. Click the **Standard option button**, click **Next**, then complete the remaining HTML Wizard dialog boxes, selecting the following options: **GIF**; **640 by 480**; **¾ width of screen**; no information page options; **Use browser colors**; **large square button**; navigation buttons **above** the screen; the **a:** drive containing your Student Disk; **Finish**; and **Don't Save**
   PowerPoint exports the slide information to HTML format and places it in a folder called Rafting, the same name as the presentation. It creates an index, or title, page that will act as a table of contents to the linked pages. Preview the Web presentation in your Web browser.

Trouble?

If you're not sure which Web browser to use, double-click the Index.htm file to see whether Internet Explorer opens it automatically.

6. Click **OK**, close PowerPoint, saving your changes, open your Web browser, then use its Open command to open the **Index.htm** file
   The index page opens and displays a Table of Contents with a hyperlink called Click here to start (at the top) followed by hyperlinks to the other slides. See Figure I-7.

7. Click the hyperlink **Click here to start** to begin viewing the presentation
   Internet Explorer displays the first presentation slide, as shown in Figure I-8. It contains navigation tools for the other pages the Wizard created.

8. Use the **navigation buttons** and the **hyperlinks** to explore the Web presentation, then click the **Index button** to return to the title page

9. Close the **Index** file and the browser

FIGURE I-7: Presentation Title page in Internet Explorer

Your browser window may look different

Click this hyperlink to start the presentation

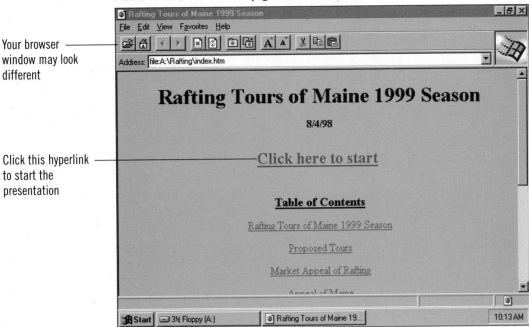

FIGURE I-8: Presentation in Internet Explorer

Index button

Navigation tools

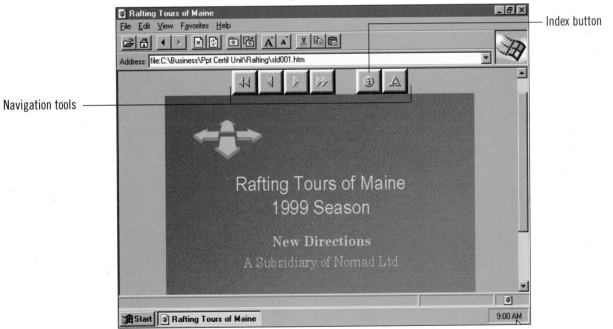

Using Frames

With frames, you can give multiple Web pages a common "look" and navigation method. However, not all Web browsers support, or allow viewing of, pages that use frames. When you create a Web page, consider the audience. If you are creating a page that will be viewed by all a company's employees, and you know that they will use the latest version of a graphical browser, it's safe to use frames. However, if your page will be viewed over the World Wide Web, and you want to make sure you don't exclude any users, you can create one version with frames and one without, and let users choose one at the publication's home page. If you have time to create only one version, choose the one that the largest segment of your audience can view.

Using Presentation Conferencing as the Presenter

Instead of displaying PowerPoint presentations to an audience assembled in a room, you also can show a presentation over a network or the Internet to individual audience members at their computers. To do this, you can use the Presentation Conference Wizard. The conference presenter uses a conference call to contact audience members. When the presenter is ready to begin, he or she instructs the audience to start the PowerPoint Presentation Conference Wizard as audience members. Then the audience members click Finish, the presenter clicks Finish, and the presentation begins. The presentation displays both the presenter's and all audience members' computers. During the presentation, the presenter can use the Stage Managers tools, such as Slide Navigator and Slide Meter, Speaker Notes, and Meeting Minder, which audience members cannot see. The presenter and all audience members can use the annotation pen to write and draw on the slides. Carrie decides to practice the procedure for being the presenter so she can show the New Directions president.

1. Start PowerPoint and open the **Rafting** presentation
2. Click **Tools** on the menu bar, then click **Presentation Conference**
   The introductory screen appears, reminding you to call all participants on the telephone.
3. Click the **Next button** to display the Presenter or Audience screen shown in Figure I-9
4. Make sure the **Presenter** option is selected, then click **Next** to display the Slide show details screen
5. Because you will show all the slides in the current presentation, make sure the screen displays **Show: All Slides**, then click **Next**
   The Connection Information screen appears. If you wanted to access the Internet through the Internet Service Provider (ISP), you would connect to it now.
6. Click **Next** to display the Connection Details screen
   See Figure 1-10. At this time, you would ask all audience members for their Internet addresses (or if you were on a network, their computer name). Next, you enter the name of the computer that each audience member is using. The computer name appears on each audience member's screen as the audience members complete the Presentation Conference Wizard. Audience members can communicate their individual computer names to you over the phone.
7. Enter the computer name of an audience member to whom you are presenting, then click the **Add button**
   If you were connecting to the Internet, you would type the Internet address of the computer you want to connect to in the text box. The computer name you typed appears in the connection list. Assume that all audience members have told you they have completed the setup and are ready to view the presentation.
8. Click the **Finish button**
   Now you connect to the audience members' computers. Slide Show in a Window appears, which lets you see exactly what your audience sees. The Stage Manager dialog box lets you control the slide show. Through the Meeting Minder window, you view speaker notes and enter any meeting notes during the show. The Slide navigator lets you go to any slide during the presentation.
9. In the Stage Manager window, click the **Next Slide button** ⬇ until **Slide 2** appears, then click the **Draw button** and draw a line under the first bullet
10. Display the rest of the slides, then close the presentation
    In the next lesson, you'll practice viewing a presentation as an audience member.

QuickTip

To show only a portion of a slide show, you must first set up a custom show using the Set Up Show command from the Slide Show menu before you run the Presentation Conference Wizard.

QuickTip

During a presentation conference, audience members cannot view video or sound clips, embedded objects, or editing of linked or embedded objects.

FIGURE I-9: Presenter or Audience screen

Step 4

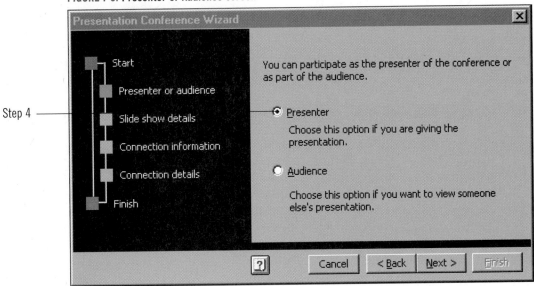

FIGURE I-10: Connection Details screen

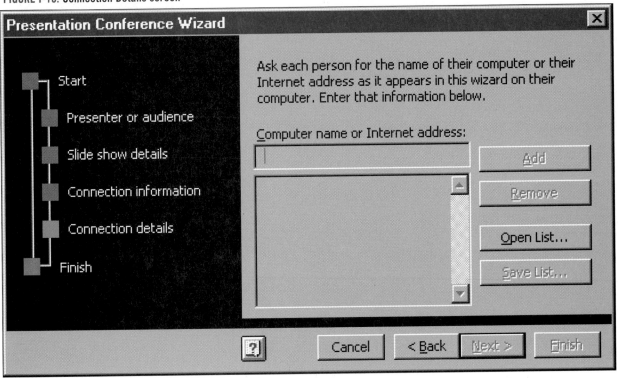

Using Presentation Conferencing as the Audience

To view a slide show as an audience member, you run the Presentation Conference Wizard. After you indicate that you are an audience member, you specify the type of connection you'll use to connect to the presenter, as well as your computer name. When the presenter contacts you and asks you to connect, you click Finish. Once audience members have done this, the presenter starts the conference, and all audience members view the presentation simultaneously on their computers. ➤ Carrie practices acting as a conference audience member, so she can show the president.

Steps

1. Click **Tools** on the menu bar, then click **Presentation Conference**
   The introductory screen appears.

2. Read the screen and click the **Next button** to display the Presenter or Audience screen

3. Click the **Audience option button** shown in Figure I-11, then click **Next**
   In the Connection Type screen, select the connection type you will use to connect to the presenter. Assume that you will connect over a corporate network.

4. Make sure **Local Area Network (LAN) or Corporate Network** is selected, and click **Next**
   Your computer name displays in the Connection Details screen.

5. Click **Next**
   Now, you are ready to connect to the presenter's computer as soon as he or she indicates on the telephone that you should do this.

6. Click **Finish** to begin viewing the show
   The Wizard prepares the connection to the presenter's computer over the network. As soon as the presenter starts the slide show, the slide presentation appears on your computer screen. See Figure I-12.

7. When the presenter has completed the presentation, close PowerPoint

QuickTip
During the presentation, you can annotate slides by right-clicking a slide and clicking Pen. Then you can drag to annotate the slide.

FIGURE I-11: the Presenter or Audience screen

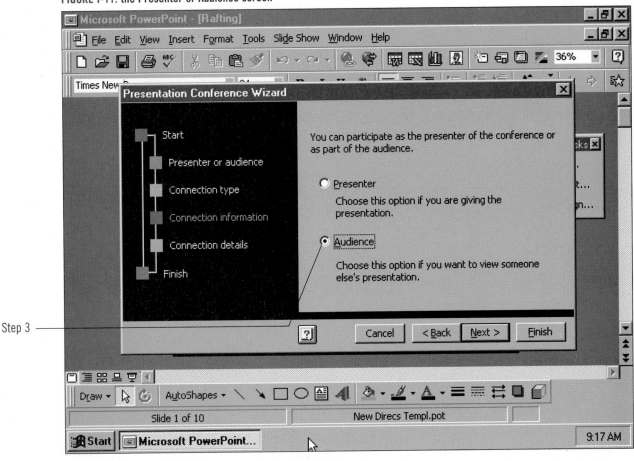

Step 3

FIGURE I-12: Presentation as viewed by the conference audience

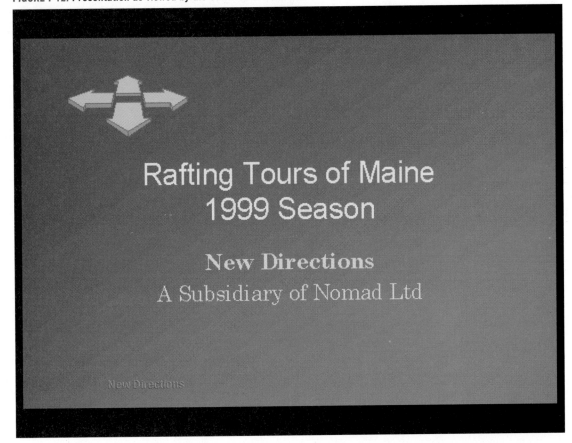

Practice

► Concepts Review

Match each of the terms with the statement that describes it:

1. Lets you send your slide show electronically from PowerPoint to have 35mm slides made.
2. A business that makes slides and provides other graphics products and services.
3. Lets you automatically create a Web page from your presentation.
4. When it converts a presentation for use on the World Wide Web, the HTML Wizard creates this automatically.
5. The host of a presentation conference.

a. HTML Wizard
b. Index page
c. Genigraphics Wizard
d. Service bureau
e. Presenter

Select the best answer from the list of choices.

6. To make a PowerPoint presentation ready to put on a World Wide Web site, you need to:
   a. Save your presentation as a .WMF file.
   b. Manually create an index page as a separate slide.
   c. Save your presentation in HTML format using the Genigraphics Wizard.
   d. Save your presentation in HTML format using the HTML Wizard.
7. When you use presentation conferencing:
   a. The presenter and the audience must gather in the same room and use computers connected on a network.
   b. Video cameras are used for each of the participants.
   c. The presenter and audience can use speaker notes and Meeting Minder.
   d. The presenter and audience can annotate slides.

► Skills Review

1. **Import text from a Word outline and apply a template.**
   a. Open the presentation PPT I-4, then save it as CoffeeLuxe.
   b. Click Apply Design on the Common Tasks toolbar, select the template PPT I-5, then click Apply.
   c. Go to Slide 3, click Insert on the menu bar, then click Slides from Outline.
   d. Under Files of type, select All Outlines. Select the Word document PPT I-6, then click Insert.
   e. Go to Slide 1, then view the slide show.
   f. View the presentation in Slide Sorter view and adjust text to fit the slides as necessary.
   g. Save the presentation.
2. **Export a presentation to 35mm slides.**
   a. Click File on the menu bar, click Page Setup, then click the Slide sized for list arrow.
   b. Click 35mm slides, then click OK.
   c. Click File on the menu bar, point to Send to, then click Genigraphics.
   d. Run the Genigraphics Wizard, selecting the following options: 35mm slides, Send via Internet connection; Plastic mounts; 1 set; Plan ahead: In by 5PM; back in 3-7 bus. days; then click Next.
   e. Click Cancel.

3. **Set custom options.**

    a. Click Tools on the menu bar, click Options, then click the View tab.

    b. Right-click Show popup menu button, then click What's This?

    c. Click anywhere on the tab, then click the Show Popup Menu Button check box to deselect it.

    d. Click the Print tab, then click Use the following default print settings option button to select it.

    e. In the Print What list box, click Handouts (six slides per page), then click OK.

4. **Save a presentation for use on the Internet.**

    a. Click File, click Page Setup, click the Slides Sized for List arrow, select On-screen show, then click OK.

    b. Click File on the menu bar, then click Save as HTML.

    c. Click Next, make sure the New Layout option button is selected, then click Next.

    d. Click the Standard option button, click Next, then complete the HTML Wizard dialog boxes, selecting the following options: GIF; 640 x 480; ¾ width of screen; Use browser colors; the large square button; navigation buttons above the screen, the a: (or other) drive containing your Student disk; click Finish, then click Don't Save.

    e. Click OK, then close PowerPoint, saving your changes.

    f. Open your Web browser, then use the Open command to open the Index.htm file, or double-click the Index.htm file in the CoffeeLuxe folder the Wizard created.

    g. Click the hyperlink Click here to start, then view the presentation, using the navigation buttons and hyperlinks.

    h. When you are done, click the Index button, then close the Index file and your Web browser.

5. **Use Presentation Conferencing as the presenter.**

    a. Open PowerPoint, then open the CoffeeLuxe presentation.

    b. Click Tools on the menu bar, then click Presentation Conference.

    c. Click Next, and make sure the Presenter option is selected, then click Next.

    d. Make sure Show: All Slides is selected, click Next, then click Cancel.

6. **Use Presentation Conferencing as the audience.**

    a. Click Tools on the menu bar, then click Presentation Conference.

    b. Click Next, make sure the Audience option is selected, then click Next.

    c. Make sure Local Area Network (LAN) or Corporate Network is selected, click Next, check your computer name in the Connection details screen, then click Next.

    d. Click Finish, then click OK.

    e. Save the presentation, then print it, using the Handouts (6 slides per page) you set as the default earlier.

    f. Close the presentation, then exit PowerPoint.

▶ # Independent Challenges

1. You are a business manager for Emerson Books, a publisher in Baltimore, Maryland. Emerson has been in business for three years. The company started out publishing how-to books for the home market, but now it publishes self-help and small-business advice books as well. Emerson has a network of independent sales representatives across the country. One of your challenges is to keep the reps informed of the latest titles so they can sell them to distributors and store managers.

You have decided to create a PowerPoint presentation called Hot Picks, containing short descriptions of Emerson's three best-selling titles in each book category, which you will make available to all reps on the company Web page. In addition, you'll show the presentation as 35mm slides at a monthly dealers meeting.

You have asked each of the three editors who work at Emerson to create a Word outline file containing three slides, describing their three hottest titles. Then you will assemble the three files into your presentation file, format it using the Emerson presentation template, and prepare it both for the Internet and for 35mm slides.

To complete this independent challenge:

1. Open the file PPT I-7, and save it as April 98 Hot Picks.

2. View the presentation, then after the second slide, import the three files submitted by the product managers: PPT I-8, PPT I-9, and PPT I-10. Be sure to go to the end of the slide show before inserting the next group.

3. Create more prominent title slides for each group: change the font to 72 point, then center the text vertically on the following slides: Car Care (Slide 3), Self Help (Slide 7), and Small business (Slide 11).

4. Apply the template from PPT I-11.

5. Set the custom options so that the Show pop-up menu does not display during a slide show.

6. Make the slides the appropriate dimensions for 35mm slides, and export the presentation using the Genigraphics Wizard, using any options you wish. Do not enter any credit card information or send the presentation to Genigraphics. Write down the options you chose.

7. Hyperlink each group title to the first slide in the group.

8. Save the presentation, run the slide show, and print the presentation using Handouts (6 slides per page).

9. Return the slide size to its original dimensions, then save the presentation in HTML format, using any options you wish.

10. Open the Index file and view the presentation in a Web browser, using the navigation buttons and hyperlinks.

2. You are a sales agent for Last Minute Travel (LMT), a small company that works with travel agents to assemble last-minute travel deals and sell them to consumers at bargain prices. LMT makes their specials available to the public on their Web page. You are working with two travel agents who e-mail you details of their latest packages in a Word outline format. You assemble the two outlines into a PowerPoint presentation, apply the company template, and prepare it for uploading to the LMT Web page.

Many travel packages can be customized for groups, and companies often call to ask you what is available so their employees can get group rates for 2- and 3-day weekends. You want to be ready to present these special packages both as group presentations in 35mm slide format and over the Internet using Presentation Conferencing. To make the packages more attractive to viewers, you'll add information about the destinations that you find on the World Wide Web.

To complete this independent challenge:

1. Create outlines for two special deals using Microsoft Word. One is a three-day trip to the Virgin Islands, leaving from Annapolis, Maryland, for $400 per person, double occupancy; the other is a four day Mountain Getaway for Singles at the Fox Mountain Resort in Virginia, for $300 per person, meals included. Each deal will be available for only one week. Add sub bullets for each package that describe the trip dates and their advantages and selling points.

2. Create an LMT company template in PowerPoint. Create masters with a customized background for the title slide and the slide itself. Use text and graphics to make a simple logo for LMT, then place it on both masters. The color scheme should be appropriate for a travel company, and the design should communicate action and fun.

3. Create a PowerPoint file containing two introductory slides, then import the two Word outlines. Apply the template you created.

4. Size the presentation appropriately for 35mm slides, then go through the Genigraphics Wizard as far as the credit information screen. Write down the options you selected.

5. Set any custom options you feel are appropriate for the presentation.

6. Restore the slide size to its default dimensions, then create at least two hyperlinks to slides in the same presentation.

7. For each trip slide, insert a hyperlink to a location on the World Wide Web that gives more information about each destination and makes people want to go there. Be sure to put text around the hyperlink that indicates why viewers would want to click that link, such as "Click this link to find out more about..." If you can't find the information you need, or to find additional information, go to http://www.course.com, click Student Online Companions, click the link for this textbook, then click the link for Unit I.

8. Save the presentation in HTML format for use on the Internet, using options of your choice. View the presentation in a Web browser using hyperlinks and navigation buttons.

9. If you are on a network, use Presentation Conferencing to show the presentation to one or more students in the lab.

Glossary

Active cell   A selected cell in a Graph datasheet.

Adjustment handle   A small diamond positioned next to a resize handle that changes the dimension of an object.

Animation   A movie that sets graphics or drawn objects to motion.

AutoLayout   A predesigned slide layout that contains placeholder layouts for titles, main text, clip art, graphs, and charts.

Cell   A rectangle in a Graph datasheet where you enter data.

Chart   The component of a graph that graphically portrays your Graph datasheet information.

Chart box   The text box in an organizational chart.

Chart depth   A chart-sizing option that changes the size of the data series markers.

Chart elements   Objects you can add to a chart to help display or highlight certain information.

Chart type   Defines how a chart graphically displays data from a datasheet.

Clip art   Professionally designed pictures that come with PowerPoint.

Clipboard   A temporary storage area for cut or copied text or graphics. You can paste the contents of the Clipboard into any Microsoft program file. The Clipboard holds information until you cut or copy another piece of text or a graphic.

Control boxes   The gray boxes located along the left and top of a Graph datasheet.

Data series   A row or column of data in a datasheet.

Data series markers   The graphical representation, such as a bar or column, of a data series in a chart.

Datasheet   The component of a graph that contains the information you want to display on your Graph chart.

Design Templates   Prepared slide designs with formatting and color schemes that you can apply to an open presentation.

Digital video   Live-action or full-motion video captured by a video camera.

Dotted selection box   Indicates that an object is selected and can be modified.

Elevation   A chart 3-D view option that changes the angle from which you view the chart.

Embedded object   An object that is created in another application but is stored in PowerPoint. Embedded objects maintain a link to their original application for easy editing.

Exception   A formatting change made on an individual slide that does not follow the Slide Master.

Folder   A subdivision of a disk that works like a filing system to help you organize files.

Freeform   A shape that has straight lines, curved lines, or a combination of the two.

Gap depth   A chart-sizing option that changes the size of the chart floor.

Gap width   A chart-sizing option that changes the distance between each group of data series markers.

Graph   The datasheet and chart you create to graphically display information.

Grid   Evenly spaced horizontal and vertical lines that do not appear on the slide.

Hanging indent   A paragraph format in which the first line of a paragraph starts farther left than the subsequent lines.

Hyperlink   A specially formatted word, phrase, or graphic that you click during a slide show to jump to or display another document.

Indent levels   The text levels in a text placeholder.

Indent marker A small triangle that shows the position of an indent level.

Interactive settings Customized actions that you apply to objects to play during a slide show.

Leading The vertical space between lines of text.

Link The connection between an object and the source file where it is stored.

Main text placeholder A reserved box on a slide for the main text points.

Margin marker A small box on an indent level that enables you to move the whole indent level.

Master text placeholder The placeholder on the Slide Master that controls the formatting and placement of the Main text placeholder on each slide. If you modify the Master text placeholder, each Main text placeholder is affected in the entire presentation.

Master title placeholder The placeholder on the Slide Master that controls the formatting and placement of the Title placeholder on each slide. If you modify the Master title placeholder, each Title placeholder is affected in the entire presentation.

Object The component you place or draw on a slide. Objects are drawn lines and shapes, text, clip art, imported pictures, and embedded objects.

Organizational chart A diagram of connected boxes that shows reporting structure.

Picture Any piece or artwork, such as a scanned photograph, line art, or clip art that is created in another application and embedded into PowerPoint.

Placeholder A dashed line box in which you place text or objects.

PowerPoint Viewer A special application designed to run a PowerPoint slide show on any compatible computer that does not have PowerPoint installed.

ScreenTip When you place the pointer over a button, the name of the button is displayed and a brief description of its function appears in the status bar.

Slide icon A symbol used to identify a slide title in Outline view.

Source file The file where a linked object is stored.

Source program The original application where embedded and linked objects are created.

Target document The file your hyperlink displays on the screen when you click it.

Text anchor Adjusts the text position in text objects or shapes.

Text box A box within a dialog box where you type information needed to carry out a command.

Text object Any text you create with the Text Tool or enter into a placeholder. Once you enter text into a placeholder, the placeholder becomes a text object.

Timing The time a slide stays on the screen during a slide show.

Title The first line or heading in Outline view.

Title master The master view for the first slide in a presentation.

Title placeholder A reserved box on a slide for a presentation or slide title.

Title slide The first slide in your presentation.

Transition The effect that moves one slide off the screen and the next slide on the screen during a slide show. Each slide can have its own transition effect.

View PowerPoint has five views that allow you to look at your presentation in different ways. Each view allows you to change and modify the content of your presentation.

View buttons Appear at the bottom of the Presentation window. Allow you to switch between PowerPoint's five views.

Wizard A guided approach that steps you through creating a presentation. PowerPoint has two wizards, the AutoContent Wizard and the Pick a Look Wizard, that help you with the content and the look of your presentation.

Index

Index

Index

Index